Tuning the instruments is a necessary prelude to any orchestral activity. The sounds may be odd, disjointed, and a bit self-conscious: but they promise rendezvous with a score. There is a performance ahead. The studies that comprise this book are somewhat of that character. They have to do with salient themes in the belief and life of Islam to-day, set down for study and action within the Christian Churches of the Middle East and beyond. Several authors have lately discussed what has been called "the coming great encounter" between the faiths of the world. These chapters concern themselves with the practice of relationship and the indispensable conditions of knowledge and perception, as these face the Christian Churches in their effort to be worthy of their Gospel in the midst of Islam.

The aim is to discover Islam from within and explore its institutions and habits of mind, in the major crises of life and the context of heritage and history in which it moves. The tiny cave beneath the Rock of Moriah and the Dome—Jerusalem's most compelling landmark—is taken as symbol and sign of inward encounter at the central points of Muslim–Christian thought and worship. These hold both likeness and contrast, identity and sharp diversity. The Christian can only hope to mediate the meaning of the Incarnation and the Cross if he meets the Muslim frankly and gladly on the ground of their mutual conviction about nature, man, and God.

Kenneth Cragg, Warden of St Augustine's College, Canterbury—the Central College of the Anglican Communion—and an Honorary Canon of Canterbury and Jerusalem, has a wide familiarity with the Islamic world. These papers for group discussion and private study are the product of many travels and much reflection, both inquisitive and hopeful.

THE DOME AND THE ROCK

The Dome and the Rock

JERUSALEM STUDIES IN ISLAM

by

KENNETH CRAGG

LONDON
S · P · C · K
1964

Mohammedanism

First published in 1964
by S.P.C.K.
Holy Trinity Church
Marylebone Road
London N.W.1
Made and printed in Great Britain by
William Clowes and Sons, Limited, London and Beccles

For much hospitality
from Jerusalem
round about
unto
Casablanca
Kano
Khartoum
Calcutta
Istanbul

Contents

Note

For reasons of economy in the transliteration of Arabic words only the ^c*ain* and *hamza* signs have been used and differentiation of consonants and long vowels omitted. Where words have a traditional English spelling this has been preferred to a pedantic correctness, except in certain special cases where judgements necessarily are somewhat personal.

Permission is gratefully acknowledged from the Editor of *The Muslim World*, Hartford, Connecticut, to reprint the major part of two extended translations of Muslim devotions at the Fast and the Pilgrimage. Other acknowledgements will be found in the footnotes.

In accordance with the publisher's usual style, capital letters have been only sparingly used for words relating to things of faith, and lower-case initial letters have been preferred for pronouns relating to God.

It should be emphasized that these chapters took their origin in a venture of corporate study. The suggestion of questions for further reflection and inquiry at the end of each chapter was part of this concern. They are local in nature and presuppose a Muslim environment. But even where this is absent (which may be less often than we think), their form may be useful for mental translation into any other contextual shape of Christian duty and alertness.

I

Introduction

"Third in excellence, God's honour be upon her." So Ibn Battuta greeting and saluting Jerusalem. The year is 1326, the occasion his wanderings between Cairo and Damascus in preface to the ultimate pilgrimage to Mecca and Medina, the first and second shrines. The Crusaders, by then, were gone even from their last foothold in Acre, their ill-starred intrusion no more than a memory, though the diarist pauses to recall that it was because of them Saladin destroyed the walls of the city "lest the Christians should seize and fortify themselves in it". He takes Jerusalem quietly in his prosaic stride, but there is no mistaking the warmth of his admiration.

> The Dome of the Rock is a building of extraordinary beauty, solidity, elegance and singularity of shape. It stands on an elevation in the centre of the mosque (i.e. the Temple Area) and is reached by a flight of marble steps. It has four doors. The space around it is also paved in marble, excellently done, and the interior likewise. Both outside and inside the decoration is so magnificent and the workmanship so surpassing as to defy description. The greater part is covered with gold so that the eyes of one who gazes on its beauties are dazzled by its brilliance, now glowing like a mass of light, now flashing like lightning. In the centre of the Dome is the blessed rock from which the Prophet ascended to heaven, a great rock projecting about a man's height, and underneath it there is a cave the size of a small room, also of a man's height, with steps leading down to it.[1]

Compared with such magnificence, the Church of the Holy Sepulchre seems to have made a poor contrast, as externally it still does, and from the traveller it invited little comment. He moved on to Askalon, merely observing that the Christians' central sanctuary was one they

[1] Ibn Battuta, *Travels in Asia and Africa, 1325–54*, translated and selected by H. A. R. Gibb, Routledge and Kegan Paul, 1929, pp. 55–6. Quoted with permission.

were "falsely persuaded to believe . . . contains the grave of Jesus". His disavowal of its validity arises, not from any dispute about the location of burial, but from the Muslim assurance that Jesus, being raptured to heaven, never died and therefore has no tomb. In the same vein, he adds with engaging frankness: "All who come on pilgrimage to visit it pay a stipulated tax to Muslims and suffer very unwillingly various humiliations."[1] We almost see his busy figure descending the western hills in a fine surge of confidence that Islam had founded glory on a rock while Christendom had no more than an edifice, and a pilgrimage, of misapprehension.

If Ibn Battuta were to return in our own day the Dome at least would deserve the same enthusiasm. Muslim devotion, aided by the wealth of Arab oil and state munificence, has regilded the shrine. After centuries of baser metal, it is newly resplendent in gold leaf. But still almost all else is sombre and grim. The western hills are now on the farther side of an enmity as bitter as any in the long history of the city. Its walls are sentinels on a frontier of irreconciliation. There are humiliations of spirit, sharp and searching, for the perceptive. But they are not those of taxation. Within its medieval suqs and market streets, the city is a pilgrims' museum, busy with modernity. Most of its visitors are airborne. Through all the retrospect of sentiment and the sheer persistence of history, to-day's generation, in its own terms, is heir to those same themes of religious relation as the contemporaries of Ibn Battuta. It is with Jerusalem as a compelling occasion of Muslim-Christian relationships that this book is concerned.

It finds its symbol where the fourteenth-century chronicler found his exhilaration. Beneath the Dome and within the Rock, he found the cave, the "small room of a man's height", where the prophet Muhammad had tarried before his night ascent to heaven. Here imagination may contract into a span the vicissitudes of biblical history and focus into a single parable the business of getting to the heart of things. There is a calling to intimate study at the centre of this meeting ground of history and religion. As Dome and Rock together represent the common and contrasted elements of Christianity and Islam, so the inner cave beneath may be imagination's rendezvous between them.

This ground is mount Moriah. Its first meanings have to do with

[1] Ibid., p. 57.

Abraham. It was, tradition says, the scene of his greatest trial, of that sharp crisis in which God's lordship claimed the same utmost sacrifice that idolatrous shrines exacted, but in compassion repudiated once devotion was unquestioned. Embodied in the mysterious restoration of Isaac into earthly fatherhood is the mercy that is correlative to human trust. This is the patriarchal meaning of the Rock.

Who is to know its further story until it emerges in Davidic times as the threshing floor of Araunah? Were the niches in the cave the housing places of the deities of Jebusites before they became the praying place of Elijah, David, and Solomon, as Muslim tradition takes them? Does the hollow floor below and the aperture through the roof of the cave into the surface of the Rock indicate a drainage system for the temple sacrifices? If so, then here was the altar of burnt offering in the outer court. What figures of Old Testament history came and went through the successive Temples of Solomon, Zerubbabel, and Herod?

Somewhere to the east of the Rock ran the ritual fence and the fortification belonging with the court of the women and the court of the Gentiles. Here, it would seem, stood the treasury where Jesus observed the widow casting in her two mites and where he often taught his disciples and other listeners. Beyond again was the eastern gate that gave access to the Kedron valley and the mount of Olives, through which Jesus frequently came and went, perhaps even in the triumphal entry itself. These Christian associations still linger around the portals, and there are traditions, too, about a house of Simeon. As now, so then, the open expanse of court which gives the Dome of the Rock its broad commanding spaces stood lifting its defiant front towards the watcher on the mount of Olives. Its huge plateau of masonry carried the precincts Jesus knew.

There to the south-east was the pinnacle tower and the temptation to spectacular messiahship. There, too, the columned hall of Solomon where as a boy of twelve he had dismayed his parents and surprised the doctors. Lately reared by Herod's builders, these were the stones that figured in the condemnation of the prophet of Nazareth. Through forty and three years a thousand priests turned masons and carpenters, since no profane hand could shape the shrine. This was the citadel of ecclesiastical privilege which finally reared his cross. At its northern perimeter stood the fortress of Antonia where after his condemnation by Pilate he set forth upon the Via Dolorosa.

So with the temple area belong the deepest issues of the Christian

Gospel. Yet, for all that, Byzantium left it oddly derelict, as any one may see who consults the famous Madeba map of Jerusalem. Eastern Christendom seems to have reasoned that the Roman destruction of the city under Titus, and the later deliberate desacrilizing of the temple area by Hadrian's heathen usages, had confirmed the divine rejection of Israel and that for this the truest symbol would be the neglect of its most holy ground. So it was left for Islamic expansion finally to rescue the sanctuary of Abraham and restore the temple precincts to active veneration and esteem. ᶜUmar, the Caliph conqueror, after whom the Dome is sometimes mistakenly styled the "Mosque of ᶜUmar", retrieved the site, and ᶜAbd al-Malik, one of his Ummayyad successors, set there his noble octagon and dome. He took his pillars from the quarry of history that lay beneath the rubble of Byzantium. None came newly from the mason to the Muslim's hand. He gave to veterans of earlier sanctities a new destiny in a resplendent monument of Islam, enriched with the new calligraphy where Muslim faith and art were most harmoniously at one.

When some three centuries later the Crusaders came, they somehow took the Dome for the Temple of Solomon.[1] On the Rock they reared an altar, the steps to which, cut by their masons' picks, may still be seen—a curious hieroglyphic on a mountain palimpsest. Ringed with the pillars of Hadrian and Herod, they celebrated the Christian mysteries and for offerings of gold gave chippings from the Rock to their pilgrims from the west.

These are the sanctities, superimposed upon each other in the sequence of the centuries, that belong with the Dome of the Rock, in its newly furbished splendour of to-day. Set in its wide stone arena reared on massive vaults from the steeply descending shoulders of the Rock itself, the edifice proclaims its open secrets to the world and asserts its authority over every traveller to Jerusalem. Yet it stands in a landscape where there is also mystery and hiddenness, and as if in symbol there is a cave "of a man's height" at the core of the splendour. There, we may say, the religions of this ecclesiastical capital may see the sign of their engagement with each other and of the truth that it can only be achieved in quiet penetration and personal exchange. Such, modestly, is the purpose of these chapters.

[1] See the fifteenth-century woodcut from Breyenbach's *Reise ins Heilige Land*, Mainz, Edward Reuwich, 1486, and the Spencer Collection, New York Public Library.

They are selected from a sequence of some fifty outlines on Islamic topics, drawn up for use among Christians in and beyond Jerusalem, whether as individuals or in church groups, during the period 1957–62. They were part of a larger Study Programme, including summer courses and local institutes of study and discussion throughout the area of the Near East Christian Council. The concern was to serve and equip the Christian communities for adventures of ministry and expression towards their fellow men in Islam. They were an effort after a surer and fuller Christian relationship to the common world of to-day and the heritage of mingled affinity and alienation from the past. The hope was that by knowing and exploring Islam they would the better arouse and inform a Muslim discovery of Christ. The intention was that the outlines might focus and foster the knowledge and sensitivity without which the Church could expect no worthy or effective meeting with Islam. They presuppose the general political and social situation but do not spell it out. Their theme is directly theological and "religious". In every case the attempt was made to take up the Muslim dogma, attitude, or institution, so as to explore its utmost range and potential, since it is to these the Christian must relate both himself and his belief. Thus the reader will find here neither special erudition in the intricacies of the Islamic heritage, nor topical reporting on its current vicissitudes. What he may find is a means of potential discoveries of service in truth and initiative in ministry.

Excluded from this context are the several studies which had to do with the Quran, its content and exegesis. These have been reserved for better maturing and possible presentation in composite form elsewhere. This will explain the absence of what might otherwise have been expected in a project of this kind. It should be borne in mind that the whole venture belonged to a wide variety of personnel with differing backgrounds, aptitudes, and concerns. There are doubtless significant gaps which any scholar can detect and any critic castigate. The plea, however, that survives all mere castigation for incompleteness and possible ineptness is the thoroughly Islamic one of "intention". The critic is invited to slant his criticism into the same central concern for the mutuality of contemporary life and the meaning for it of our often combative, partly common, always related, theologies. If he does not share this commitment, his criticism will be the more total and the less relevant.

In that event it is perhaps wise to add one other point. It is the old suspicion that any intention of mediation of belief must of necessity compromise the ventures of understanding. Or, in other terms, a Christian community aiming in this way to educate itself by painstaking reflection on Islam, is thereby disqualified from knowing it because it lacks the paramount detachment and "disinterest". In this sense, it is claimed, there can be no "missionary" studies of other faiths. The intention to communicate precludes the will to see impartially. I cannot truly see the Dome of the Rock if I have one eye on Gethsemane. I must somehow be suspended in indeterminate neutrality above the Kedron valley, like the souls in the tradition on the day of judgement, walking their tightrope.

But is decision only in suspension? Is detachment ever more than partial? Can we in fact dispossess our minds of all criteria of approach even if they be supposedly merely those of scholarship? Will it not be sounder, not to say more feasible, if we confess our interests, take conscious control of their "prejudice", and by discipline and hope release their potential assets of affinity, humility, perception, and involvement? It is a curious notion that studied vacancy of mind about God, or law, or life, or men, could feasibly equip the student for the discovery of all that is Islamic. Nor would Muslims have ever thought it so, had not a legacy of Christian obtuseness or aloofness left the sort of suspicions which the studies here are set to repudiate and replace. Neither as Muslims, nor Christians, nor as men and contemporaries, can we afford the luxury of isolation, or the folly of distrust. In the last analysis this issue of integrity in study and integrity in soul is one. We are the more likely to make truth-learning exploration if we attempt truth-bearing relationships. And in any event there is that irreversible mixed-upness of which the central temple-mosque-shrine of the hill across from the mount of Olives is here the token.

The arrangement of the chapters that follow is intended to conform to the essential nature of a mosque, which as we saw was the name Ibn Battuta gave to the entire area of the Temple. For any mosque is a focus of historical, institutional, personal, and social community. It is these which have been intended in the "Pillars of the House", "Temple Area", "Precincts and People", and "Streets of Jerusalem". These belong naturally with the physical setting of the whole: they correspond with the essential structure of Islam as *Din*, its shape of devotion and view of the world. From the area of its dogma and devotion, so represented, its people move out into the business of their living, as men and women, in families, as citizens and fellows, in the burdens of their being, their superstitions, their associations, their goings out and in, their mortality, and the final loneliness of death. All this is the purpose of "Precincts and People". Both belong with "Streets of Jerusalem". Under this head we turn to three studies of the practical interrelationships of Christians with their Muslim neighbours. The community which now possesses the Dome and the Rock cohabits the city with the folk of Christ. What that cohabitation, in and beyond the walls of Jerusalem, should mean for either community can only be answered from within its own resources of soul and doctrine. It is a situation in which all that we can offer is a minority report.

PILLARS OF THE HOUSE

2

The Muslim's Worship

"When a man prepares for ablution the angels come to his right and the satans to his left. If he makes mention of God when he begins the ablutions the satans flee from him and the angels spread over him a pavilion of light, having four ropes, at each rope of which there is an angel glorifying God most high and praying forgiveness for him. . . ." So runs the answer of the slave girl, Tawaddud, to Harun al-Rashid, in the catechism on Prayer that occurs, of all places, in *The Arabian Nights*. Those four ropes symbolize our present theme, the aim of which is to assess the Muslim's worship and so enter that "pavilion of light", as the writer calls it, which Muslims understand as their ritual rendezvous with God.

It is the *Salat* proper which is our concern. We are not here dealing with the other wide area of prayer in its full sense, namely petition and intercession, known as *duʿaʾ*. Nor are we directly concerned here with the general atmosphere and nature of the mosque. In treating of *Salat*, there is hardly need to take up detailed description of the postures and phrases, which can readily be found in any sound manual of Islamics. Our objective is rather to take the measure of the whole institution of prayer, the second of the Five Pillars of Religion in Islam and the duty which along with *Zakat* identifies a Muslim.

The slave girl gave the Caliph no precise interpretation of what were her four ropes. But Muslim precept and practice leave us in no serious doubt at least as to the imaginative borrowing we can have of them in outlining what *Salat* is and means.

THE ROPE OF DUTY

Prayer in Islam is obligation. It is a duty enjoined and incumbent on every believer, to neglect or abandon which is to forfeit Islamic status.

He who wilfully avoids prayer without excuse has no place in Islam. So run the traditions. The injunction of course has quranic origin, though the actual practice of five daily prayers became "statutory" only after the Prophet's death.

It is clear from the Quran that performance of *Salat* was the sign of submission. The new adherent became Muslim in this act and in the *Shahadah*, or witness. Performance is the proper word, since prayer in Islam is *done*, not merely said. Its fivefold recurrence daily can be traced back to passages like 4.103 which mentions fixed times of prayer but specifies no number. Surah 17.78 speaks of sunset and dawn and 11.114 of "the two ends of the day and at night". Surah 2.238 refers to "the midmost prayer" as the one Muslims are most likely to forget and 24.58 also mentions three times.

In its repetition the prayer is the fulfilment towards God of what he has laid upon the faithful as expressing their recognition of his sovereignty and the prophethood of his messenger. Prayer in Islam is thus essentially a religious duty. It does not arise from psychological considerations having to do with the value of repetition, though these have been subsequently adduced by modern writers.[1] Nor is it primarily an outflowing of devotion or an exercise of religious initiative, a seeking of God in desire. Nor yet is it an occasion of articulation of need, welling out of despair or aspiration. It may occupy in part, in Muslim experience, the place that these sources of adoration and petition have elsewhere. But essentially *Salat* is the fulfilment of a statutory duty: it is an act of homage Godward, a performance of what God has laid upon the faithful. This is its legal and only basis.

This aspect is eloquent in the postures themselves, which are the biggest occasion of the sacramental in Islam. No witness of Muslim congregational *Salat* can miss its impressive quality. The ranks of the devout, their unison in movement behind the *imam*, the concentration of attention on the precise sequence of gesture and of phrase, the heart of the *rakᶜah* in the *sujud* or prostration bringing the pride of man, his brow, to the humble earth—all these express in a profound and moving symbol the attitude of surrender unto God. The positional equality and the collective reverence suggest a single common allegiance Godward.

It is also to be remembered that the core of the Muslim's utterance in each *rakᶜah* is the *Fatihah*, or opening Surah. Its burden is not petition

[1] Cf. Syed Amir Ali, *The Spirit of Islam*, p. 162.

or request, save as noted below. It is occupied with the offering of praise and the acknowledgement of undivided sovereignty and undiverted worship:

> Praise be to God, Lord of the worlds, the merciful Lord of mercy, Master of the Judgement Day. Thee it is we worship, thee it is we implore for aid. Guide us in the straight path, the path of those whom thou hast favoured, not the path of those upon whom thy wrath abides nor of those who go astray.

The *Takbirs* (i.e. saying *Allahu akbar*) and the *Subhans* ("Praise to my Lord most high") further proclaim that the worshipper is first and foremost acknowledging his Lord in tribute of reverence, of which no small part is the meticulousness of his obedience. The *Salat* is *mafrudah*, that is, obligatory—the Prayer of the Morning (*Subh*) with two *rak*ᶜ*ahs*, the Prayer of the Noon (*Zuhr*) with four, the Prayer of the Afternoon (ᶜ*Asr*) with four, the Prayer of the Sunset (*Maghrib*) with three, and of the Evening (ᶜ*Isha*ʾ) with four.

The careful prescriptions of the ritual build up this element of the meticulous as part of the form of duty and reverence. Among the *Mubtilat*, or things which disqualify the acts of devotion, are ill-discipline, unseemliness, chatting and laughter, eating and drinking, "hemming and hawing" or unnecessary coughing, and neglect of the niceties of the ritual, as well as ritual impurity (on which see below). The cumulative effect of this precision and propriety is to emphasize that tribute is being paid to one who in enjoining these acts has decreed and ordained his proper recognition as Lord.

The whole may well be described by the name of one of its parts, namely the *Tasmiyah*, or saying of the words, "In the Name of God". It is essentially an act in the Name of God, in the sense that it is according to his precepts and in homage to his lordship. The central fact about the acts of Muslim devotion in *Salat* is that the believer is ceremonially expressing the meaning of his whole status under God. He is fulfilling the obligation to offer the prescribed homage and submission to God most high. The primary fact informs and permeates the whole ethos of the ritual. It is, we may say, the main guy-rope of "the pavilion of light". "Thee it is we worship."

THE ROPE OF PROTECTION

Precisely because the *Salat* is the point of man's recognition or rendezvous with the divine greatness acknowledged in these terms, it is also a sacrilizing thing for the participant believer. It hallows him by encounter and so casts a protective mantle around him. Yet like many sacred things it requires itself to be carefully "protected" from contamination. These two facts together are a second strand of its strength.

The *Fatihah* itself clearly suggests this idea of the Muslim pray-er being one who enjoys the divine protection. He is not among the incurrers of the divine wrath. Often in the Quran, prayer is linked closely with patience and the connection of thought seems to be that in the practice of *Salat* there is that which "defends" the spirit and the person of him who prays from evil so that he can afford to be patient. The recognition of God in homage begets the sense of God in his guardianship of the believer. For prayer and patience, see Surah 2.45, 153 and 22.45.

In her response to the Caliph's questions, the slave girl said: "Prayer makes Satan wroth, it wards off trial, it spares one from the evil by enemies, it defends against vengeance and it restrains from lewdness and what is disapproved." There may have been in her sense of prayer's effect, or in the earlier origin of these ideas, some connection with *Salat* as actually marking Islamization, so that it certainly brought the new pray-er into the protection of Islam and freed him from those disabilities which attached to non-Muslims. It made his testimony in a court admissible, according to the law of evidence, as a non-Muslim's was not. It would also materially alter his status in such things as blood-price and recoverable damages for injury.

But though these were material and tangible consequences of *Salat* in circumstances of new adherence, their significance for our study lies more in their being a sort of parable of a larger immunity which the practice of religion conferred. Belonging to Islam, one enjoyed a political corporateness of protection, and entered into a collective entity, a house of existence. What this was in imperial expansion, it also afforded in emotional security. He who joined with the ranks in the mosque and shared in the rhythm of worship knew himself part of a community which in its totality was the people of God and the special object of the divine favour. That communal participation was reinforced by the greeting to left and to right of *al-Salamu ʿalaikum* with which prayer ends. Addressed to all fellow-Muslims in time and place it is a greeting renewed in the frequent *Tasliyah* with its calling down of blessing upon the Prophet, his companions, and his people. In some usages it runs: "Peace be upon thee, O Prophet, with the mercy and blessing of God, and peace upon us and upon the good worshippers of God."

This "sacrilizing" of the Muslim in the *Salat*, his undergoing, so to speak, a ceremonial state that will serve and symbolize his immunity from the divine wrath and from evil, has itself to be ritually ensured. The rite that protects is, therefore, the rite that is protected. This phenomenon is discernible elsewhere too. The recital of the Torah, for example, the most sacred occasion of Jewish life, must therefore be itself safeguarded by meticulous provision. If a Shefer Torah has the slightest inexactitude from a scribe or copyist, or even if its ink fades, that fact will automatically invalidate the reading. Likewise Muslim *Salat*, the preserver from evil, must be carefully preserved from contamination.

So the first condition of *Salat* is *Wudu*ʾ, or ablution, in which the devout, after "intending the ablution", wash both hands to the wrists, rinse the mouth three times, take water up into the nostrils three times, wash the face three times, wash both arms to the elbows, wipe the head once, wipe the ears once, wipe the head and neck once, and wash both feet to the ankles. The directive behind this is in Surah 4.43 and 5.6. In this way ceremonial purity is established, together with the fulfilment of other conditions, such as the avoidance of garments or of exposures ritually impure, the use of a place that has been rendered ritually clean by a prayer mat and the facing of the *Qiblah*, with the *Takbirah* of consecration. The ceremonial purity remains until the salutation of peace at the end of the final *rak*ᶜ*ah* desacrilizes the pray-er.

An accompanying prayer at this point of *Wudu*ʾ clarifies its symbolic meaning: "Make me one of those who repent, make me of those who have purified themselves." It is also customary to use the *Ta*ᶜ*awwudh* or formula of seeking refuge with God from the menaces of evil that beset the sacred acts. In immunizing himself ritually the believer represents to himself the inward hallowing which the *Salat* accomplishes, given of course, the *Niyyah*. One may note also Surahs 29.45 and 31.17.

This concept of "intention" applies to all the Five Pillars of Muslim religion and is to be noted in all their constituent parts. Thus the Muslim announces his *Niyyah* of the *Wudu*ʾ or of the particular prayer according to the hour, just as he mentions the *Niyyah* of the fast every dawn of Ramadan. Without this intention the "office", though perfectly recited and performed, remains invalid. That confession of intention can itself become formalized, just as one can say, "Lest we forget" in what is in fact a substitute for remembering. But "the intention of the intention", so to speak, is to inaugurate the sacrilized state and in it to focus attention on the status of the pray-er as within God's realm. And in the same sense is the requirement of many of the manuals of prayer instruction that the devout shall not turn sidelong glances towards their neighbours but concentrate on their own *Salat*.

THE ROPE OF MERIT

It follows from this that there is another element for the student to note, which has, however, to be stated with care. No observer of Muslim *Salat* can fail to sense the feeling of merit or, if the word were not so clumsy, meritoriousness, about it. We must beware of stating this over crudely and there are other features to be set over against it. But it follows from the obligatory character of Muslim ritual that its performance is praiseworthy. Men's standing with God turns upon their works, and this being the first of them its accomplishment creates worth before God. Ritual acts take their emphatic place in the totality of what a man performs, as it goes into the scales whose verdict, as graphically told in Surah 101, is decisive on the day of judgement. Given sincerity and propriety, the works of Muslim obligation, including worship, avail in relation to one's standing with God and one's expectation of Paradise.

It is difficult for minds schooled to Christian concepts of grace and redemption to appreciate fully the extent to which this is inevitably the case in the Muslim soul. The resultant contrast is one of the sternest issues between the two faiths. "Thou . . . dost assure us *thereby* of thy favour and goodness towards us" runs one of the phrases of a Christian liturgy for Holy Communion. Its reference is to "receiving these thy creatures of bread and wine". The whole basis of our acceptance with God lies in that of which we are no other than repentant recipients. God's is both the initiative and the accomplishment of our salvation and our works of gratitude follow, not that we may qualify with him for favour, but because undeserved favour has already been bestowed, in a context commensurate with his holiness.

The absence of this dimension in the Muslim reckoning alters the entire divine-human situation. The shifting of the onus for our relationship with God to a fulfilment of obligation, a bringing of tribute, a performance of ritual duty makes meritoriousness central. It is not that God is not gracious in Islam. He is gracious to accept our doings and favour us with his reward. In the Gospel he favours us with his compassion and accepts us in his own initiative of compassion and sacrifice.

This is why no Muslim worship requires the sacramental dimension aside, of course, from its own postures. That to which it is responsive in God is majesty and law, authority and greatness. The Christian sacrament of "the body and the blood" makes us the very guests of God. Noteworthy in this sense is the provision the prayer manuals contain against eating and drinking in mosques. In the general sense that the place of worship is not to be turned into a place of picnic or a restaurant, it would be apposite to mosque and church and synagogue alike. But, taken imaginatively, there is a world of contrast in that veto and the Christian participation by faith in Christ crucified through the breaking and the taking of the bread.

In trying to wrestle as Christians with the Muslim notion of merit in prayer, arising from its status as a duty performed, we can, perhaps paradoxically, find allies in Muslim attitudes themselves. Here we reach the proviso with which these paragraphs began. Fulfilment of the ritual obligation in Islam does qualify for God's favour, but gives no ground for presumption about its being granted. This is the striking feature that should never be overlooked. It arises perhaps from the Muslim sense of the sovereignty of God's will, in that favour can never be presumed. So the Muslim pray-er keeps always within the spirit of the *Fatihah* with its plea for guidance in the straight path.

It may be useful in this connection to note the extra-ritual form of prayer (*duʿaʾ*) of the *Qunut*. This is the term that describes the standing posture at the end of the final *rakʿah* when the Muslim prays, speaking towards his upturned palms held almost at chin level. The petition reads: "O God, I ask thy succour, I implore thy guidance, I pray thy forgiveness, I repent unto thee. In thee I believe, upon thee I rely. To thee I ascribe all praise: I thank thee and am not among them who belie thee and thy gifts." Elsewhere there are parallels, not least in Sufi devotion, to these protestations of unworthiness and penitence. Thus it is clear that Muslim reliance on the merit of religious performance does not obviate self-reproach and humility. On the contrary. Still, the Christian task is to carry these merciful instincts after self-abasement into their full and real significance as tokens of the truth in

Christ that our relationship with God cannot be other than one of dependence upon mercy. It will be found in the end that loyalty to that principle must take us to the cross. Islam has halted at a half-way house, reaching to the recognition of unworthiness yet relying on the accrediting of worth, remaining in the status of creditors Godward and yet using the language of debtors.

THE ROPE OF COMMUNION

What Tawaddud called "the pavilion of light" is held together by a fourth rope. Among the ten virtues of *Salat* as she listed them for the Caliph is that "it brings the servant near to his Master". So doing "it illumines the heart and brightens the countenance". It is interesting that some manuals put among the *Mubtilat* that disqualify prayer, "weeping over the affairs of the world, whether out of fear of God or hope of his mercy". If laughter is unseemly in the mosque, so also are tears. For in the awareness of God is peace and tranquillity.

All prayer is the expression of a relationship. The pray-er is responding to the fact of God. Worship is the recognition of worth. Tested by this criterion there is no doubt that Muslim *Salat* is the expression of the Muslim sense of God.

The two final verses of Surah 7 read: "So remember thy Lord in your soul with devotion and reverence and without ostentation, in the morning and the evening, and do not be negligent. Truly those who are with my Lord are not too big with pride to do him worship. They laud his praises and adore him." It is this communion and adoration which the Christian must be at pains to understand. "Thee it is we worship" says the *Fatihah* in its emphatic way. Through and beyond all duty, protection, and merit, the *Salat* is set for the adoration of God within and through the concepts of him known in Islam.

As such, it has been remarkably successful, perhaps because of its simplicity of ritual, in actualizing devotion among its masses. In one respect the fact that attendance at mosques is not necessary to worship, except on Fridays at noon, has helped to this result. Every and any Muslim, wherever he chooses to stretch his prayer-mat, has this immediacy of access. The sacrament that expresses his meaning, namely postures of body, is wholly within his own individual power and aegis. The words are few and in their ritual setting dramatic and impressive. He has no need of the apparatus of art and music, book or vestment, except the characteristic chanting of the sacred text. The numinous in his religion is, so to speak, entrusted entirely to himself.

All these aspects of Muslim prayer, which have to be seen and experienced by the outsider who would understand, underline this final quality of *Salat* as that wherein and whereby the Muslim seeks communion with God. We must not be deterred (as we would wish students of our Christianity not to be deterred) by formalism, unworthiness, or absenteeism. These exist, witness the Quran's own warning: "Woe unto them that are careless (heedless) in their praying" (107.4, 5). It is by its own criteria that we must understand what it should be. What is it that the Gospel says to men whose allegiance calls them to the utmost in surrender to God, without allowing them to receive the utmost in grace from God? If that correctly sums up our Christian situation vis-à-vis the Muslim's worship, can we meet it other than as we dwell with a wondering worship where God meets us in Christ?

QUESTIONS FOR STUDY AND DISCUSSION

1. What would you say, from observation and discussion with Muslims, is the intention of the Muslim's worship? What does he mean in his *Salat*?

2. Why is the Christian Gospel incompatible with the idea of meritorious worship? How may this issue be constructively interpreted to Muslims?

3. What possible relation can a Christian interpretation have to the rôle of ablution in the Muslim scheme?

4. The ritual acts of the Muslim's worship, aside from the *Qiblah*, or direction, in which he does them, are not associated with something historical, as are the Passover and the Holy Communion. They are symbols of a status without a redemption. In view of this, how would you set about explaining to a Muslim the nature of Christian worship with its roots in history?

5. What perplexities or criticisms does Christian worship arouse in the average Muslim? How do you meet them?

6. "Prayer insures against evil" (Surah 29.45, lit. "wards off",

"interdicts", "forbids"). How, then, does one explain the state of the Pharisee in the Parable (Luke 18.11, 12)?

7. There are no tears in the mosque. Consider the rôle of Muslim worship in the Muslim qualities of fortitude and doggedness. Has anything been forfeited to achieve them?

8. How do the "times", or, in Christian language, the "hours", of prayer fare in the circumstances of the modern world, with shifts and schedules and time-tables? Is there a "spirit" that can be fulfilled when the "letter" is abandoned?

9. The Muslim has six "mosques" or points of prayer in his body: two palms, two knees, and two great toes. These support him in *sujud* or prostration. His walking and his working are thus with his kneeling. Any parable here? How do we get our mind, heart, and will, moving with and on our knees?

3

The Meaning of Ramadan

Our theme, like its predecessors, is ambitious. For who shall say what is the meaning of Ramadan? Shall we ask the aspirant after the ultimate degree of fasting, in which the fast is broken by any thoughts that concern other than God and his judgement and the world under both? Or shall we think in terms of the apprehensive concern of an ignorant woman who fears for an infraction of the fast because she cannot control a physical function which is traditionally within the *muftirat*, or things that invalidate Ramadan? Each have their place in this inclusive fourth pillar of religion in Islam. There are endless diversities of attitude between these two extremes.

Shall we follow the many traditions that hallow this time as a veritable fast from every kind of inward evil—from lust, from every intemperance of word and deed and desire, from slander, gossip, and envy, from ill-temper and arrogance? Or shall we assess the meaning of the fast in the languid yet easily provoked, half-sulky, half-apathetic, folk who wait in the shade of the evening sun for the gun that brings the food? Ramadan in truth means all these, according to how we elect to regard it. Is it essentially the body's endurance or the spirit's supremacy: the community in ritual conformity or the soul in disciplined command?

The questions in a way are academic, since the answer must be both. In this human world of flesh and blood, of body and spirit, there is no spiritual aspiration that does not require a physical demand. The perversions or depravities of the external and the bodily—the superstitious or superficial forms—are inseparable from the possibility of the valid and ennobling. The very means to man's expression of victory over his lower self can subtly become the victims of it, so that a fast becomes no more than an occasion of hunger, and the discipline that shaped it an irksomeness generating pride in the observing or weariness in the suffering. But such attitudes do not belong to a valid Ramadan.

Tested by its intention, they are features of the dangers from which no spiritual objective can be naturally immune and by which it may be overborne.

THE IMSAK OF RAMADAN

Let us find a clue through the wealth of detail, both of theory and of practice, concerning Ramadan by the help of an interesting term belonging with it, namely *Imsak*. Some two hours before the dawn of a Ramadan day, or less in some cases, a gun or other signal announces the time of the predawn meal with which the night closes. The predawn meal itself ends with another signal which introduces the daylong state of *Imsak*. "Holding", "withholding", "restraint", and perhaps even "tenacity" are all among the meanings or associations of this word. (Behind it lies a fruitful root. *Tamassuk*, a further derivative, means "grasp".) Combine the word "hold" with different prepositions and there are varieties of sense: hold off, hold on, hold to, uphold. Muslims do all these, at and in the fast. But first it would be right to study its hold or claim on them.

There are numerous Muslims, not least in Negro Africa, for whom Ramadan is much the most significant, and sometimes almost the only, attachment to Islam. While some moral theologians taught that it was the most spiritual of the pillars of religion because it was evident only to God himself, many ordinary people take it as the most evident form of allegiance. *Saum*, or fasting, is observed by some who have virtually no other outward allegiance to Islam, not even *Salat*. As an unmistakable social and communal institution, it provides some Muslims with their first and most ready expression of Muslim adherence. Islam in this way spreads as something done before it is something believed. It thus initiates into the other pillars.

For those also who are habitual and articulate Muslims Ramadan provides a potent visible reminder of their being such, and like any other "sacramental" thing focuses and fosters what they are, through what they do. The special Ramadan arrangement of the day and night, taking hold upon the most elemental business of life, namely food and drink, makes for intense corporate feeling. It is an immediate discriminator between those who are, and those who are not, within the whole. Christian faith has no such total and inclusive, outward and social, occasion of "belonging".

The hold of Ramadan goes back to its specific institution recorded in Surah 2.182–7, by which the traditional month of the Quran's first descent is honoured and by which also the Jewish, Christian precedents for fasting are pursued in distinctively Muslim form. The original Muslim ᶜAshuraᵓ, a sunset to sunset fast, on the Day of Atonement, was displaced, at least as the central expression of religious fasting, by a month-long dawn to sunset fast. It is interesting that in the Meccan Surahs the only reference to fasting is in Mary's vow (19.26). The ritual institution is Medinan.

Special sanctity attaches to this period. Ramadan itself was one of the sacred pre-Islamic months, at which time it always fell in summer—as may be judged from its name, which implies the scorching sun. Not only is there the hallowed *Lailat al-Qadr* of the beginning of the quranic *Tanzil*, but Surah 97.3–5 describes this time as one of angelic visitation and celestial peace on earth. Thus fasting is thirty times more meritorious during the month of Ramadan than when performed at any other time. Tradition has many benedictions on these twenty-nine days and hails them as a period in which the gates of hell are closed and those of heaven are opened wide.

The *Imsak* of Ramadan, its hold upon its people, has been well described of late in an article, "Le Ramadan au Caire, 1956".[1] The fast "bouleverse en effet tout le rythme de la vie individuelle et sociale. Même ceux qui ne jeûnent pas . . . n' échappent pas à son emprise." There are the special preparations of the merchants, the ceremonies having to do with the "sight" of the new moon, the excitement of the *ᶜId al-Fitr*, and the intensified emotion in which the children participate. Though Islam has little rôle for children prior to the age of discretion, save that of spectators, Ramadan strikes the imagination, in the lengthened hours of activity, the special sweets at night, the anticipation of the age of fasting, and some of the features of the Christian Christmas. Thereby it becomes a mighty portal into Islam for the oncoming generation. There are moreover all the factors related to the state of *Iᶜtikaf* (see Surah 2.187) or "being much in the mosque" for prayers and quranic recitation. Ramadan radio programmes and special visits by shaikhs to local mosques for instruction and recitation all contribute to the atmosphere of the month and give social and moral force to its observance.

[1] *Mélanges*, no. 3, pp. 1–75, by J. Jomier, O.P. and J. Corbon, P.B., Institut Dominicain d'Etudes Orientales du Caire. The quotation is from pp. 1–2.

Without attempting here any estimate of the total numerical incidence of fasting (which readers must do for themselves in their own locality—always being alert to the question of whether the sources from which they attempt even approximate judgements are representative) we may note that the virile persistence of Ramadan is itself a fact of great significance. For clearly the fast is a point of encounter between Islam and modern conditions. The old amalgam of fast and sleep which tended to characterize Ramadan days in pre-twentieth century times is not now generally feasible. The currents of contemporary life, of mechanized production, and technology, of politics, and the attitude to time, have all combined to make Ramadan a more strenuous business than when night could be turned into day without being too exacting on the day following.

THE IMSAK OF THE BODY

Against the background of these reflections on the hold of Ramadan as a Muslim institution, we must ask: What is the withholding of the body during these days? Specifically it is the cutting off of all intake into the body, whether food or drink, even to the extent of not even swallowing saliva, during the daylight hours of the month. Those exempted, other than children and aged, such as travellers, the sick, and nursing or pregnant women, must make good their omitted days, when the special circumstances end. The fast has been traditionally held to include also any unnatural intake such as medical injections, though the sense of the incompatibility of this with the real intention of the fast has more recently led to *fatwas* permitting them.

Strangely (to the stranger) Ramadan also traditionally includes certain physical functions in which the body gives rather than takes—vomiting (unless involuntary), sexual relations, and menstruation.

There can be no doubt that a strong "holding" of the body, a serious *Imsak*, is demanded by these provisions or prohibitions. A *Sahur* or pre-dawn meal and night food at the day's end, however festive, cannot blunt the force of these day-long privations. Nor does it aim to: the teaching is that these meals are not to be in such excess as might be calculated to soften the fast's rigours. He has not made a pure intention who tries physically to circumvent what he intends. The exactingness of Ramadan has especial force when the incidence of the

Muslim lunar calendar brings it into the height of summer.[1] But it is not the physical realities of the fast that are its ultimate meaning. They have their place—as the physical must in everything "sacramental". It is that to which their discipline points which is the real *Saum*.

Moreover, Ramadan ends. There is an *ᶜId al-Fitr* or Feast of the Breaking. Islam is not essentially ascetic, only purposively so. God is not over-exacting. It is vulgar and churlish to refuse the good things of nature—life, sex, appetite, and body—always provided these are regulated and proportioned. Islam, in its proper expression, is not Manichaean, has no rooted hatred of the body, and refuses to imitate the partisans of asceticism for asceticism's sake. All the meaning of Ramadan is unto the "thing signified".

THE IMSAK OF THE SOUL

The *Imsak*, as the term goes, inaugurates the day. It puts away the plates and cups, the pans and briques, and bids the body wait, wait, wait, until the evening. In the meantime it is educating and symbolizing the *Imsak* of the soul. Ramadan, you may say, is a parable in discipline. It is an acted subordination of the body and a practised authority over the soul. It is like the drill of a regiment, or the roll-call of a school, in which each takes stock of himself and confesses where he belongs in responding to whether he is present. In answering he is reminded that he is present "under authority".

The soul, then, is to rule the body: the body is to acknowledge itself the servant of the soul. Yet beyond this, which is the admitted teaching of all the Muslim theorists of Ramadan, is the soul's own discipline. For in a sense, even in voluptuousness or evil-doing, the body is subservient. The lustful eye, the sharp tongue, the lazy or aggressive body—all these are therein and thereby serving a soul that is indulging itself by these devices. Some sins, it is true, are almost wholly spiritual though few of them can be practised without some involvement of senses and members. But in either event the discipline of the soul is not attained merely by physical abstentions. "The inward man", a New Testament phrase for the meaning of which Ramadan has some relevance, must be concurrently controlled by his own sense of personal self-responsibility. Thus the fast is not truly kept if the

[1] In the present decade, Ramadan is retreating through the winter months, at least in the northern hemisphere.

only consequence is hunger. There must be a fast from the sins of the soul for which the body merely provides the instrument. If as instrument its docility and amenability are strengthened, the question of instrumentality for what becomes all the more urgent.

Ramadan in popular tradition is a time when the devils are chained and evil spirits held in check. This must be a parable of the restraining of the evil in the spirit of man—his self-seeking, his jealousy, his pettiness, his disloyalties to the good, and his proneness to the bad. In its characteristic way, Islam supposes that this worthy end of self-restraint in the hidden springs of action can be served by the means of ritual observance, *Ictikaf*, and the influence of quranic memoriter and traditional recital. Ramadan, in this sense, partakes of the general Muslim confidence in a "conditional" goodness of which man is capable—"conditional" in that it results from the acceptance and performance of the right conditioning factors. Of these Ramadan is perhaps the most obvious.

Here we come upon that very central Muslim concept of the *Niyyah* already briefly referred to. The doctrine of "intention" relates to all the pillars of religion. A confession of faith, without the deliberate focusing of attention upon it, is not valid. Nor is an act of *Zakat*, or a single *Salat*, or a performance of pilgrimage, unless they have been properly prefaced with this assertion of intendedness or sincerity. Likewise with each day of Ramadan. This necessity of the *Niyyah* in Islam should give pause to the outsider inclined to accuse Islam of ingrained externalism and formalism. For it is just these which the *Niyyah* has to exclude—though of course anything designed to make you real can be involved in unreality, like the man who could not remember what it was he ought not to have forgotten!

As well as the theme of the spiritual mastery of bodily needs and desires, another aspect of Ramadan and the soul of the Muslim is the sense of obedience to God that fulfilment mediates. To a degree all the pillars of religion in Islam serve as occasions in which the faithful may be aware of performing what God has required. Ramadan in this respect is perhaps the most evocative of such joy of achievement. Each night and the closing festival of the first of Shawwal bring this release of satisfaction which, though usually coupled with expressions of humility, exhilarates for its own sake and as a promise of the rewarding hope of Paradise. Ramadan prayers have frequent reference to the Garden.[1]

[1] See following chapter, "Prayers of Ramadan".

It would seem, however, that there is in general no very close or conscious connection in the minds of Muslims in Ramadan between the fast and the relation it might bear to sin and forgiveness. Though sin and pardon are frequent words, say Fathers Jomier and Corbon, "nous n'avons pas recontré de conference ou d'article entièrement consacrés au péché".[1] The pattern seems rather the other way round. The fast serves to focus, not so much a sense of sin as of satisfaction. It seems clear that the closing feast or *ᶜId al-Fitr* for many Muslims is an occasion of genuine accomplishment which, while physically and psychologically understandable, may contain within itself the seeds of self-approbation. In keeping Ramadan one has, with endurance and carefulness, fulfilled what one understands to be a divine demand. It would be more than human to subdue a consequent sense of being right and proper, of being, as it were, in ethical credit. Yet all such emotions, at least by Christian criteria, are dangerously invalid. We are never in a Christian relation if we suppose that our relationship with God has ceased to call primarily for repentance. It is of course true that all forms of religious "dutifulness", as Pharisaism so clearly shows, are open to this deadly danger of complacence. Perhaps to be forewarned is to be forearmed. But if the above quoted observation is typical, and if the year and the city observed are representative, it would appear that Ramadan is more an occasion of testing and of vindication after testing, than a sacramental focus of an abiding "undoneness" to which a seasonal outward recognition is brought. This leads into a final realm of study.

QUESTIONS THAT REMAIN

What should be the pattern of Christian relation to this *Imsak* of Ramadan? How, if the play on words may be allowed, are we to lay hold of this situation? It is clear that just as Ramadan is a great test of Muslim adherence and of Muslim supremacy over circumstances, so it is a big test of Christian relationship. It goes without saying that Christians will avoid any ostentatious or insensitive patterns of eating and drinking. Some have felt that, while asserting the freedom of the Christian man, it might well be within a Christian relation to experience the Ramadan fast-day as a token of alongsidedness and the will to take its measure. Some might by that means find a new realism in their

[1] Op. cit., p. 39.

assessments. But in the end the Christian relation to the meanings of Ramadan will turn upon the wise expression of certain insights—always remembering that Christ speaks to "those who have ears to hear".

The first issue is the ethical compromise of a *proud* performance of religious duty. This we have already anticipated. Evil in the human situation has a devious and subtle way of permeating even the fulfilment of the admitted good. The Pharisee's meticulous and exacting discharge of (legal) obligations makes him superciliously thankful that he is not like the Publican. This corrupts all his fastings. We should beware therefore of the inverted reproach of him which preens itself on being non-Pharisaical and proceeds to "thank God we are not as this Pharisee". The only remedy here is the acceptance of discipline and obligation with the recognition that no discharge of them suffices. The sense of unworthiness *within* our goodness is the only safeguard of their worth. This paradox it is, or should be, the responsibility of every religious system to understand and proclaim. If we can help Muslims to the force of it, it will be because the truth of the situation finds a kinship in their souls. The point is not, and cannot be, met in depreciation of the law of Ramadan, since the danger only arises when the fast is appreciated and discharged.

Akin to the above is the question which may be summed up in St Paul's call: "Mortify therefore your members" (Col. 3.5). His "therefore" takes the reader back to the redeeming events of the cross and the resurrection and to the vocation of the Christian to participate in the very pattern of his redemption, in the context of the ongoing work of hope, God's hope, in the soul of man. In other words the purposiveness of Christian self-control lies not alone in the impulse of law or legality, but in the setting of gratitude and the energies of divine love at work. This gratitude is the perspective that forbids self-righteousness: and grace is God's workshop of humility.

The fullest Muslim interpretation of Ramadan as a fast from evil deeds, from impurity of thought, from self-will, raises the question which, in one form or other, confronts all study of the Muslim concepts of man. Is "control" enough? Is "discipline" feasible? Can we achieve an *Imsak* that really holds the self in proper truth? God requires truth in the inward parts (Ps. 51.6). Is there not a sense in which the truth he requires *he* must also supply? So in Christian faith, man's "truth-in-being" is not achieved by the *Imsak* of man's self-discipline but rather by the *Imsak* that happens when Christ takes hold of man. Only the Indweller is adequate: discipline is no doubt one of the features of his rule, but not without him the ruler. In this sense, the New Testament proclaims a Gospel of which the call to self-discipline is a part within the wholeness of self-surrender to a personal saviour. Ideology, in the realm of the person, as in that of society, points to a need beyond itself. The more seriously we take the ideology, the more realistically must we proceed beyond it. This is the logic of Christian truth, as distilled, for example, into the experience of St Paul which stands as a central clue to New Testament meanings.

Belonging in Ramadan can be a figure of men's involvement with each other. The whole power and theme of the fast is communal. Men in Islam participate because they are "in Islam". This is a form of their membership and the fact that others, with strong communal sanction, are fulfilling it also both commands and fosters the individual's conformity. In a sense the realization that we live among fellows, among a common humanity, can become a force in the conquest of self-will. There is clearly an intimate connection between what the individual ought to do and the fact that he is part of a whole, a human whole. Ramadan recruits the second fact and makes it a sanction of the first. In a wider sense being with our fellow-men, not simply in a pattern of conformity but in an identity of love, should dictate our personal bodily existence. Like everything else in Islam, then, Ramadan can be a large occasion of that crisis which Christ brings into all religious form and fulfilment.

These four aspects of a Christian response to Ramadan will be illuminated by the contents of the prayer manual of the fast, translated in the next chapter. The petitions and the minds that feel and frame them must be set in the framework of liberation through Christ if we are to discern both their wistfulness and their constraint.

QUESTIONS FOR STUDY AND DISCUSSION

1. What is the Christian meaning of an unworthiness within goodness itself and of the "righteousness which is by faith"?

2. What is meant by the insistence that the fast is not real if hunger is its only consequence? How is this deeper implication ensured in the month and outside it?

3. What impressions has actual resident experience of Ramadan and the ᶜ*Id al-Fitr* left with you? Would they lead you to conclusions, both for analysis and relationship, different from those outlined here?

4. No (Christian) picnics during Ramadan is a rule or law (in Kuwait for example). What other duties, would you say, belong to an alert and sensitive Christianity in the month of fast?

5. "Blessed are they that hunger and thirst . . ." (Matt. 5.6). What is the full meaning of this Gospel beatitude? How might it relate to Ramadan and how might the relationship be shown and exemplified?

6. The fasting ordinance also brings problems of personal integrity, conformism, sincerity, to thinking Muslims. What is a proper Christian relation to Muslims who ignore, or who pretend, or who compromise, the fast, in the variety of their personal interpretations of what being a Muslim involves?

4

Prayers of Ramadan

If we are to discover Muslim devotion in its native quality it will best be by direct translation of its manuals. One such, published at Sidon, Lebanon, in A.H. 1349, or A.D. 1930, is *Mukhtasar Ad^{c}iyat Ramadan*, or selection of petitionary prayers for the fast.[1] In the rendering that follows, the temptation to abbreviate and exclude repetitive material has been, for the most part, resisted. For otherwise the reader would have less access to the emphases and preoccupations of the users. Only at a few points in the conclusion have reiterated phrases been elided, as also has the *Tasliyah*, or calling down of blessing upon the Prophet, after its first few occasions. It should be borne in mind that the manual is a *Shi^{c}ah* text and therefore in measure coloured by *Shi^{c}ah* prepossessions. But it is for that reason no less a mirror of the devout soul through the days of the sacred month.

In the name of God, the merciful Lord of mercy. Praise be to God, the Lord of the worlds. Praise and blessing be upon Muhammad and his people, noble and blessed.

These are the more important prayers for the blessed month published with vowelled letters so that the benefit of them may be the more widespread.

And may God prosper our purpose. In the name of God, the merciful Lord of mercy.

NIGHT PRAYERS

Opening Petition: to be recited each night of Ramadan.

O God, I begin my adoration with the praise of thee, for thine it is by thy gifts to direct me in the right way. I am truly persuaded that thou

[1] The translation, by the author, is reprinted from *The Muslim World*, vol. 47, no. 3, July 1957, pp. 210–23.

art the most merciful in all that relates to pardon and forgiveness, and the most fearful of punishers when it comes to retribution and requital of evil. Thou art most exalted in splendour and majesty.

O God, thou hast permitted me to call upon thee and to make request of thee. Then hear, O thou hearer, my praise. O most merciful, attend unto my prayer. Forgive my fault, O thou pardoning one. How many griefs, O God, hast thou freed me from; how many cares hast thou banished; how many evils hast thou brought to nought; how many mercies hast thou bestowed; what links of affliction hast thou broken.

Praise be to God, taking neither partner nor son, with whom there is no fellow in sovereignty and no patron condescending to him. Magnify him truly. Praise be to him for all that demands he should be praised, for all his benefits. Praise be to God, whom none can resist in his sovereignty and none contest in his authority. Praise be to God, alone in his creating and unapproached in his exaltedness. Praise be to God, whose command is manifested in his creation, whose honour is evident in grace and whose glory is seen in the outstretched hand of goodness: he whose storehouses never fail, whom excess of giving cannot enrich save in graciousness and splendour. For he is the all-powerful provider.

O God, I seek of thee a very little out of what is so vast—though my need thereof is great indeed, while thou, without it, art rich from of old. With me it is a great thing but for thee it is a simple trifle. O God, (it is) thy pardon for my transgression, thy forbearance for my sin, thy mercy for my wrongdoing, thy covering of my unworthy deeds, thy indulgence for my multiplied iniquity, whether done in error or knowingly. Let me have boldness in beseeching thee for what I have no right to seek from thee, who hast bestowed upon me thy mercy and shown to me thy power and hast caused me to know thy attentiveness unto me.

Here I am taking upon me to call upon thee believingly. Unafraid I pray unto thee, awaiting thy favour, looking unto thee in respect of those things which I have purposed. And if they have been too slow for me and I have been discontented with thee in my ignorance, what seemed slow to me was truly better for me, as seen in the light of thy knowledge of the issue of things.

I know no gracious patron more patient with an unworthy servant than thou hast been with me, O Lord. Thou callest and I, replying, make thee my Lord. Thou dost endear thyself unto me even though I make myself hateful unto thee. Thou comest unto me in love and, as if I were weary of thee, I do not respond unto thee. Yet all that has not prevented thy having mercy upon me, nor from being gracious unto me and favouring me with thy kindly goodness. Then forgive thine ignorant servant and be kindly unto him, according to thy tender goodness, O thou gracious and compassionate.

Praise be to God, sovereign Lord, author of the universe, who raisest the winds and orderest the morning, who art worshipped in religion and Lord of the worlds. Praise be to God for his forbearance when he knows all. Praise be to God for his pardon though he be all powerful. Praise be to God for his long suffering in displeasure, though he is well able to do all he chooses. Praise be to God, Lord of creation, source of all livelihood, who orders the morning, Lord of majesty and honour, of grace and beneficence, he who is so far that he may not be seen and so near that he witnesses the secret things. Blessed be he and for ever exalted.

Praise be to God, he has no competitor to equal him and no peer to compare with him, and no helper to aid him. With his might he subdues the mighty and by his greatness the great are humbled.[1] Whatever he wills, by his power he attains. Praise be to God who hearkens unto me when I call upon him, covers my unworthiness when I have been rebellious, and magnifies his grace upon me: I will not more transgress. How many a joyous gift has he bestowed upon me, against how many a great and fearful thing has he protected me, how many a delightsome pleasure has he shown me. I will sing unto his praise and make mention of him in thanksgiving.

Praise be to God whose veil is never rent, whose door is never barred, who repels none who seek him, nor disappoints their hope. Praise be to God who preserves those who fear him, delivers the faithful and the welldoers, lifts up those that are despised and sets down the arrogant, who causes things to perish and replaces them by others. Praise be to God who destroys the mighty and brings the ungodly to an end, who lays hold of the fugitives and punishes the reprobates. He it is unto whom the pleaders cry aloud, he is the place of the petitioners' need and the reliance of believers.

[1] It is interesting to note here the strange identity of thought between this paragraph and the next with the *Magnificat*: "He hath put down . . ." etc. It is idle, however, to speculate on the source of the likeness.

Praise be to God in awe of whom the heavens thunder with their inhabitants, while the earth and her habitable hamlets quake and the seas rage with all that swims within them. Praise be to God, who creates and was not created, who sustains and was not sustained, who nourishes and yet was not nourished, who brings the living to death and the dead to life. He is the living one, who dies not. In his hand is good and he is mighty over all.

O Lord, send down blessing upon Muhammad, thy servant, thy messenger, thy faithful, chosen and beloved one, the choicest of thy creation who holds thy secret and makes known thy message. He is most beautiful, perfect, sagacious, honourable, pure, and exalted. Send down blessings, more than thou hast blessed or mercied or favoured or greeted any other of thy servants, thy prophets and apostles, thy chosen ones, the gracious among thy creation.

O God, send down blessing upon Ali, commander of the believers and appointed one of the apostles of the Lord of the worlds, thy servant and thy protégé, the brother of thy messenger and the manifest sign to thy creation, thy great token, thy glorious proclamation, and thy straight path.

Send down blessings also upon Fatimah, his pure companion, the most honourable lady, queen of the worlds, and send down blessing upon the two grandsons of mercy, the two Imams of true guidance, Hasan and Husain, the two lords of the youth of the people of Paradise, from among the whole creation.

Send down blessing upon the Imams of the Muslims (here are recited the names of eight Imams following Husain) and the successor Al-Mahdi who are thy signs upon thy servants and faithful ones in thy realm. Send down blessing, O Lord, plentifully and perpetually, and bless the trustee of thy command, the one who is the hope of men, the just one, the expected. Surround him with thy protecting angels who draw near unto thee and aid him with thy holy spirit, O thou Lord of the worlds.[1]

O God, let him be one calling to thy book and performing thy religion. Grant him to succeed in the earth, just as thou didst bring into the succession those who preceded him. Establish unto him his religion

[1] The reference is to the Hidden Imam for whose appearance Shiʿahs look at the end of time to inaugurate the Judgement. Theories have differed sharply as to what happens after the Hasan here named and the status, past and to be, of the Mahdi who followed him.

in which thou hast made him to find joy. Grant him security instead of fear, that he may worship thee and never associate with thee anything. O God, make him strong and a means to strength. Grant him victory and make him to be victorious. Bring him through triumphantly, grant him a ready and manifest conquest, and bestow upon him victorious authority. O God, make manifest through him thy religion and the path of thy prophet, so that he may not conceal aught of thy truth, out of fear of any within thy creation.

O God, our desire is unto thee, that thou wilt grant unto us a gracious government by means whereof thou mayest bring strength to Islam and its people and bring low hypocrisy and the hypocrite. Grant us, therein, to be among those who are called to thy obedience, leaders in thy way, that thou mayest enrich us therein with the good things of this world and the next.

O God, whatsoever of the truth thou hast caused us to know, lay it upon us as a charge and, wherever we have come short of it, bring us unto it. O God, by the same truth, order our disorder, repair our fragmentations, and reconcile our disunity. Increase, thereby, that in which we have little, and strengthen our abased condition, enrich our poverty, settle our debts, make good our privations, provide for our destitution, make easy our difficulties, and thereby also cause our countenances to be radiant. Loosen our captivity, prosper our petitions, make good in fulfilment our pledges, and hear our prayers. Grant unto us our request and cause us to attain our hopes both here and hereafter. Bestow upon us, O Lord, beyond our deserving, for thou art the beneficence of the seekers and the most bountiful of bestowers. Heal our hearts thereby and take away their wrath. Guide us unto the truth which is therein brought forth by thy will. For thou guidest whom thou wilt into a straight path. Grant us victory thereby, over thy enemy and ours, O thou God of truth. Amen.

O God, I complain unto thee of the absence of our prophet, the withdrawness from us of our leader, the number of our enemy, the fewness of our numbers, the intensity of the plots against us, and the way in which the times seem to be against us. Send down blessing upon Muhammad and his people. Aid us against all these things with speedy victory from thyself, by a triumph thou shalt bring to pass, by the authority of truth manifested by thee and by the mercy wherewith thou wilt cause us to be prospered and by the strength with which thou wilt clothe us through thy compassion, thou most merciful of all.

Pray also this prayer:

O God, I ask of thee, in thy decree and determining within the irreversible command, to bring it about by thy wise ordering, as something that will neither be revoked nor changed, that thou write me among the pilgrims to thy house, the sacred and inviolable. Thankful is their pilgrimage: unto forgiveness is their endeavour, their misdeeds and iniquities being pardoned them. Grant also within thy decree and determination, the lengthening of my years, in blessedness, mercy, and enlarging favour. Render me among those through whom thou makest thy religion victorious and do not let me be supplanted by another. Send down blessing, O God, upon Muhammad and all his people.

Pray also this prayer:

O my God, the petitioners stand before thy gate and the needy seek refuge in thy courts. The ship of the wretched stands on the shore of the ocean of thy grace and goodness, seeking passage into the presence of thy mercy and compassion. O my God, if, in this blessed month, thou forgivest only those whose fasting and performance is right, who will take the part of the transgressor in his defaulting, when he perishes in the sea of his transgressions and sins? O my God, if thou art merciful only towards the obedient, who will take the part of the rebellious? If thou receivest only those who have done well, what then of those who have fallen short?

O my God, those who fast have surely gained, the faithful doers triumph, and the sincere are delivered. But we, thy guilty servants, have mercy upon us out of thy compassion. Liberate us from damnation by thy pardon, forgive us our trespasses and with us the rest of the believers, men and women, through thy mercy, O thou most faithful. Send down blessing, O God, upon Muhammad and his people.

Pray also this prayer:

O God, by thy mercy towards those who do rightly, bring us in and exalt us among the inhabitants of heaven. Grant us to drink from a cup of the celestial fountain: grant us marriage with the fair-eyed ones and let us be served by the immortal ones who are like unto hidden pearls. Feed us with the flesh of birds and with the fruits of Paradise. Clothe us with garments of brocade, silk, and gold embroidery. Grant us the blessings of the night of power and of pilgrimage to thy house. Grant us to fight, with him who is thy representative, in the path of thy cause. Hearken unto us in what is worthy in our petitions and prayers. O thou Creator, hear and answer us and when thou gatherest all together, the first and the last, on the day of resurrection, then have mercy upon us. Write down for us a release from the fire and safe keeping from torment. Cause us not to fall into hell and cut us not off in retribution and damnation from thee. Feed us not from the bitter *Zaqqum* and *Dari*ᶜ.[1] Let us not be among the devils nor make us to be cast upon our faces in the fire, nor clothed in the garments of fire and of the *Qatiran*.[2] Deliver (us), O God, from every evil thing, O thou who truly art God alone. There is none save thee. Amen.

Pray also this prayer:

I seek refuge in the majesty of thy gracious countenance. May this month of Ramadan not pass, nor the dawn of this night of mine break, while thou hast before thee any deed or guilt of mine for which thou dost requite me.

PRAYERS FOR THE LAST TEN NIGHTS OF RAMADAN

1. O God, send down blessings upon Muhammad and his people. Grant or apportion unto me a vision which will close up for me the door of ignorance. Bestow upon me guidance from every error; wealth that will bar the door to all poverty; strength whereby thou wilt remove from me all weakness; power whereby thou wilt ennoble me above all unworthiness. Grant me also the exaltation by which I may be lifted above humiliation; the security to repel from me every fear; mercy whereby to be defended from all calamity; knowledge to open unto me all certainty; and certainty to banish all doubt. Grant me that prayer by which thou mayest extend unto me, on this night of Ramadan and at this hour, a gracious answer, O thou who art kindly. Give me that awe whereby thou wilt bring me all mercy, and a protecting virtue between me and my transgressions, so that I may

[1] *Al-Zaqqum* is the bitter tree of hell, which bears galling fruit (Surah 56.52); *Al-Dari*ᶜ no animal will eat. A foul, stunted growth, it is the symbol of frustration and despair, and contrasted with the luscious fruit-bearing trees of Paradise.

[2] The original is *Sarabil al-qatiran*, "shirts (?) of resinous pitch". *Qatiran* is a brown, viscous liquid, derived from trees, and very combustible. The sense of the petition is clear—escape from fiery damnation (cf. Surah 14.50).

prosper thereby and be among those who enjoy security with thee, by thy mercy, O thou most merciful.

2. O thou aid of those who seek refuge, send down blessing upon Muhammad and the people of Muhammad. Be unto me a fortress and a sure haven, O thou shelter of those who have recourse unto thee. Send down blessing upon Muhammad and the people of Muhammad. Be unto me a shelter and a succour and a helper, O thou who comest to the aid of those who cry unto thee in need. Send down. . . . Be unto me a hiding place and a champion, O thou Lord of the believers. Send down. . . . Be thou unto me a sovereign, O thou who savest the believers from overwhelming sorrows. Send down. . . . Aid my sorrow and cheer my grief, make me glad in this great month with a happiness that will have no sequel of wretchedness for me, O thou most merciful.

3. O God, extend my years, enlarge my livelihood, make healthy my frame, bring to pass my hope. If I have been written down among the wretched, blot out my place with the wretched and write me down among the blessed. For thou annihilatest what thou wilt and what thou wilt thou establishest. With thee is the Mother of the Book (the dossier of decrees?). O God, upon thee do I rely in my need this night. From thee I have accepted my poverty and lowliness that the night may enlarge me, through thy mercy and thy pardon. I have more hope in thy mercy than I have in what I do. For thy forgiveness and thy compassion are more ample than my transgressions. Do thou supply my every need as is good for me and acceptable unto thee, by virtue of thine ability so to do, seeing it is so easy for thee. For verily I shall find no good whatsoever save from thee. None other than thou will ever rid me of evil. My hope for my religious duty-done, for my place in this world and the next, for the day of my destitution and abasement and the day I lie in the grave, and people are sundered from me, is not in what I have done. My hope is none other save thou, O Lord of the worlds.

4. O God, O my Lord, I beseech thee, as one who is poor and needy, who fears and supplicates thee; I beseech thee my Lord, to send down blessing upon Muhammad and his people and to protect me from disgrace in this world and from retribution in the next, to double unto

me that which I do this night and during this month. Have mercy upon my dwelling place and protect me from the punishment of those things which thou hast reckoned against me, the things which are concealed from thy servant and which thou, of thy mercy towards me, hast veiled from me, delivering me from their shame and disgrace and reproach in this transitory world. Unto thee be praise for this mercy. In every circumstance, I beseech thee, O Lord, to send down blessing upon Muhammad and his people and to fulfil upon me thy grace, under the protecting shield thereof, in the world to come. Save me from shame and disgrace by thy favour unto me, O thou of all most merciful.

5. O God, I pray thee to make complete according to my finest hopes the reward of thy mercy. Rid me of all that is evil. Verily I cannot ward off the things I must beware of, save by thee. Indeed I have come to be like a mortgaged man by the things which I have done and the disposition rests in thy hands. There is no suppliant more beggarly than I. So send down blessing upon Muhammad and the people of Muhammad and pardon me my wrongdoing, my ignorance, my deserts, my follies, and every transgression that I have committed. Cause me to attain my inheritance without toilsome obstacles. Do not let me perish in body or soul in seeking anything that is not decreed for me, O thou of all most merciful.

6. O God, thou hast warned peoples by the mouth of thy prophet (may the blessing of God be upon him and his people). Thou didst say: "Say: 'Call upon those whom ye claim to be gods beside him, they are powerless to deliver you from harm or to turn it aside.'" (Surah 17.56.) O thou who alone art able to turn away evil from us and avert it send down blessing upon Muhammad and his people. Alert me to anything that may harm me and avert it from me. During this great month cause me to pass from the shame of transgression to the strength of obedience, O thou of all the most merciful.

7. O God, grant me to be preserved from the house of evil and selfishness unto the abode of immortality. Grant me a readiness for death before the time arrives. O God, I beseech thee and call upon thee solemnly by every name of thine that any of thy creatures have ever named thee by, or by which, in the knowledge of the unseen as it is

with thee, thou hast ever been invoked. I call upon thee by the greatest name that is most truly thine, that thou answer him who thereby calls upon thee. Send down . . . and make me happy this night with a happiness that hereafter I shall never find turned to wretchedness, O thou of all most merciful.

8. O God, I pray thee to send down . . . and to grant unto me a reverent heart, a sincere tongue, and a patient flesh and add the reward of Paradise thereto, O thou of all the most merciful.

9. Enrich me, O Lord, with an ample inheritance by thy majesty and inviolability. Grant me soberness of body and pleasure. Relieve me of all stress and strain. Let not my enemy rejoice over me. Make the night of power to be a blessing unto me, even as one of thy creation saw it, let it be blessed to me as thou didst bless it to him, Muhammad and his people. Upon him and them be peace. [Here follows a directive for the reiteration of petition.]

10. O God, Lord of the month of Ramadan and sender down of the Quran, this month of Ramadan is at its end. O Lord, I seek refuge in thy gracious countenance that the dawn beyond this night may not break nor this month of Ramadan pass with any guilt or transgression, for which thou wouldest punish me on the day I meet thee, unforgiven by thee through thy kindliness and goodness, O thou most merciful. O God, send down . . . for thou art glorious, worthy of praise.

PRAYERS AT THE DAY-BREAK

Pray this prayer which is the prayer of Invocation.

O God, I call upon thee by thy majesty at its most radiant, for every splendour of thine is truly splendid; O God, I call upon thee by thy entire glory; O God, I call upon thee by thy beauty at its most beautiful; O God, I call upon thee by thy complete beauty. (This formula is repeated using an almost constant pattern of a descriptive noun, superlatively understood, affirmed to be veritably so and inclusively pleaded, with the following sequence of nouns and the derivative superlatives—majesty: greatness: light: mercy: word: perfection: names: might: will: power: knowledge: speech: honour: authority:

rule: exaltedness: favour and signs. These sentences are here abbreviated into this list for reasons of space. In the centre of the sequence is the phrase "All things suppliant unto thee are beloved of thee, so O God I call upon thee by all things suppliant unto thee".)

O God, I call upon thee by that which thou art, in power and greatness, calling upon thee severally by every element of that power and greatness. I ask thee these things, O God, in the name of that wherewith thou dost answer me when I call upon thee, O God. Do with me . . . so and so . . .

(Plead your needs here: it shall indeed be done if God wills.)

THE LITTLE DAY-BREAK PRAYER

It is well to use this prayer at the day-break after every night in Ramadan.

O thou who art my stay in trouble, O thou my companion in distress, my friend in well-being, thou who aidest me in my desire, thou art he who covers my disgrace and secures my fears and annuls my faults. Pardon my sins, O God. I pray thee for the reverence of faith rather than the reverence of abasement in the fire, O thou sole God, thou one alone, thou ever-subsisting, thou who begettest not nor art begotten, thou who hast no equal, thou who givest to him that asks of thee out of compassion and mercy and initiates good even for him who has not asked it of thee, out of thy goodness and in conformity to thy perpetual grace. Send down blessing upon Muhammad and the people of his household. Grant me a wide and inclusive mercy, whereby I may attain unto the good of this world and of the world to come.

O God, I seek thy forgiveness for those things which I have repented of before thee and then have returned back to them. I seek thy forgiveness for every good deed wherein I have sought thy face and things unworthy of thee mixed themselves in therewith (Or: What was not unto thee compromised me therein). Send down . . . and forgive my wrongdoing and my evil by thy long suffering and gracious favour, O thou kindly Lord, whose suppliant is not disappointed and whose benefits fail not, thou who art exalted above all, who art so near that there is none nearer than thee. Send down . . . and have mercy upon me, O thou who dividest the sea for Moses.

O God, cleanse my heart from hypocrisy and my actions from evil, my tongue from lying, my eye from deceit, for thou knowest the things that deceive the eye and what men's bosoms hide. O Lord, this is the standing of one who seeks refuge with thee from the fire, from the danger of the fire, asking thy succour against the fire. It is the standing [this phrase is repeated after each plea but is not translated here every time] of one who flees unto thee from the fire acknowledging his sins, confessing his transgression, and repenting of his sin unto his Lord. This is the standing of a poor and despairing soul, of one who fears and pleads for help of the sorrowful and distressful. It is the standing of the troubled and harassed spirit, of the stranger who is overwhelmed, of the desolate and lonely, of him who can find none to forgive his evil-doing save thou, who has none save thee to refresh him in tribulation, nor any to strengthen him in weakness save thou, O gracious God. Let me not burn in the fire after my worship of thee and my abasement before thee as one who has no merit of himself. Thine, rather, is the praise, the honour and the goodness that come to me.

Say, as long as one can:

Have mercy, O Lord, O Lord, O Lord. . . .

Then with a new breath say:

For my weakness, the poverty of my powers, the worthlessness of my person, the dissipation of my members, the sickness of my flesh and body, my whole being and my solitariness in the grave, my grief at the least calamity—I beseech thee O Lord to grant me consolation and blessedness on the day of sorrow and regret. Let my face, O Lord, be white on that day when men's faces are black. Preserve me on the day of awful dread. I ask of thee gladness on the day when men's hearts and eyes are downcast, gladness at the time when the world is sundered. Praise be to God upon whom I call. Unto none other do I have recourse. If I did invoke any save he, verily my prayer would fail.

Praise be to God in whom I hope. My hope is in no other. Were my hope elsewhere it would be denied. Praise be to God who deals in grace and goodness and bestows beauty and grace. He is the Lord of majesty and honour, Master of all mercy and sovereign over all that is worthy. He fulfils every desire and supplies every need. O God, send down . . . and grant me assurance and a good hope in thee. Establish what I long for in my heart and cut off any hope of mine that is in any save thyself, that I look unto none beside thee and have no confidence outside of thee, for thou art kindly in what thou willest. Deal graciously with me in everything, according to thy will and pleasure.

O Lord, truly I am weak: torment me not in the fire. O Lord, be merciful unto my prayer and my entreaty, unto my fear and low estate, upon my wretchedness and my seeking of refuge and shelter. O Lord, I am too weak to seek the world to come but thou art of wide compassion. By thy power, might, and riches, I beseech thee, O Lord, by my very need thereof, to grant me in this year and month of mine, in this day and hour of mine, thy goodly favour, whereby I may be independent of things right and good given by thee into the hands of others.

O Lord, thee it is I implore: unto thee is my desire: in thee is my hope. Thou art worthy that it should be so. I have hope in none save thee: I will have no other confidence, O thou most merciful. O Lord, I have indeed wronged my soul. Forgive me, therefore, and have mercy upon me. Pardon me, O thou who hearest every voice and gatherest all that passes away, O thou who dost recreate souls after death, whom darkness hides not, whom no voice can mistake, whom nothing can preoccupy and distract. Grant unto Muhammad . . . the best of his request unto thee, of what is asked for him and is sought of thee on his behalf until the day of resurrection.

Grant me health that may prosper my livelihood and seal me with thy blessing, lest transgressions ruin me. O God, make me glad with the portion I have from thee that I seek nought of anyone. O God, send down . . . and open unto me the storehouses of thy mercy. Have mercy upon me with an irreversible mercy both in this world and in the world to come. Grant unto me, of thy wide grace a sweet and valid blessing, by virtue of which I will hereafter be beholden to none save thee, causing me to grow thereby in thankfulness. Grant me poverty and destitution unto thee and in thee, the capacity to abstain and to withhold from all save thee, O thou who doest well and makest beautiful, thou fount of goodness and favour, who reignest and rulest in power. Suffice me with all that is necessary and supply me with good things. Bless me in all my affairs and grant me all things needful.

O God, make easy unto me those things the difficulty of which I fear. It is an easy and ready thing for thee to do so. Make convenient for me the griefs I am afraid of and dispel the troubles I fear, ridding me of toilsomeness and calamity, O thou of all the most merciful. Fill my heart with love toward thee, with awe of thee and with acceptance of the truth of thy book, with faith and detachment unto thee and longing for thee, Lord of majesty and honour. O God, thine are the things that are right, bestow them upon me, O God, and as for the consequences that result from those who came before me, let me not be made to bear them. For I have done my duty in hospitality to every guest. I am thy guest, let my guest-portion this night be Paradise, O thou whose it is to bestow Paradise, thou Lord of forgiveness. There is neither power nor might save in thee.

ANOTHER PRAYER TO BE RECITED AT DAY-BREAK

(*It is said that Hasan, son of the beloved, used this as a daybreak prayer.*)

O thou my succour in trouble, my help in adversity, I seek refuge in thee; of thee I ask aid; unto thee do I have recourse and unto none other. Of none else do I ask for rest save of thee. Do thou then succour and relieve me. O thou who passest over what is slight and pardonest what is grievous, receive of me the little and forgive the great, O thou merciful pardoner.

O God, I seek of thee a faith with which my heart may be occupied and a true assurance that I may know nothing will befall me save what thou hast ordained for me. Make me content with that life thou hast determined for me, O thou most merciful of all, my refuge in my need, thou my companion in distress, my patron in grace, my succour in my desire. Thou it is who coverest my misdeeds and preservest my spirit, who dost blot out my faults. Forgive me my sin, O thou most merciful.

PRAYERS OF THE DAYTIME

To be recited every day of Ramadan after the prayer of the Prophet, upon whom with his people be peace and blessing.

O God, bring happiness to those in the tombs, make rich every poor man; O God, satisfy with food every hungred; O God, clothe every naked one, settle the debt of every debtor, relieve every distressed one, bring back every stranger. O God, liberate every exile, reform everything that corrupts the affairs of Muslims. O God, heal all who are sick, supply our poverty from thy riches, transform our evil case with good of thine, set us free from debt, and enrich us so that we be no more poor, for thou art mighty unto all things.

Pray also as follows:

O God, this is the month of Ramadan in which thou hast sent down the Quran as a guidance to men—manifest signs of guidance and the *Furqan*.[1] This is the month of the fast, the month of performance. This is the month of coming back unto thee, of repentance, forgiveness, and mercy. This is the month of deliverance from the fire and of the gaining of Paradise. In this month is the night of power, which alone is better than a thousand months. O God, send down . . . and make me careful of the fast and its fulfilment. Preserve it unto me and I therein. Aid me also with thy most gracious help and prosper me therein unto the obedience of thee and of thy prophet and thy favoured ones. In this month let me be free of cares that I may worship thee and call upon thee and that I may read thy book. Give me therein a mighty blessing: make good unto me the issues (of Ramadan) and preserve me in repentance. Grant me now health of body; increase me in riches; set a term to the things that trouble me. In this month hearken unto me when I call, that I may attain my hope and aspirations.

Banish from me drowsiness and sloth, weariness and languor, hardness, negligence, and heedlessness. Here let me find escape from disease, sickness, trouble, sorrow, obstacles, sins, and transgressions. Here banish from me evil, shame, fatigue, calamity, pride, and hardship.

Thou art the hearer of prayer. O God, send down. . . . Defend me from the accursed Satan, his madness and devices, his blasts and enchantments, his whisperings and assaults, his crafts and wiles, his diversions and snares, his deceits and desires, his ambushes and emissaries, his polytheism, partisans and followers, his dissidents, leaders, partners, and companions, and all his tricks. O God, send down. . . .

[Here follow prayers in the sense of the above for a good fast and a prospered pilgrimage.]

Let there be no obstacle between me and those blessings, nor any sickness, distress, strain, trouble, negligence, forgetfulness, but rather mutual concord and fidelity unto thee and in thee, following thy truth and fulfilling thy covenant and promise according to thy mercy, O thou most merciful. Let the best of what thou decreest for thy loyal servants be mine this Ramadan: bestow upon me mercy and unending forgiveness, health, pardon, and compassion, grace that hearkens, release from the fire, the triumph of Paradise, and the good of both

[1] One of the titles the Quran uses of itself, meaning "the criterion, the touchstone of truth, that by which all valid distinctions are known" (cf. Surahs 2.185; 3.4, and 25.1).

worlds, more than thou bestowest upon the foremost of thy servants who draw near unto thee.

[There follow several pages of reiterated petition on the same pattern, the translation of which is not here reproduced for reasons of space. The section ends with the following paragraphs.]

Our desire is unto thee, O God; thine are the beautiful names and the exalted attributes, the supremacy is thine, the glory and grace. I call upon thee in the name of the merciful and compassionate. Be pleased on this night, wherein the angels and the spirit came down, to send down blessing . . . and to set my name tonight among the blessed and my spirit among the faithful and my good deeds in the high heavens, let my evil deeds be forgiven. Grant me assurance to rejoice my heart and a faith no doubt can compromise, and satisfaction with my portion from thee. Bring unto me here and hereafter good things and preserve me from the torment of the fire (repeated).

Rouse thine anger this night, for the sake of Muhammad and the righteous ones, his family. Slay their enemies with might; count their number and leave none upon the face of the earth; never forgive them, O thou best of lords, thou Caliph of the prophets. Thou art the merciful, the original, the glorious, the unmatched, the abiding, the never-negligent, the living, the undying. Every day thou art at work. Thou art the Caliph of Muhammad, giving him victory and granting him blessing. I ask thee to prosper his deputy and successor and him who holds the right among his loyal ones. Grant him and them all victory, O thou who art God alone. There is none save thou. Make me to be with them in this world and the next and may thy forgiving mercy rest upon all that I will, O thou most merciful.

5

Zakat and our Neighbour

"A Dieu foy: aux amis foyer." So runs an intriguing inscription over the fireplace of the old medieval castle at Farnham, Surrey. "For God a heart; for friends a hearth" might be a ready English venture on the French. Faith in God must in some sense be a hospitality to man. Hence the unity of the twofold commandment of love to God and love to neighbour, the one in and because of the other. *Zakat* is the pillar of Islam which, as a social and religious institution, embodies in economic manward form the outward obligation of belief in God.

Though the inter-penetration of the Godward and the manward has always been admitted, the range and intensity have varied. Or in other terms, the significance of "our neighbour" receives ambiguous definition. Hence, no doubt, the lawyer's question: "And who is my neighbour?" which found answer in the parable of man, priest, levite, and Samaritan en route from Jerusalem to Jericho. "Every living creature loveth his like" says Ecclus. 13.15, "and every man loveth his neighbour." Here the implication is that neighbour presupposes kin—a conclusion that seems to be corroborated when the same writer observes elsewhere: "The mercy of a man is upon his neighbour, but the mercy of the Lord is upon all flesh" (Ecclus. 18.13). Yet in this very contrast is the hint that may transform the whole. For as men learn the God of all flesh there is the claim that their neighbour also may be seen in all flesh. So it is that whereas in Lev. 19.18 the injunction, "Thou shalt love thy neighbour as thyself" is linked with "Thou shalt not bear any grudge against the children of thy people", in our Lord's parable it becomes the positive obligation to serve all men according to their need. So the meaning of "neighbourness", as in the Samaritan story, becomes a kind of reciprocal humanity and the very term is interchangeable. The victim is taken as "neighbour" by the compassionate, and the rescuer plays "neighbour" to the stricken stranger.

The form and range of these inter-human duties as arising from the sovereignty of God are the theme of *Zakat*, the third pillar on which Islam rests. Our most profitable approach to the study of its place and meaning will be in this setting of the sense of God and the sense of the neighbour. For it is as a divine behest, within a structure of obligation, that *Zakat* exists for the Muslim. And it is central to social ideology in the Islamic world.

ZAKAT AND EARLY ISLAM

Like several other institutions of early Islam, *Zakat* can be traced back into the *Jahiliyyah*, or pre-Islamic time. Al-Bukhari relates a tradition in which a new adherent of Islam asked the Prophet if his practice of almsgiving in his pagan past would still be reckoned to him after his embrace of the faith. The answer was in the affirmative. Certainly the acceptance of the obligation of alms, or poor rate, belonged with *Salat*, or worship, as marking entry into the new religion. (See Surah 2.43, 83, 110, 177, 277, *et al.*) Deliberate rejection of it was tantamount to idolatry (Surah 41.7).

It is probably fair to link the Islamic form of alms with the early circumstances of the Muslim community, which, as is well-known, was a relatively despised and economically depressed group. Surah 11.28 describes a similar circumstance in Noah's day which is no doubt a significant parallel. Thus there was both great need for, and incentive to, mutual help. This may well be reflected, for example, in Surah 76.7 and 8, where the godfearers "give food to the distressed, the orphan, and the captive, out of love for God, feeding them for God's sake only, and desiring neither reward nor thanks".

The Hijrah also, focal as it is in Islamic formation, can be seen as an event within *Zakat*, in that it turned upon the hospitality of Medinan Muslims, the *Ansar*, who re-propertied the emigrant *Muhajirun* on their arrival and in the ensuing months. A virtue so crucial to the very survival of Islam and exemplified in its pivotal event passed in that way most appropriately into the structure of Islamic ideology. It was not, of course, by Medinan *Zakat* alone that the losses of the emigrants were made good. But at least they had in the heart of their history an exemplification of a principle central to their economic life.

When the dual community of *Ansar* and *Muhajirun* in Medina became stronger and more affluent, the logic of the same economic solidarity was extended to those "whose hearts were ready to be won over". In Surah 9.60 a list occurs of the proper recipients of alms, set out to silence complaining or defamatory criticism about its distribution. These are: "the poor, the distressed, the officials engaged in alms collection, near or intending adherents, captives for their ransom, and wayfarers", and also any purpose covered in the wide and general phrase: *fi sabil Illah*, "in the way of God". Similar categories are mentioned in Surah 2.177 with the addition of the near of kin, orphans, and beggars (cf. also 2.215).

Zakat had thus an intimate place in the development of the community. Receipt of it from new believers sealed and confessed their allegiance. "Take alms of their wealth", the Prophet was directed, "whereby thou mayest purify them and mayest make them to grow and mayest pray for them" (Surah 9.103). Evidently the benefit of the Prophet's intercession and even of interview with him (see Surah 58.13), as well as the general advantages of participation, turned upon this material commitment.

But at times the significance of *Zakat* operated the other way. Much has been written on precisely what is implied by the recipience of alms on the part of those who were minded to confess allegiance. The well-disposed among the pagans might become even more so by tangible experience of the brotherhood of Islam. A judicious generosity was calculated to turn the scales. Bounty which had derived from God could thus be properly utilized "in his way". Better to induce surrender than to battle for it. Mutual help might well anticipate the final decision, the more so as afterwards it was to be its pattern.

The long section of Surah 2 which deals with *Zakat* insists that payment should be neither grudging nor disparaging. It should not be done to "be seen of men". Nor should it be niggardly. God will certainly requite the unworthy, ostentatious giver with penury, but the true alms-payers, especially the secret ones, will be like a well-watered garden and their alms will atone for their evil deeds. The same passage (2.263–77) links the praise of *Zakat* with the condemnation of usury, as if to say that in a society fully permeated with genuine *Zakat*, usury would be eliminated. Usury means taking personal advantage of another's extremity, whereas *Zakat* means its relief at one's own cost. Over all must stand the fear of God. They give of their substance "who are fearful of a day the evil whereof is near at hand" (76.7).

Since paying *Zakat* was always a mark of being Muslim, a privilege for those within Islam, or about to be, it may be asked how far *receiving* it was also limited to Muslims. The phrase about paying *Zakat* to intending adherents seems to imply that it was not generally available for those who stayed outside Islam. The general categories of needy and destitute presumably covered non-Muslims, since they all shared the common Arabian setting, and this is implied in the very idea that help from alms might be an inducement. But, at least as far as the Quran is concerned, *Zakat* is within and not beyond the community of faith. It must be seen as one of the major factors in the cohesion, the early survival and the ultimate triumph, of the first Muslims in their tale of the two cities. What remained as a pillar of *Din*, or religion, was first a pillar of its own emergence into history.

ZAKAT AND MODERN ECONOMIC THOUGHT

These seventh-century origins and their twentieth-century translation into current sociology are separated by many vicissitudes of legal and administrative history, for the intricacies of which there is neither place nor point here. Fiscal patterns under the Ummayyads and Abbasids are matters of complicated research. There is wide variety and ramification in the story of *Zakat*, the proportions paid and payable, the rates on varying types of property and profit, whether movable or immovable, agricultural or manual, earned or unearned.

What is important for our purpose is the way in which the whole institution has become a main source of ideology in what relates to social and economic life to-day. This has doubtless been stimulated by the new political independence of the Islamic world and the live options that thus exist for Islamic thought when destinies are no longer under imperial control. At the same time the accentuating problems of contemporary life have given the pundits more strenuous occasion than they have often recognized. So it is that Marxism, capital development, industrialization, and other modern factors, have thrown up questions and problems for which the answers are sought in the implications of *Zakat*. It is seen, in some quarters, as undergirding the Welfare State, and justifying large, sometimes visionary, proposals for banking reform and a classless society. There is much exhilaration in this apology and it is often unrealistic. But its ideas, even where pretentious, are important.

Zakat, these writers say, witnesses to the social responsibility of property and possession. What is yours, they remind the owner and the wage-earner, is also not yours. This doctrine is often linked with the labour theory of value and with the truth that all material wealth necessarily derives from the fact of community. A Robinson Crusoe can get no pay for his services and his products have no market value. Things can only be bought and sold and services become remunerative in the setting of society. So society has a stake in all possession. The legitimacy of the private, whether landed estate, inherited capital, or personal income, is only ensured when this fact is recognized. Things are rightly mine when I see them as not mine and do so in a concrete way.

Here the institution of *Zakat* comes to our aid by laying on us the legal obligation to pay alms with a fifth, a tenth, a sixteenth of our property, according to the manner in which we came by it. In honourably accepting this obligation and maintaining payment, we legitimatize what we retain. But refusing or neglecting it, we arrogate to ourselves what is socially owed and in so doing disqualify our ownership.

It is easy to see how this general idea merges into current concepts of the Welfare State and of social responsibility. There have been efforts in some quarters, notably in Pakistan, to have the duty of *Zakat* seen in State action and to argue that it is fulfilled in the payment of taxation. For in modern fiscal practice almost everywhere taxes serve to a compulsory redistribution of incomes, with graded rates falling heaviest on the rich and allowances or social benefits accruing for the poor. It may be claimed, further, that the State alone has the facilities for securing and disbursing tax revenue amid the complexities of contemporary life, and that the original ends of *Zakat* are in our circumstances to-day far beyond the competence of a purely voluntary and religious system to attain.

But suggestions for any formal merger of *Zakat* in fiscal procedures have been strongly disapproved. The reasons have been summarized in a *fatwa*, or legal opinion, by the present Rector of Al Azhar, Dr Mahmud Shaltut.

> *Zakat* is one of the religious obligations and of the five pillars upon which Islam is built, and is in one category with Prayer, fasting and the confession of the Unity, by which faith is reinforced and souls purified, and the Muslim fulfils it in accordance with his faith and his religion. Taxes, however, have

quite a different status. They derive from the fact that the nation represented in the ruler, or the ruler as representative of the nation, has insufficient resources for the carrying out of services essential to the community, such as the provision of education, hospitals, roads, irrigation canals, factories, and national defence, and accordingly, when the rich in the nation, who are able to assist in the performance of such public enterprises, hold their hands and draw back from expenditure and assistance, has the right to lay upon them the taxes which will bring these things about. . . .

There is another difference between taxation and *Zakat*, namely that the latter has rates that are limited and laid down in the text of the law which it must not exceed or fall short of . . . whereas taxes may rise or fall or even be abolished altogether.[1]

So continues the Shaikh:

Zakat being thus one of the divine ordinances and duties of faith, it must be forthcoming whether or not there is a need for it, and it will thus be a constant source of supply for the poor and needy whom no nation or people lacks. And since taxation derives from government ordinance according to necessity, it is clear that neither can dispense with the other. They are two distinct entities both in their legal origin, their purpose, their range, sanction and continuity.[2]

If State taxes become too exacting and coercive, the remedy, he says, is to press upon the State the duty of economy in public expenditure, rather than deprive the poor of their rights in *Zakat*. And at all costs the religious significance of the alms as a purification of the devout must be preserved, as it could hardly be if State "levies" came to be thought to have displaced it. Shaikh Shaltut is clearly concerned for the humanitarian sensitivity of the believer, which God has willed to embody in the pillar of the faith, and to immunize this religious quality from the inroads of the secular and coercive.

While he is doubtless arguing for something which no perceptive critic would wish blithely to discredit or exclude, the pietism of this approach remains suspect for its lack of realism. How familiar in the west also are these debates about the dispensability of dogma and the eclipse of "religion" by the broadening interventions of the State that tend to substitute tax-gathering for philanthropy. Yet, priceless and precarious as are the values of compassion which "religious" self-taxation with the sanctions of divine injunction is intended to enshrine, the demands of efficiency, not to say complexity, would seem

[1] *Al-Fatawa*, Cairo, 1959, pp. 116–17. [2] Ibid., p. 117.

to swing heavily in the direction of the State. This should perhaps, in the end, be seen as an Islamic trend, for it renews the decisive instincts of the Prophet and the Hijrah and their appeal to the political. Yet the pietist insistence on the religious nature of *Zakat* struggles gamely among the canonical lawyers against the all-engrossing State.

It would seem, however, that the zealots for *Zakat* will have to see in general fiscal practice both a tribute to, and a fulfilment of, its institutional witness to social responsibility. This may prove to be one of those occasions where institutions win a general fulfilment as ideology only by foregoing their formal patterns. If so, the phenomenon is not new in history. State taxation does at least solve the problem of non-payment of *Zakat*, if by the same token it destroys the truly religious, i.e. the voluntary, principle. If this perplexes the purists it at least saves them from the potential dishonesty of mind which champions what they know to be all too often a dead letter. "The system of *Zakat*", writes Shaikh Ata Ullah, "is practically extinct."[1] Admittedly, this author calls strenuously for "State action" as a means of ensuring that *Zakat* is paid—an action which he believes the inauguration of Pakistani Islamic statehood has made both imperative and feasible. Yet he is at once involved in the dilemma that if *Zakat* was enforced and collected by State action, we should compromise or destroy religious "purity" and spontaneity. It is here that we move into deeper ranges of our study in the "philanthropy of man".

ZAKAT AND THE DIVINE MIND

We began with the relation of *foy* and *foyer*, our duty to our neighbour as belonging with and acting through our love to God. These, in their implications in the present context, can be set down under four heads.

1. What is the ultimate sanction of compassion? It seems evident that *Zakat* does not obtain, or even always survive, merely by standing as a religious "ought", a pillar of *Din*. That this "sufficient" sanction suffices is the burden of arguments against its being identified with State taxation, as made by Shaikh Shaltut and many others. Yet do religious injunction and exhortation avail to actualize? And if these do not energize, what else rightly will? Shaikh Ata Ullah writes: "Its

[1] *Revival of Zakat*, Lahore, n.d., p. 100.

acceptance as an article of faith and its payment must go hand in hand." Yet he promptly adds: "In its original form it is hardly to be found in any Muslim country to-day. . . .", and continues: "A Muslim who does not honour this obligation is by common consent a *fasiq* and a *fajir* (a violater and a rake) and is to be proceeded against by the State, even to the extent of declaring him an enemy of the State."[1] Yet so often "common consent" remains indifferent or concurs in the neglect. What then?

Here Islam, with the rest of faiths, confronts the final problem of human intractability, only the more sharply for its characteristic confidence that "to know is to do". The Christian student of Islam continually finds himself meeting these aspects of the Islamic assurance about the once-born perfectibility of human nature. The dilemma of the law lies in its very claim: *what ought to be* is its meaning, *what is not* its frustration. Nor can State action compel what ought to be without, as Shaikh Shaltut observes, making it something other than the religious thing it is.

In the end is there not one solution only to this elemental problem of the good law and men's perversity, namely to allow the issue to fall into two clearly recognizable parts: a relative, partial, imperfect, but enforceable, modicum of social justice, maintained by State imposition and political sanction? This on the one hand; and on the other a recognition that there is a reach of neighbour "love", of rightness by man for man, which the State can neither bring about, nor enforce, for which it can only "hold the ring" while other factors, spiritual, "religious", and non-compulsive, operate.

This is the basic Christian distinction resting, in the second sphere, on the necessity of divine grace in the remaking of human nature. The first is in many places happening by State initiative along the lines of an ideology deducible from *Zakat* as a pillar of faith. As such it fulfils by its compulsions what *Zakat* is after, though forfeiting the freedom. But the second will always lie beyond the realm that State action can attain, for it turns on human will to be self-expending. Ideology is not enough. It finds only a hollow echo in the wilderness of human pride and sin unless it be set in the context of grace and regeneration. "We love", says the apostle, "because he first loved us" (1 John 4.19). What he has in mind is not merely the force of a great example but

[1] Ibid., p. 99.

also the power of a divine activity which, entering in us, brings the power for its own imitation. This remains the Christian witness to the sincerity of the intention of *Zakat* and to an honest realism about actualities.

2. Does the obligation of *Zakat* not in fact take a contemporary response far beyond its assumptions? For is not this pillar of religion, as the authorities of faith expound it, still within the old, conservative structure of human inequality? Does it not suppose, as Shaikh Shaltut suggests, that there will always be distinctions of rich and poor in the form that requires *Zakat* of the one for the other? This is confirmed by the frequent form in which *Zakat* is argued as a rebuttal of Communism. It would of course be impossible to pay if private property were thoroughly abolished. And in a fully Communist society it would be impossible to receive. So, for rendering inoperative and inoperable a pillar of the faith, Communism is manifestly condemned. A philosophy which sees private almsgiving, dependent on the goodwill of the wealthy, as the meeting of the poor's needs, does not thus refute a philosophy that denies the right to be rich and the means to be "charitable". Indeed it only plays into its hands and leaves both flanks exposed. To allege the duty of alms is not to create the dignity of equal opportunity. If the duty is neglected there is hypocrisy: if it is fulfilled there is antiquated palliative and continuing injustice.

So it is that Marxism compels a radical reassessment of a social order that is understood, theologically, as static, however genuine the compassion it proposes. Do not current problems of population as well as the new capacities of technology require and enable an approach to "the poor always with us" wider than *Zakat* and more drastic? Professor Wilfred Cantwell Smith makes the point well in discussing an article on the theme of alms in the Al Azhar Journal, *Majallat al-Azhar*.

> . . . that there are rich and poor, and a great gulf between them, is accepted as presumably inevitable and even as ordained of God . . . There is simply no awareness that modern applied science has revolutionized the possibilities before human society in this respect. . . .[1]

Zakat as an institution compels us to ask: What is the meaning of human dignity in the modern world? But in the hands of most of its

[1] W. C. Smith, *Islam in Modern History*, Princeton University Press, 1957, p. 155. Quoted with permission.

interpreters, it fails either to recognize or harness the contemporary technological resources for the tackling of social evils and holds religious duty to the static pattern of benevolent wealth and recipient poverty.

3. With and beyond *Zakat*, what of a human fraternity that transcends the frontiers of religion? This is, or will be, the increasing test of all faiths, namely their posture towards mankind *as a whole*. *Zakat*, in conception, is an Islamic institution operating within Muslim society. Though non-Muslims are supported by the State and poor relief for them is not unknown, *Zakat* proper does not relate to them, unless within the category of *muʾallafat qulubuhum*, i.e. those about to Islamize. Malikite jurists add the category of spies, while the Caliph ʿUmar is said to have practised help to *dhimmis*, or non-Muslim tributaries, out of *Zakat* and to have related *fuqaraʾ* and *masakin* (general descriptives of the needy in Surah 2.176 and 9.60) to Muslims and "people of the Book" respectively. But in general full fellow humanity was not acknowledged within *Zakat*. The question also arose among jurists whether it could be paid *to* a non-Muslim ruler, making the possibility of mutual help among Muslims contingent upon the ruler having the right religion.

Most religio-cultural entities manifest parallels to this situation. Yet the whole point of the parable of the Samaritan on the Jericho road lies in the fact that his love ignored, in its spontaneity, the barriers of people and creed. There was a similar indifference to race the other way round when Jesus, to the marvel of his disciples, talked with the Samaritan woman (John 4.27). To-day in this twentieth century of one earth tenancy, are we not compelled to find a basis for a purely human compassion? If so, must *Zakat* not be interpreted beyond itself, even as the early Church had to follow Christ beyond Jewry?

4. Is there, finally, or can there be, a *Zakat* of the self? This notion that what is mine is not mine—does it apply only to my property and not to my person? Does it attach to what I possess and not to me possessing? This equation which *Zakat* implies between owing and owning, should it not include me as well as mine? The same arguments would seem to apply, *a fortiori*. "Brethren we are debtors", said St Paul. In his mind was the debt we owe to divine grace. The self, and the family, are reserved in the *nisab*, or minimum income figure below which *Zakat* is not payable. The point of this, of course, is for reasonable personal and domestic maintenance, the care, one may say,

of the self which is the basis of the capacity to earn and to pay. Yet this, by its focus on the me at the heart, presumably reserves that me for the sort of decisions about myself which are consistent with the nature of *Zakat*.

But this calls for a certain dispossession of ourselves, the kind of self-disappropriation which the President of Egypt wrote of as being the supreme requisite on the morrow of the 1952 Revolution and "the new régime".

> If I had been asked in those days what I most desired, I would have immediately answered: To hear an Egyptian speak fairly about another Egyptian, to feel that an Egyptian had opened his heart in pardon, forgiveness and charity towards his Egyptian brothers.[1]

Only this would reverse that "confirmed individual egotism" in which "the word 'I' was on every tongue".

It is in these terms that any *Zakat* of our goods argues a call to the offering of ourselves. This is the more so if we reflect upon how easily external payments can in fact mean the contrary. Since Chaucer's Friar, and before, there have been those who prefer to give alms that they may the more complacently retain themselves. The very gifts become a substitute for the giver and almsgiving a social soporific. How significant in this connection is the declension in the popular sense of the English word "charity", truly a terrible fall from the *caritas* of 1 Corinthians 13. How like it also the absorption of the Hebrew meaning of "righteousness" in the word for "alms". May not personal compassion in fact diminish when we hand over conscience in a fully personal sense to the operations of a Welfare State or by piety contract out of poverty?

We discern this final truth of our human relationships as calling for all we are, as well as part of what we possess, if we meditate on the divine pattern and God, self-giving and self-given in Christ, God who is fully ours in not being self-regardingly his own. This is the *foy* to make the *foyer*: and over each is the fashion of the cross.

QUESTIONS FOR STUDY AND DISCUSSION

1. What articles, discussions, or views have you met of late about *Zakat*? How is it seen by Muslims of your acquaintance and what is their practice?

[1] *Falsafat al Thaurah*, Cairo, 1954, pp. 22–3.

2. "Do not render your righteousness vain by upbraiding and wrong" (Surah 2.264). The word used is *tubtilu*, from the same root as the *Mubtilat* which disqualify worship. In what senses is almsgiving spiritually disqualified? How can we make charity in fact the negation of a true love and an actual serving of ourselves? Where and how is deliverance from this inverted evil?

3. How does *Zakat* figure in current Islamic ideology, as undergirding the Islamic view of property and as a reply to Marxism?

4. What positive parallels do you find in New Testament teaching and that of the Quran in what has to do with alms (cf. Surah 2.263–77 and Matt. 6.1–4).

5. In what senses does almsgiving cleanse? (Surah 9.103.) How is almsgiving itself cleansed when this is necessary?

6. How far does being a co-religionary affect the status of a fellow man as neighbour?

7. To what extent is it true to say that modern developments of science and technology on the one hand, and of State action and responsibility on the other, have altered the whole problem with which *Zakat* was instituted to deal?

8. How in Christian faith does the principle of the cross relate to our understanding of the pattern and cost of God's relationships to men and to our inner attitude to ourselves?

9. What bearing might the idea of *Zakat* have on our communication of the Christian directive, "Ye are not your own"?

6

"Labbaika": A Study in Pilgrimage

With this ejaculation, *Labbaika*, the Muslim pilgrim greets Mecca and each of the sanctuaries he visits during the pilgrim state of ceremonial cleansing. "At thy service doubly I stand", he says. The English phrase is a single Arabic word. It invites us into the meaning he finds and intends in the fulfilment of this, the fifth, of the "Pillars" of religion in Islam.

The word itself has a possessive attached, and is used in the accusative, probably as the absolute object of the cognate (but unstated) verb. The dual indicates intensity. "Here I am intent upon your obedience", "Waiting I still wait and standing I still stand", make some approach to the sense. The meaning is that the pilgrim is doubly God's—by dint of the divine claim and of his own response thereto, by the fact of revelation and the act of recognition. Due devotion to God can never be other than sustained, renewed, perpetuated. "Before thee I am, in all I am" might be a dictionary paraphrase, if a mere dictionary could express a personal reality.

To make the Hajj in the month of Hajj is the duty of a lifetime. "These", wrote Doughty in his *Arabia Deserta*, "lay up devoutly of their slender thrift for many years before, that they may once weary their lives in this great religious voyage." Doughty knew in his bones the weariness of those Arabian caravans. "I was certainly assured that there rode some amongst them whose homesteads lay in the most backward mountains . . . and that ascending and descending the sharp coasts they marched first three months in their own difficult country; so they have nearly twelve months journey from the setting out to the Holy City."[1]

To-day the old arduousness, at least for many, has gone from the pilgrimage, with the sharp increase in airborne travellers. Nor is it

[1] C. M. Doughty, *Arabia Deserta*, vol. 1, p. 59.

only the rigours of the way that have been lightened. The menace to life and health of insanitary conditions has been much diminished by measures taken in the last decade. The deterrents to the sophisticated, of which Muhammad Husain Haykal wrote in his monumental study of the pilgrimage, *Fi Manzil al-Wahy*, have been mitigated through such criticism as that which he there voiced. As a result, pilgrimage to Mecca has renewed itself in the vigour of contemporary Muslim life and experience, an ancient, and yet also a twentieth-century, institution.

The definitive quranic passage on the Hajj is Surah 2.196–203. It takes place in the last month of the Muslim calendar *Dhu al-Hajj* (though 2.196 refers to the "months" of pilgrimage. Any visit to Mecca outside the pilgrim month constitutes a "lesser pilgrimage" or *ᶜumrah*—a usage based on Surah 9.3). The duty of Hajj is incumbent on every adult Muslim once in a lifetime, if "he can find his way thither". (See 3.97.) This proviso has been the subject of prolonged debate among canonical lawyers, seeking definition of valid disability. Factors like poverty, insanity, slavery, and having no escort (for women) have been cited as proper deterrents. Trade may be carried on during the journey but not within the actual pilgrimage ceremonial. There has been considerable debate of late years as to the propriety of using the pilgrimage for political consultation, to which bodies like the Islamic Congress have been inclined, whereas conservative elements insist that a purely religious intent should not be combined with other activity, however convenient may be the presence of several heads of state at the one time and place.

Our task here is to group a few ideas on the meanings of the pilgrimage, with a view to our relation with Muslims in the midst of this experience, whether in prospect or retrospect, or vicariously through their fellows who return.

FOCUS OF HISTORY

The *Qiblah* of daily prayer, which Mecca was declared to be, instead of Jerusalem, in Surah 2.142–5, becomes the *Qiblah* of life's biggest journey. What the *Mihrab* is to the mosque, pilgrimage is for the life, namely the direction of its orientation. All that Mecca was, and is, in the genesis and pattern of Islam, it is to be also in the awareness of the individual Muslim. The pilgrimage is calculated symbolically and sacramentally to link the two.

Several strands of Islamic history come together in the pilgrimage. There is the dominant fact of Mecca, or its adjacent Mount Hira, as the point of the Quran's initial descent. Here is the matrix, in so far as a city can be, of Islam. Here is the focal point of that *Tanzil* which, continued in Medina, acquainted man with the divine will in what Islam receives as the revelation to end revelation. It is to this fact, with its implicit demand upon his obedience, that the pilgrim's *Labbaika* replies. He comes because he stands, and in order to stand, within the history of revelation.

But there is further associated history involved in the Hajj. Many of the rites of the pilgrimage, like the whole institution, go back into the *Jahiliyyah*, or pre-Islamic time. The prophetic decision to incorporate pilgrimage to Mecca into the pattern of Islam was no less formative than the decision in the Hijrah to migrate from Mecca. That migration was, in fact, only the beginning of the campaign for its re-possession. The Treaty of Al-Hudaibiyyah, by which, in the fifth year of the Hijrah, Muhammad arranged the right to enter Mecca, pilgrim-wise, the year following, was the most formative document of policy in the intervening years. As Surah 48.1 puts it, God therein "opened a great opening". The subsequent pilgrimage of Muhammad in A.H. 6 served notice that Mecca would, within Islam, be the same focal point of the tribes, the same mart and metropolis, it had ever been. The final victory of Islam, no doubt facilitated by these developments, integrated the purged, but ancient, sanctuaries into the heart of Islamic ritual and devotion. This sustained continuity with the past was a most powerful factor in the Arabian consolidation of Islam. It supplied the one thing for lack of which the pre-Hijrah evolution of Islam had gone so hardly, conflicting as that did with the as yet un-quieted fears of Meccan vested interest.

But the history within the focus of the pilgrimage goes back beyond the *Tanzil* and the *Jahiliyyah* into the distant "Islam" of that great father of the faithful, Abraham. The Quran, in repeated passages, links Mecca with Ibrahim, the prototype of all *Hanifs*. (See 2.125–31; 3.97 (Becca); 14.37; 22.26.) In the pilgrimage is the *Maqam Ibrahim*, the standing or station of Abraham, while the running between Safa and Marwah is associated with Hagar's search for water. The Kaᶜbah is not only the focal point of Muhammad's victorious symbolic purging of

Arabia's idols, but also of the pioneer of human rightness before God. The Muslim thus greets what he holds to be his Abrahamic foundations, both in stone and heritage.

FOCUS OF COMMUNITY

This incorporation in the Islamic history has its present counterpart in the active sense of community which informs the pilgrimage. It is this factor to which numerous contemporary participants bear witness. Familiar enough in Islamic history is the fact that pilgrimage was, so to speak, the Muslim means to cosmopolitanism. Tradition-seekers met here and compared their notes, while architects and artists, in the course of their religious duty, brought their minds and crafts into contact, because they were all pilgrims. To the pilgrimage both art and architecture in Islam owe much of their integrity.

Yet it is in personal experience that the cohesion wrought through pilgrimage evidences itself most clearly. There is the common character of pilgrim garb, throughout the state of ceremonial *ihram*, or sacrilizing, during the pilgrim rites. There is the common ground of the *tawaf* where the whole conclave fulfils its single course in the circumambulation of the Ka^cbah. In this and other pilgrim *manasik*, or ritual acts, the entirety of the pilgrim concourse enters into a sense of solidarity.

There is also the geographical range of the pilgrim origins. The contingents are often proportionately larger from the remoter areas. Indonesia and Malaya have for long been sources of a vigorous pilgrim interest. Most Muslim accounts emphasize this feature of an intermingling "world" of Islam at the focal Meccan points. Pilgrimage, we may say, is, in that sense, a mediated experience of commonwealth and provides a symbol of unity which no other religion affords so inclusively. Pilgrimage has long filled a dominant rôle in religious cohesion. But Mecca, in this capacity, has a centrality that Meshed, Karbala^ↄ, Ajmer, and the rest cannot rival.

Nor is the pilgrim cohesiveness of Islam, from Nigeria to Samarkand and the Balkans to the Timor Sea, limited only to those who physically make the pilgrimage in any one *Dhu al-Hajj*. For the ^c*Id al-Adha* coincides throughout the Muslim world with the sacrifice by which on the tenth day of the month the pilgrims mark the end of the state of *ihram*. At ^cAqabah, where Abraham is believed to have prepared himself to sacrifice Ishmael, or elsewhere in the vicinity of Mina, the pilgrims sacrifice each a sheep or goat, or, with partners, a camel. The simultaneous fulfilment of these rites gives the pilgrimage a general impact throughout the extent of Islam.

This is reinforced and renewed with the return of the pilgrims to their scattered homes, carrying with them the holy water of Zamzam and telling of the fulfilment of various vicarious vows and intercessions. The returned pilgrim has a status in the community which serves to extend both the fame of the act and the range of its significance. It may be that the speedy return of many contemporary pilgrims and the facility of their travels make them less awe-inspiring folk than their counterparts of earlier generations. But there is no doubt that pilgrimage still lives in more imaginations than their own.

FOCUS OF ALLEGIANCE

Mecca, as the famous promulgation of Surah 9 warned the heathen, has been out of bounds to all but Muslims since before the Prophet's farewell pilgrimage. Thus the pilgrim rites have never been experienced by non-Muslims, unless by subterfuge like that of Richard Burton. The Kaᶜbah remains inviolate to all curious or pagan eyes. All is *terra incognita* and forbidden territory, even to the people of the Book. It is idle to speculate when this exclusion may be terminated. Meanwhile it serves as a vivid reminder that pilgrimage has to do with belonging in Islam. Our final study must be in the pilgrim rites as a focus of participation.

The best place to pursue it is in the language of pilgrim prayers[1]—a more important subject than the pagan antecedents of the rites or the topography of Mecca.

With the repeated *Labbaikas*, from the initial *Niyyah* (or intention), until the end of the sacrifice that terminates *ihram*, goes, in the prayer language, a confessed sense of the presence and immediacy of God. "This is thy sanctuary", "I take refuge with the Lord of this house", "I seek thy gracious countenance, O thou Lord of the worlds". Sundry *Takbirs* and *Taᶜwidhs* and *Talbiyahs* punctuate these devotions (ascribing greatness to God, taking refuge in him, and saying *Labbaika*).

[1] See the translation, *Manasik al-Hajj* (*The Muslim World*, vol. 45.3, July 1955, pp. 269–80), reprinted here in the following chapter.

Various sentences connect this divine majesty with what we may call the recognition of Meccan prophethood.

But there is also a deep emphasis on pleas for forgiveness associated with the performance of the rites. This is in line with injunctions of Surah 22.26–34, where cleansing and sacrifice and the shunning of idolatry, in all its abomination, are related to pilgrim fulfilment. The devotional language of the Hajj prayers is characterized by self-reproach, but also by a pleading of the efficacy of the pilgrimage performed. "I consecrate unto thee my manhood, my body and all my members. I withhold them from enjoyment, from women, from everything which thou hast made unlawful to whoever enters the sacred state. Thereby, I seek thy gracious countenance."

It would be hard to say how closely the state of pardon is consciously linked with the sacrifices made. Rather these would seem to be a fulfilment of the divine will (as is the whole venture) on the ground of which, in the total context of the divine mercy which can never be presumed, the pilgrim pleads his hopes and fears, and stakes his anxious claim. The sense of being, for good or ill, in the hand of God is sharply conveyed by the closing petitions for a safe return and for God, as the pilgrim's representative (Caliph), to guard and preserve his family and his journey.

Another large preoccupation is "the fire". "I take refuge with thee from the fire and from whatever in deed or word or work would bring me nigh to it."

The quranic background and temper of all these petitions is unmistakable. Their meaning and the spirit of their use differ widely from Muslim to Muslim. But the sense of them all is obedience within the framework of a divine command and an associated experience of belonging with the right.

From time to time the solemnity and crisis-nature of a pilgrimage may prove the occasion of even deeper issues of soul. There is a story current in Isfahan of a man who decided to make the Hajj and browbeat his debtors and neighbours in order to secure his expenses. Shortly before he was due to leave, his wife, then pregnant, smelled a savoury odour coming from down the street and requested some of the dish being cooked. When the husband went to investigate he found a poor woman cooking a chicken for several ragged children who stood around. The man was told that, as the chicken had died, she could not let the neighbour eat it, though it was all she had for the children. The man returned home and later brought to the woman the money he had collected for the pilgrimage, saying: "You have more need of this than I."

When his friends called for him to start out he feigned illness and they went without him. Returning weeks later, they came to congratulate him on the pilgrimage he had made. "But", said he, "I did not go." "You did", they replied, "we saw several times your face among the crowd, and we had a vision in which God told us that you had made an acceptable pilgrimage."

The Algerian author, Malek Bennabi, in a French novel, *Lebbeik: Pélèrinage des Pauvres*, describes an habitual drunkard who had betrayed the memory of his godly parents and was a shame to his uncle. A divorced husband, we find him ridiculing in the port of Bone a group of intending pilgrims whose boat puts in there. But a dream resolves him suddenly to join himself to their venture and he boards the ship with dramatic determination in the nick of time. His subsequent conversations and experiences end in the abandonment of his old life, in reconciliation with his wife, and in the decision to stay a citizen of Mecca.

Whether in life or in fiction, such stories are a witness to the potential crisis-in-soul a pilgrimage may constitute. Doubtless the same occasions have no more than a formal meaning to multitudes, being perhaps an essay in self-righteousness and esteem, just as in the parable, when men went templewards to pray, there was a contrast both in what they meant and with what they returned. While being alert to all that is potentially of the Pharisee in the annual influx to Mecca, in the yearly "standing" in the Kaᶜbah's precincts, we must watch for, pray for, work for, all that may be, however inarticulately, of the publican.

Early in the Hijrah's sequel the direction of Muslim prayer forsook Jerusalem in order to face Mecca. From Medina one has to have one's back on Jerusalem if one is to look towards Mecca. Islam then received a new "Temple Area". The pilgrimage has perpetuated that decision in a symbol that preoccupies the Muslim mind away from the cross and God in Christ.

There are, nevertheless, certain directions from which one cannot face Mecca without also facing Jerusalem. Could this be in some sense a parable? Things Christian are not at the core, but they are within the radius, depending on the attitude from which Mecca is approached. Everything turns upon what it is in God, or of God, to which we are responding and in what terms he bids men seek him. If we are to serve the Christian meanings beyond Dome and Rock, we must live in the power and evidence of that history which was the place and crisis of God's encounter with us through Christ, and where ours with him is ever renewed.

QUESTIONS FOR STUDY AND DISCUSSION

1. What, in your experience, do Muslims mean in and by the *ᶜId al-Adha* (*Bairam*)?

2. What factors and attitudes have you found in the impulse to, experience of, and results from Muslim pilgrimage, as far as your acquaintance goes?

3. A journey has often been a figure, or symbol, of spiritual meaning and experience. What, then, would you say is the real content, ground, and goal, of the Christian pilgrim's progress?

4. The original Islamic pilgrimage was to Mecca de-idolized (of which the changed *Qiblah* was a pledge). By it, Islam retained ritual and practice from the old time under its own new conditions. In so doing it "converted" the old to its own pattern. What was the New Testament attitude to the heathen world that Gentile Christianity displaced?

5. What, as you understand them, are the implications of the *Tawaf*, the running, the standing, the stoning, and the sacrificing, that take place in Mecca, Safa, Marwah, Al-Muzdalifah, and other pilgrimage points?

6. What is the Islamic account of the Kaᶜbah, its history, meaning, structure, and significance?

7. What are the problems and opportunities created for Christian witness and interpretation to Muslims by the Islamic attitude to Abraham?

8. "I seek refuge with God" says the pilgrim. From what, and by virtue of what, is God our refuge in the sense of Christian faith?

9. What, for the Muslim, makes an acceptable pilgrimage? What, for the Christian, is the place and crisis of a man's acceptance with God?

7

A Pilgrim's Prayer Manual

The devotions and rubrics of a pilgrim's prayer manual translated below afford the surest access to the temper of devout pilgrimage.[1] The text has been fully rendered[2] except in the final memorial prayers, where the identical sentence is used in every case, since the patterns of refrain are a significant part of the whole. No attempt is made to annotate the text or indicate the frequent quranic references that echo there. The prayers of commemoration used in visiting the tombs of Al-Maᶜla, a sacred cemetery close to Mecca's western walls containing the tombs of the son of Abu Bakr, the first Caliph, of Khadijah, the Prophet's wife, and Aminah his mother, are of course outside the pilgrim rites proper. Between the cemetery and city is the Mosque of the Jinn, traditional site of Muhammad's encounters with the archangel Gabriel at the descent of the Meccan portions of the Quran. Abu Qubais is a hill on the eastern side commanding an excellent panorama of the Kaᶜbah and reputedly the burial place of Adam, Eve, and Seth. Jabal al-Thaur holds the cave in which the Prophet and Abu Bakr sheltered during the Hijrah to Medina.

Bare notes such as the foregoing on the topography of the holy city of Islam's origin do nothing to capture the exaltation it raises in the pilgrim soul. But the spirit of that landscape is in these prayers.

This prayer shall be recited at the entering of the gate of peace (Bab al-Salam).

O God, thou art peace. Peace comes from thee. Unto thee peace

[1] Translated by the author from *Manasik al-Hajj wa Adᶜiyat al-Tawaf*, Cairo, edition of A.H. 1357. For a general introduction to pilgrim ritual and geography, see G. E. von Grunebaum, *Muhammadan Festivals*, New York, 1951, pp. 15–49.

[2] Four short extracts, included in *The Call of the Minaret*, pp. 122–3, are omitted here.

returns. Then make us alive, O our Lord, with peace. Bring us into paradise, thy abode of peace. Blessed art thou, O Lord, and exalted, thou fount of majesty and honour. O God, open unto me the doors of thy mercy and forgiveness. Bring me into them. In the Name of God unto whom be praise and blessing, and peace upon the Apostle of God, with whom may God be gracious.

Upon beholding the noble sanctuary, let him bless God thrice and recite the Takbir (the ascription: God is most great) thrice, and say:

There is no god save God alone. He has no like and unto him is the power and unto him the praise. He is mighty over all things. I take refuge with the Lord of the house from unbelief and poverty, from the torment of the grave and from a narrow heart and an anguished bosom. May the blessing of God be upon our Lord Muhammad, upon his people and his companions. Peace upon them all.

O God, let this house increase in honour, reverence, grandeur, awe, exaltedness, and righteousness. Increase, O Lord, those who do it honour, who magnify and esteem it among those who have made pilgrimage hither and who resort hither in veneration, honour, worship, in awe, dignity, and righteousness.

On coming to the gate of Banu Shaiba, let him say:

O Lord, cause me to enter in with truth and to go forth with truth. Grant me power from thy presence to aid me. And say: The truth has come, falsehood has passed away. Verily falsehood is a thing that goeth away. We bring down of the Quran that which is a healing and a mercy to the believers. It does not increase the wrongdoers save in loss.

This is the confession of intention to circumambulate the Kaᶜbah:

O God, I desire the circumambulation of thy holy house: enable me thereto and accept of me seven circuits, the circuits of the pilgrimage, of the holy visit, seeing it is performed unto God, the Exalted, to him be power and majesty.

Then he kisses the Black Stone and raises his hands saying:

In the Name of God; God is most great: unto God be praise.

Prayer of the First Circuit.

Praise be to God, glory to God. There is no god save God. God is most great. There is no might and no strength save in God most high, the great. Blessing and peace be upon the Apostle of God, may God send blessing and peace upon him. O God, I come unto thee out of faith in these and belief in thy words, in reliance upon thy covenant and in obedience to thy law, the Sunnah of thy Prophet and thy beloved, Muhammad, may peace and blessing be upon him. O God, I ask thee for pardon and favour and constant clemency in the things of religion, in this world and in the next, safety in paradise and escape from the fire.

And he says in every circuit:

O our Lord, bring us good things in this world and in that which is to be. Keep us from the torment of the fire. Bring us into paradise with the righteous, O thou mighty, thou forgiver, thou Lord of the worlds.

Prayer of the Second Circuit.

O God, truly this house is thy house, the sanctuary is thy sanctuary, the security is thine. The servant is thy servant. I am thy servant and the son of thy servant. This is the doing of one seeking refuge with thee from the fire. Then make our flesh and our frame inviolate from the fire. O God, cause us to love faith and adorn it in our hearts. Cause us to detest unbelief, transgression, and disobedience. Make us to be among the rightful. O God, defend us from thy punishment on the day when thou raisest thy servants. O God, cause me to inherit paradise without a reckoning.

Prayer of the Third Circuit.

O God, I take refuge with thee from doubt, from *shirk* (polytheism), separatism and hypocrisy, from evil character and evil outlook, from calamity of substance or kindred or child. O God, I ask thee thy favour and paradise. And I seek refuge with thee from thy wrath and the fire. O God, I take refuge with thee from the terror of the grave and I take refuge with thee from danger in living and danger in dying.

Prayer of the Fourth Circuit.

O God, cause it to be a righteous pilgrimage and a grateful striving. Let guilt be forgiven. Let this be a righteous and accepted deed, a transaction which is never voided, O thou who knowest what is in the heart. Lead me forth, O God, from the shadows into the light. O God, I ask of thee the things that properly belong to thy mercy and the sureness of thy forgiveness, security from all iniquity and a full share (booty) of righteousness, safety in the garden and escape from the fire. Lord, make me assured with that wherewith thou hast endowed me and bless me in thy gifts. Cause everything of which I am repentant to be retrieved by good from thee.

Prayer of the Fifth Circuit.

O God, shelter me under the shadow of thy throne on that day when there is no shelter save the shadow of thy throne, and nought abides save thy countenance. Give me water from the reservoir of thy Prophet, our Lord Muhammad—may the blessing and peace of God be upon him—a joyous, health-giving draught, after which we shall never thirst again. O God, I ask of thee the good which thy Prophet our Lord Muhammad asked of thee—may the blessing and peace of God be upon him. I take refuge with thee from the evil from which he sought refuge with thee, he, thy Prophet our Lord Muhammad. O God, I ask of thee paradise and its favour and whatever will bring me nigh unto it—of word or deed or work. I take refuge with thee from the fire and from whatever, in word or deed or work, would bring me nigh to it.

Prayer of the Sixth Circuit.

O God, thou hast much against me in respect of my relation with thee and with thy creation. O God, forgive me what is due unto thee and unto thy creation and take it off from me. By thy gracious glory make me well-satisfied without what thou hast disallowed. By obedience unto thee keep me from rebelliousness against thee and by thy goodness keep me from any save thee, O thou who art of wide forgiveness. O God, verily thy house is great and thy countenance is gracious. Thou, O God, art forbearing, gracious, and great. Thou lovest to pardon: therefore, pardon me.

Prayer of the Multazam.[1]

O God, Lord of the ancient house, set free our persons and the persons of our fathers, our mothers, our brethren, and our children from the

[1] The place where pilgrims press their breasts, arms outstretched, against the wall of the Kaᶜbah, near the eastern corner and the door. The prayer has this pressure in mind in one of its petitions. *Barakah*, or blessing, is had by this contact.

fire, O thou of all goodness and grace, kindliness, favour, bounty, and beneficence. Let the issue in all things be good for us: protect us from shame in this world and punishment in the next. O God, truly I am thy servant, the son of thy servant, standing beneath thy portal leaning hard upon thy favour, and humbled within thy hand. I crave thy mercy and dread thy fearful punishment, O thou of age-old goodness. O God, I pray thee to lift up my remembrance of thee and to lay aside my fault, to prosper my affair, to cleanse my heart, to shine upon me in my tomb, and to pardon my transgression. I ask of thee the high places of the garden.

The Prayer of the Stone of Isma^{c}il, upon whom be peace.

O God, thou art my Lord. There is no god save thou. Thou hast fashioned me and I am thy servant. As far as I am able I rely upon thy covenant and thy promise. I seek refuge with thee from the evil of what I have done. I return unto thee by thy grace toward me and I return because of my sin. Therefore, forgive me. For there is none that forgivest sins save thou only. O God, I ask of thee the good which thy righteous servants have asked of thee and I seek refuge with thee from the same evil from which thy righteous servants have sought refuge with thee. O God, by the dignity of thy chosen Prophet, thy blessed Apostle, cleanse our hearts from every characteristic which would separate us from the vision of thee and from the love of thee. Let us die in loyalty to the Sunnah and the community and in longing to find thee, O thou Lord of majesty and honour. O God, enlighten my heart with knowledge and employ my body in thy obedience. Save my secret thoughts from rebellion and my mind occupy with reverence. Protect me from evil and from the whisperings of Satan and save me from him, O thou most merciful, so that he may have no power over me. Our Lord, verily we have believed, so forgive us our trespasses and guard us from the torment of the fire.

Prayer to be recited at drinking the water of Zamzam.

O God, I ask of thee profitable knowledge and a plentiful weal, and healing from every disease and sickness, through thy mercy, O thou supreme among the merciful.

Prayer of Al-Safa.

I begin as God and his Apostle began. Verily Al-Safa and Al-Marwah are rites of God. He who makes a pilgrimage to the house, or performs the lesser pilgrimage (Al-ᶜUmrah), it is no fault in him that he makes the circuit of them. He who volunteers a good thing, God is a receiver of thanks and he knows.

The Intention of the Running (Al-Saᶜy).

O God, I desire to run between Al-Safa and Al-Marwah, seven circuits (either the Hajj or the ᶜUmrah) unto God, mighty and glorious, O thou Lord of the worlds.

Then he mounts the steps of Al-Safa and says:

God is most great: God is most great: God is most great. Unto God be praise.

The Prayer of the Running.

God most great, God most great. Praise be to God indeed. Praised be God the mighty, in his excellent glory morning and evening. By night worship him and in the long night praise him. There is no god save God alone. He fulfils his promise and aids his servant. Alone he puts to flight the confederacies. There is nothing before him, nor anything after him. He brings to life and he brings to death. He lives for ever and he dies not. Nor does he ever pass away. Good is in his hand; destiny is with him. He is mighty over all things. Lord, forgive and have mercy. Pardon and be gracious.

Do not require what thou knowest of, for thou knowest what we know not. Thou art God, most mighty, most gracious. O Lord, save us from the fire, as those who being preserved take the spoil and rejoice in gladness with thy righteous servants, with those upon whom God has been gracious of faithful prophets, martyrs, and good men. Good companions indeed are these and that by the favour of God. God knoweth well. There is no god save God. In truth, in truth, no god save God for worship and for glory. There is no god save God and we worship none save him, being sincere unto him in our religion, despite the hatred of the unbelievers. There is no god except God, the one, the sole, the eternal. He takes unto himself no companion and no child. There is no partner like him in authority, nor does he, out of weakness, need any patron. Then call him great in the *Takbir*.

O God, verily thou hast said in thy descended book: "Call unto me and I will answer you." We have called unto thee our Lord. So forgive us in accordance with thy command, for thou dost not break a promise. Our Lord, verily we have heard the caller calling us to faith: Believe in your Lord. And O Lord we have believed. Then forgive us our trespasses and rid us of our iniquities. Let us be called hence with the righteous. O our Lord, bring us what thou hast promised by thy messenger. Let us not be confounded on the day of resurrection. Verily thou dost not break promise. O our Lord, in thee have we trusted. Unto thee have we returned. For unto thee is the ordering. O Lord, forgive us and our brethren who have preceded us in the faith. Let there be in our hearts no rancour towards those who have believed. For thou art kindly and merciful. O Lord, make our light complete. Forgive us, thou art powerful over all things.

O God, I seek of thee the whole good, present good, and future good. I seek refuge with thee from evil in its entirety, both present and to be. I crave of thee pardon for my guilt and ask of thee thy mercy. O God, O Lord, increase me in knowledge and lead not my heart astray any more, for thou hast mercifully granted me favour before thee. Verily thou art the bestower. O God, I take refuge with thee from the torment of the grave. There is no god save thou. Praise be unto thee. Indeed I was among the wrongdoers. O God, I take refuge with thee from unbelief and poverty. O God, I take refuge with thy good pleasure from thine anger, and with thy pardoning grace from thy retribution. I take refuge with thee from thee. I will not withhold the praise of thee. Thou art as thine own praise sayeth. Glory then be unto thee until thou art well pleased. O God, I ask the good which thou knowest and I take refuge with thee from the evil thou knowest. I pray forgiveness of thee for everything known to thee. Thou verily knowest the hidden things. There is no god except God, the King, the truth, the enlightener. Muhammad is the messenger of God; the trustworthy, the faithful promise.

O God, I ask of thee that as thou hast given to me Islam so thou wilt not take it from me until thou dost call me hence as a Muslim. O God, let there be light in my grave and light in my hearing and light in my seeing. O God, enlarge my heart and facilitate for me what concerns me. I take refuge with thee from the evil of the whispers of my bosom and from distraction and from the ambush of the grave.

O God, I take refuge with thee from the evil that comes in the night and the evil that comes in the day, from the evil the winds blow upon (me). O thou most merciful of all, praise be to thee. We have not truly worshipped thee, O God. Praise be to thee. We have not recollected thee with a true recollection. Praise be to thee. We have not thanked thee with a right thanksgiving, O God. Praise be to thee. We have not sought thee with true purpose, O God. O God, make faith a thing we love and adorn it in our hearts. Let us truly hate unbelief and corruption and rebelliousness. Make us rightly guided. O God, guard me from thy punishment on the day thou raisest up thy servants. O God, guide me with guidance and cleanse me with piety. Forgive me the last and the first. O God, stretch forth upon us thy blessings and mercy, thy goodness and thy bounty: O God, I ask thee, the gracious one, the establisher who never changes and never passes away. O God, I am refuging in thee from the evil thou sendest us and from the evil thou prohibitest to us. O God, call us hence as Muslims and join us to the good, neither shamed nor afflicted. O Lord, let things be easy not arduous. Fulfil what is good, O Lord. Verily Al-Safa and Al-Marwah are rites of God. He who performs the pilgrimage or the ᶜUmrah, there is no fault in him that he makes the circuit of them. He who volunteers a good deed, God is the receiver of thanks and he knows. O Lord, accept of us: preserve us and pardon us. Help us in our obedience unto thee and our gratitude towards thee. Let us all die in the faith, in complete Islam, thou being with us well-pleased. O God, have mercy upon me that I may evermore forsake misdeeds, as long as thou causest me to live. Have mercy upon me that I may expend wealth that belongs to me and of thy bounty grant me right insight into what on my part will please thee, O thou most merciful.

The Intention of the ᶜUmrah (the Lesser Pilgrimage).

O God, I wish to perform the ᶜUmrah; so facilitate it unto me and receive it from me. I have intended the ᶜUmrah and I have become consecrated for it unto God, most high; to him be majesty and strength.

The Intention of the Pilgrimage.

O God, I wish to perform the pilgrimage, so make it a ready thing unto me and accept it from me. I have intended the pilgrimage. I have consecrated myself for it unto the Most High; unto him be strength and majesty. Here I am before thee, O Lord, here before thee. Before thee who hast no partner unto thee. Here at thy service. Praise and grace are thine and power. There is no partner with thee. O God, I consecrate unto thee my hair, my manhood, my body, and all my members. I withhold them from enjoyment, from women, from everything which thou hast made unlawful to whoever enters the sacred state. Thereby I seek thy gracious countenance, O thou Lord of the worlds.

The Prayer of the Farewell Circuit.

Verily he who enjoined upon thee the Quran is he who bringeth thee to a place of returning. O thou bringer back (of men), cause me to return. O thou hearer, hear me. O thou all powerful, restore me. O thou who hidest (men), hide me. O thou merciful one, have mercy upon me. O thou bringer back, let me return unto this house of thine. Be bountiful unto me in the returning unto it multiplied times thereafter, repentant, worshipping, wayfaring towards our Lord with praise. God fulfils his promise and prospers his servant and alone confounds the confederates. O God, write down for us peace and pardon and wealth and also for thy pilgrim servants, the guests, the victors, the travellers, and all who dwell in thy land and sea, of the nation of Muhammad.

O God, preserve me on my right hand and on my left, from before and behind, from above and below, that thou mayest bring me unto my people and my country. When thou hast brought me unto my country and my people, I ask thee not to abandon me from thy mercy, not even for the twinkling of an eye, and there is nothing less than that.

O God, be a companion unto us in our journey and a "Caliph" among our people. Blot out the faces of our enemies. Enfeeble their condition and they will be unable to pass and come upon us. O God, let it not be the last time for this house of thine. O God, have mercy upon me through my forsaking evil-doing as long as thou preservest me alive. Have mercy upon me that I may expend wealth that belongs to me and bestow on me a good insight into what is pleasing unto thee in me. O God, let me long enjoy my sight and let it last all my days.

Let me see my revenge upon mine enemy. Make me victorious over those who wrong me. O God, I seek refuge with thee from grief and sorrow; I seek refuge with thee from feebleness and sloth; I seek refuge with thee from faintheartedness and avarice. I seek refuge with thee from being overwhelmed with debt and from the spite of men.

O God, we ask of thee, in this our journey, righteousness and devotion and deeds that will please thee. O God make this our journey easy and shorten for us its distance. O God, thou art the companion of the way and the "Caliph" among our people.

O God, I seek refuge with thee from the hardship of the journey, from distress of prospect, from the evil of catastrophe to property or family or child. O God, accompany us with thy counsel and take us in safe conduct. O God, shorten before us the land and make the way easy for us and ease the tedium (or depression) of the journey. O God cause us to reach our journey's end by thy goodness and protection and by thy favour. For good is in thy hand and thou art mighty over all things. O God, make our journey easy for us and shorten the land for us. O God, accompany us in our journey and be in our stead among our people. O God, protect me from between my two hands, from behind me, on my right and on my left, and above me. I seek refuge with thy greatness that I be not treacherously dealt with from below, O thou most merciful of all, thou Lord of the worlds.

The Prayer at ᶜArafah (the place of the "Standing" east of Mecca).

Here I am before thee, O God, at thy service, doubly at thy service and at thy pleasure. Good is in thy hands, is from thee, and is thine. I have walked before thee according to all that I have said in word, or sworn in an oath, or vowed in a vow. What thou willest comes to be: what thou willest not will not be. There is neither strength nor power save in thee. Thou art mighty, O God. Whatever blessing I have called down it has been upon him whom thou blessest. Whatever curse I have cursed with it has been upon him whom thou cursest. Thou art my protector in this world and the next. Let me die as a Muslim and join me to the good.

The Friday Prayer and the Visit to Al-Maᶜla and the lady Khadijah, the lady Aminah and all the memorial places and visits.

Let him say: Peace be upon you, O people. There is no god save God: people of the house of a believing folk. You are those who have gone before: and we, if God wills, are joined with you. Rejoice in that the hour of which there is no doubt is coming and that God doth bring back from the tombs. I confide with you the testimony that there is no god except God and that Muhammad is his servant and his Apostle. (Then the *Surat al-Fatihah.*)

Prayer to be said at every saint's shrine if a visit is desired.

Peace be upon you, O friend of God. Peace upon you and the mercy of God and his blessings. We have come unto you as visitors and stand upon your place of life. Do not send us back disappointed. I entrust with you the testimony that there is no god except God and that Muhammad is his servant and his Apostle. (The *Fatihah.*)

Prayer (to be said at the grave) of ᶜAbd al-Rahman ibn Abi Bakr the faithful.

Peace be upon you my lord ᶜAbd al-Rahman, son of Abu Bakr the faithful. Peace be upon you, O son of the faithful (friend) of the Apostle of God. May God most high be pleased with you and make you glad with the best gladness. May he make the garden your abode and resting place. I entrust in you . . . (as above).

Prayer to be said at the visit of the lady Khadijah the great.

Peace be upon you, lady Khadijah. Peace be upon you, wife of the blessed one. May God most high be pleased with you and make you glad with the best of gladness. And may he make the garden your abode and your resting place. I entrust in you . . . (as above).

[Identical words are used for Aminah, substituting the title "mother of the chosen".]

Prayer at the Mosque of the Jinn.

He shall say after two rakaᶜhs: O God, thou seest me and seest where I am. Nothing that concerns me is hidden from thee. I am the poor, unworthy servant who confesses and acknowledges evil and shortcoming. O God, I have entrusted in this honoured place from this our day to the day of resurrection, a pure and sincere friend. I confess that there is no god save God and that Muhammad is his servant and his Apostle.

Saturday: Visit to the Mount of Abu Qubais

Prayer of Dar-al-Khaizaran.

O God, I ask of thee a perfect faith, gladdening my heart, and a sincere assurance so that I may know that nought shall happen to me except what thou hast written for me. Thou art my protector in this world and the next. O God, I entrust in this honoured place . . . (as in the previous prayer).

Prayer at the Memorial of our lord Bilal.

O God, protect me from Satan, so that he may have no power over me. O God, I have entrusted . . . (as in the two previous prayers).

Prayer of the Birth Celebration (Maulid) of the Prophet. May the peace and blessing of God be upon him.

O God, by the honour of thy chosen Prophet and thy blessed Apostle, the trustee of thy heavenly revelation, cleanse our hearts from every feature that would remove us far from the vision of thee and the love of thee. Let us die, O God, in loyalty to the Sunnah and the community and in desire for meeting thee, O thou Lord of majesty and honour. O God, I have entrusted . . . (as in the three previous prayers).

Prayer at the Birth Celebration of our Lady Fatimah. May God be pleased with her.

O God, I ask thee by that fair one who is part (of Muhammad) and her children, Al-Hasan and Al-Husain, make our affairs easy: enlarge our bosoms and seal our deeds, O God, with good things. O God, I have entrusted . . . (as in the four previous prayers).

Prayer at the Memorial Place of Abu Bakr the faithful. May God be pleased with him.

O God write for me, thy servant, a release from the fire and a reprieve from the fire, security from punishment and transit on the straight path, a portion in the garden and a blessed end. Call me hence as a Muslim, a believer, and join me to the righteous. O God, I have entrusted . . . (as in the five previous prayers).

Prayer of the Memorial of Jabal al-Thaur.

O God, by the honour of Muhammad and his intimate and friend, make our affairs easy, enlarge our bosoms, and enlighten our hearts. Seal our deeds with good things. O God, thou knowest my secret and my open things. Receive my plea. Thou knowest my need. Thou knowest what is in my soul. Forgive me my sins. None forgiveth sins save thou. O God, I have entrusted . . . (as in the six previous prayers).

Prayer of the Memorial of Mashaqq al-Qamr.

O God, send thy blessing upon a Prophet who has repeated the *Shahadah* and said the *Takbir* and performed the pilgrimage and the ᶜUmrah and for whom the moon was sundered, who commanded the recognition of the religion of God and prohibited what is immoral and illicit. O God I have entrusted . . . (as in the seven previous prayers).

Prayer of the Birth Celebration of ᶜAli. May God be pleased with him.

O God, illumine my heart with knowledge and let my body be used in thy obedience, save my inmost self from discordant things. Let my thoughts be occupied in reverence. Guard me from the evil whispers of Satan and protect me from him. O thou merciful one, seal our deeds with good things. O God, I have entrusted . . . (as in the eight previous prayers).

Prayer to be said in every memorial.

O God, our Lord, accept of us and be gracious unto us and pardon us. O God, call us hence as Muslims and bring us alive again Muslims and join us to the righteous. O God, I have entrusted in this honoured place . . . (as in the nine previous prayers).

The Petitionary Prayers of the Pilgrimage and the Circumambulation are ended.

TEMPLE AREA

8

The Names of God
A Study of the Asmaʾ Al-Husna

William Temple once concluded an address to the Central Council for Health Education with the phrase "the dreadful astonishment of God". His theme was the duty of a Christian society to the physical consequences of irresponsible sex conduct. He was not, of course, quoting consciously from the Quran. But a similar sentiment breaks through its pages from time to time, when the divine "astonishment" contemplates the capacity of men for that irreverence which is the final stuff of atheism.

Some theorists may find it difficult to reconcile "astonishment" with deity. But there can be no doctrine of creation which does not include a divine expectation in respect of it, and no understanding of man the creature which does not leave that expectation in his hands. It is here, precisely, that the trusts wherein man's dignity consists become decisions about the divine ends. Hence the involvement of God in the behaviour of man to that final length of vulnerability which is the other side of the fact of idolatry. *Shirk*, as the Quran affirms it, is in the end just this willed negation of God, in his gifts and in himself. The God with whom we have to do is one who has so ordered things that men, if they choose, need have nothing to do with him. Yet divine love is never indifferent about their indifference. Thus his "astonishment" is simply the truth of his sovereignty and his compassion.

These reflections may seem an odd preamble to the Islamic theme of "the names of God". But when the Quran implies this "astonishment" it says (of the faithless): "God is bountiful to men, but most of them give no thanks" (Surah 10.60 and 27.73). Here in its double sense is the situation between God and man, the initiative of grace and the response of recognition. In this relation is the whole of religion. For Islam it hinges upon the Beautiful Names by which God is at once denoted in his goodness and acknowledged in gratefulness and dependence. In his names he is described and by his names he is invoked. They are then the crossing points in a divine manwardness and a human Godwardness. They are at once clues of theology and the stuff of prayer. Their study is the most necessary introduction to the meaning and habit of the mosque.

It begins, of course, with the *Bismillah* itself. "In the name of God, the merciful Lord of mercy." But that address is enriched and fulfilled in the variety of terms by which men in Islam both call, and call upon, God. The invocation of God in his names is enjoined in Surah 7.180: "God's are the beautiful Names, so call upon him by them", while Surah 17.110 repeats the injunction to call upon the *Rahman* by any of his names.

Plainly there is no invoking God, which is not also a describing of him. Or in more abstract language, there is no religion without theology. This study is the practical, devotional context in which all consideration of Islam must begin.

There has been much controversy in Muslim scholasticism about the *Asma᾽ al-Husna*, and this has made some contemporary writers impatient of them. In this simple outline, it would be inappropriate to try to enter into the intricacies of this debate. Nor need we lose our way in the sort of sentimentalism which characterized Edwin Arnold's *Pearls of Faith*, whose versified illustration of the meaning of the Names, first published in 1882, may be consulted for certain insights it has to offer. The need for critical caution may be illustrated by quoting the extraordinary passage in the Preface, where Arnold speaks of "the camel-driver, Muhammad . . . abolishing all the idols of the Arabian Pantheon, except their chief, *Allah Ta῾alah*, God the Most High"!

Eluding both the scholastics and the sentimentalists, what ought the sober student to know about the divine names? The phrase *Al-Asma᾽ al-Husna* is found in the Quran in Surahs 20.8 and 59.24, as well as in the two passages above. In 59.22–4 we find the fullest single quranic listing of them. The figure, ninety-nine, is traditional. About two-thirds of that number actually occur quranically. J. W. Redhouse, in the *Journal of the Royal Asiatic Society*,[1] collected from various sources no less than five hundred and fifty-two. But ninety-nine is the devotional number, fixed in the beads of the *Subhah*, or Islamic rosary.

[1] 1880, No. 12, New Series, pp. 1–69.

It also makes the sum of the Arabic numerals ٨١ (81) on the left-hand palm and ١٨ (18) on the right-hand palm—a fact which passes into symbol when, in devotion, the outstretched, upturned hands are lifted to God in prayer.

One ready way of becoming versed in the Beautiful Names is to note them in the personal or family names of Muslims. Almost invariably any name in the form ᶜAbd al- . . . uses one of the *Asmaᵓ al-Husna*. Occasionally one may meet a name like ᶜAbd al-Khalifah. But for the most part the status of *ᶜabd* (servant) is one that can only properly be had in relation to God. So we have the very frequent nomenclature: ᶜAbd al-Nasir, ᶜAbd al-Munᶜim, and the rest. The names of God, properly in construct with the word *ᶜabd*, play as large a rôle in Muslim naming as they do in Muslim praying.

The names have an equally central place in Islamic art. The visitor to the tomb of the Emperor Jahangir near Lahore will find the *Asmaᵓ al-Husna* around the plinth itself. Examples are legion, in *mihrabs*, around domes, and in innumerable illuminated manuscripts. One may also find single names, or pairs, inscribed in places where their special significance belongs, like the *Ya Fattah*, "O thou Opener", on the fly-leaf of a schoolboy's copy book, or *Ya Hafiz*, "O thou Preserver", on the lintel of a dwelling: while *Al-Rahman al-Rahim*, "O thou merciful Lord of mercy", prefaces all works of Islamic philosophy and law. A quranic concordance is a great help in noting the setting in which the names are used and what they signify in the context, as well as in comparing their incidence.[1]

Here our study takes four themes: Invocation, Relation, Involvement, and the Soul's Vocabulary. No attempt can be made to deal with the significance of grammatical forms, nor to classify the names by reference to power, knowledge, mercy, unity, judgement, worshipfulness, in God.

INVOCATION: GOD IN HUMAN ADDRESS

The primary purpose of what we may call God's namability is that he may be invoked. This we have seen already. Significant in this

[1] A useful source for the student of the Beautiful Names is the article in the *Encyclopedia of Islam, Asma al-Husna*. Zwemer's *Moslem Doctrine of God*, 1905, contains a list and analysis. Mention may perhaps be made of a discussion in the writer's "*The Call of the Minaret*", 1956, pp. 40–4 on some aspects of their use, especially their relative frequency and their unity.

connection is the very ambiguity in the word *daʿa*. It means, at once, "call" and "call upon". This is implicit, as reflection confirms, in any names in any context. They denote, in order that their possessors may be addressed. Names, human or divine, would not be necessary unless there were intercourse. They are the vocabulary of converse and relationship.

So, both biblically and quranically, we find that God's names are the ground of his accessibility. Calling him, for example, *Ya Razzaq*, "O thou Provider", and calling upon him to provide, are synonymous. They mean precisely the same thing. The mention of the name is in itself the plea. So it is that much of Muslim prayer, outside the ritual worship, is the simple ejaculation of his names, with no further petition. In terms of aspirations explicitly phrased and uttered, Muslim prayer strikes the Christian student as very inarticulate. Long invocatory phrases are often followed by the barest, baldest pleas, like "Save us from the fire", or by none at all. Yet, in part, the explanation is that in simply naming God, one is calling upon him "in that Name", and awaiting his answer to the description.

Thus the utterance of the name is plea as well as worship. In effect the suppliant is saying: "Be, O God, what thou art". The situation may be loosely likened to that in Christian liturgy where the initial ascription of praise to God provides the ground on which the later petition is based: "O God, who art the author and giver of all good things . . . graft in our hearts the love of thy Name. . . ." In calling upon God, we must know whereby he is called. Our pleas rest upon his character, as such character, delineated in his names, comes within our knowledge. Prayer is thus an intelligible relationship and God's attributes are a practical reality.[1]

RELATION: GOD IN HUMAN CONCERN

We are assuming in all such address to God that he takes cognisance of us. He has given us names to invoke him because he is in vital relation to our lives. If this were not so familiar a statement, it would seem the remarkable wonder that it is. God's having names, usable of him and to him, by man, means that our knowledge of him has living significance.

[1] This is precisely what Christian devotion means in the final phrase of any act of prayer: ". . . through Jesus Christ our Lord". Christ is to us the inclusive assurance and expression of what God is in his manifold names and, as such, the ultimate ground and access of our Godward relationships.

He is not a formula with which to conclude a debate, nor an abstraction to grace a theory. He has names! His significance has to do with our experience.

Study the variety of these relational descriptives. He is *Al-Qabid wa-l-Basit*, "the closer and the opener"; *Al-Khafid wa-l-Rafiʿ*, "the abaser and the exalter"; *Al-Samiʿ wa-l-Basir*, "the listener and the seer"; *Al-Ghafur wa-l-Shakur*, "the forgiver and the cognisant of gratitude", *Al-Hasib wa-l-Raqib*, "the reckoner and the watcher". He is *Al-Wasiʿ*, who comprehends all being, *Al-Samad*, unto whom all beings have recourse. The relational quality of his names is evident in a whole sequence that have to do with human dependence. Our recipience is the other side of God's providence: thus *Al-Wahhab*, "the bestower"; *Al-Muhyi*, "the life-giver"; *Al-Muʿid*, "the restorer"; *Al-Qahhar*, "the subduer"; *Al-Musawwir*, "the fashioner".

In all these senses God's nature is for us a nature in relationship. What he is becomes known in the setting of what he does—the principle which lies also behind the central Christian doctrines of God in the incarnation and the Trinity. Our awareness of him, in other words, is the consequence of his awareness of us. To this fact the New Testament refers in one of those rare occasions where a writer actually changes his words in the act of writing them: "Now that ye have known God, or rather, are known of God . . ." says St Paul (Gal. 4.9). Our knowledge of him, in short, is our side of a divine initiative. What we know of him is experience of his relatedness to us.

The far-reaching significance of this fact, and its implications for Christian expression of Christ to Muslims, take us into the deepest reaches of the divine names. It can be illustrated by those in particular that have, in themselves, a reciprocal quality, in the sense that they cannot be true without mutuality. Consider *Al-Wali*, "the friend" (or "patron"), *Al-Muʾmin*, "the trusty", and *Al-Shakur*, "the cognisant of gratitude". All are terms applied to men in the corresponding relation to God. They then mean, in order, "the protégé", "the believer", and "the grateful".

It cannot then be too strongly emphasized that the divine names bring the Godness of God into direct association with humanity. He is not defined, still less experienced, in aloofness and dissociation. On the contrary, we know him in being known of him. Revelation is relation; truth is experience; theology is doxology. The biblical faith in God as active in history, of God at work in his Messiah, of God as self-given to and among men, is an enlargement and fulfilment of the implications of his names. Indeed, it may truly be said that God's capacity to be named of men involves his capacity to dwell among them. If "words" (like these *Asma*ᵓ *al-Husna*) can meaningfully refer to God, then God himself can become the Word. No one can intelligently use these names and at the same time deny the possibility of his incarnation in fulfilment of them, though of course it will be another matter, beyond this possibility of incarnation, confidently to identify the fact of it. But whether actual or not, it cannot be denied as a possibility without jeopardizing God's namability in general.

INVOLVEMENT: GOD IN HUMAN MEANING

Granted that God, as bearer of these names, is in active and manifold relation to us and all men, we are led into the further fact that we describe such relation in vocabulary that is in general use of men and among them. We could not, of course, do otherwise. For nothing can be described for us except in terms that are already familiar. Such terms necessarily have their human sense and import. In naming God, intelligibly, we are involving him in human meanings. The question at once arises as to the sense in which terms and adjectives, current of men, can be truly and rightly applied to God. Or, in other words, the problem of what the names *mean*.

This takes us into much the biggest issue attaching, in Islamic theology, to the *Asma*ᵓ *al-Husna*. Some of the reaches of it may seem strange and forbidding to readers unaccustomed to think theologically but who may be patient with a cursory summary of what is, seriously, at stake. When one says, for example, that God is *Latif* and *Halim*, and that man is *latif* and *halim*, does one mean the same thing?

As and when the theologians answered a straight No! to this question, they jeopardized the whole reality of religion, revelation, prayer, worship, and theology. For if one cannot use human meanings in speaking of God, one cannot have a meaningful theology at all. And without a meaningful vocabulary one can neither pray nor believe. Yet, if one gave an unequivocal answer Yes! one seemed to do violence to the truth that God is essentially other than man. How can one say that for God to be *Latif* and for man to be so are remotely similar or even comparable at all? Would not such an idea be a sort of *Shirk*, in that man would, allegedly, be sharing what was God's?

Clearly, the dilemma is a real one. The instinct of classical Islamic theologians was to escape from it into a negative theology. Fearing the unthinkable implications of Yes! they took refuge in formulae like the famous *Bila kaif*, *bila Tashbih*, and *Al-Mukhalafah*. God could be denoted in human terms "without asking how", and "without similarity", insisting always on the doctrine of "the difference". Broadly, these phrases meant that the names were to be used without conceding that when they were used they meant, divinely, what they meant humanly. In this way, it was supposed, the dangers of *Shirk* were neatly eluded and the way of devotion left fully open. Men used terms because they had to, or else renounce religion. But they used them with a refusal to say what, if anything, they positively meant.

The "rescue" here of the validity of theology, and of religion, is a highly artificial one. What is given, with one hand, is taken away with the other. "Go on talking of God and continue calling upon him by his names, but do not inquire what they mean." It is little wonder if practical religion found this "solution" unsatisfying. The situation can only be truly satisfied if one sets it within a real belief in the real knowability of God. In the end, if faith and theology are to be significant at all, it can only be in the confidence that God is ready to be involved in human meaning.

Reflection shows that Muslim use of the *Asma' al-Husna* confronts Islam with the same kind of situation as Christian faith in "the Word made flesh". Though Islamic thought roundly rejects the Christian faith in the incarnation, it does not thereby escape the issues that go with it. For, if God is described at all by man in any meaningful and religious sense, he is thereby within the human realm. The Christian faith of God in Christ is simply that because God is love (and therefore self-giving), he gladly undertakes his self-revelation, in those human terms without which no revelation to man can occur. This he does in Christ. We do not need, then, to think of the human realm as something incompatible with God and its terms such that we can only use them of him with the sort of negative, and disqualifying, provisos we have noted. Rather, we believe that the conditions of our knowing him are precisely the conditions his revealing of himself has savingly accepted. Christ is for us the divine assurance of what the Names of God mean, and of the fact that their meaning we can positively know and love.

We apologize to non-theological readers if there is difficulty in this part of the exposition. What emerges is an opportunity to invite the thoughtful Muslim to a new openness of mind to Christian faith. The things in the latter which he often very blithely rejects have more to do with the inner heart of his own thought than he often knows. The more earnestly and honestly we all face the question: *What does it really mean* that God is called by these names? the more we shall be facing something like what Christianity believes about Christ—namely a divine involvement in the things men can recognize because they are in life.

For in the end this question of the sense of the names is deeply practical and spiritual. We do not merely want to have descriptives in order to talk about God, we need them because we depend on him. We do not merely want to debate the possibility of discussing what can be said of him: we yearn to know him "with whom we have to do". A negative theology cannot suffice a living soul.

There are also lesser problems of intelligibility within the names themselves. What, for example, is the exact connotation of *Al-Latif* or *Al-Mutakabbir*? How is God "subtle" and "proud"? And even the names that are seemingly the simplest, like *Al-Malik*, "the king", by what criteria should we interpret? Edwin Arnold wrote a poem on this royal name. Its burden is the kingliness of a monarch who throws open his palace to a potter:

> Consider if a king should call thee "friend"
> And lead thee to his court,
> Roofed large with lazulite, and pavemented
> With flow'rs on green floors wrought:
> If he should bid thee sit at meat; and spread
> A table served so fine
> There lacked not any pleasant food or fruit
> But came at call of thine. . . .

So far, so good. But may there be a royalty which in fact goes out of the palace and dwells in the potter's cottage for sublimely royal ends? And more, what, as Arnold goes on to wonder in his poem, if the potter proves graceless and

> . . . loved him not
> Whose kindness was so strong?
> If Ebn Solul kept not the palace laws,
> Had not the Sultan wrong?

How will the divine kingship then react? For it is just this eventuality which, in the biblical view, as well as in the quranic idea of *Zulm*, or wrong doing, has in fact happened. What, then, will be the reactions and criteria of the divine king-likeness?

These are fair questions. Are the divine names primarily bases for invocation to action on God's part, or requirement for action on ours? Take, for example, the name *Al-Quddus*, "the holy" (see Surah 59.23 and 72.1). Is it a descriptive which denotes "apartness" which men must recognize by ideas of *haram*? Or is it a holiness which in active righteousness goes forth to redeem and sanctify? How are we to understand and where are we to recognize the actions which make good and substantiate the names? These are issues which no sincere use of them can escape. In part, of course, the answers lie in nature and in history. Some are fragmentary answers and others, in the natural realm, are equivocal. Yet in circumstance, in natural law, in the patterns and vicissitudes of our human life, we must read, mark, and learn what it is that God is gracious, wise, able, benign, compassionate, mighty, and strong.

Yet beyond all these meanings of God's attributes discernible in the natural order, the Christian relation to the divine names goes further. It believes that God, involved as he is with us, in being "named" at all, has caused the totality of the significance of his names to be discernible, verifiable, definable, in that supremely divine enterprise of God with and among men, which we know in the person of Christ our Lord. In him the concern of God manward so fulfils itself that the meaning of what it is that God is God comes home, via the manger and the cross, to all who see and hear.

GOD AND THE SOUL'S VOCABULARY

Thus the divine names pass into a living currency, where abstract problems of their import are lost in the living reality of him they describe. We need not stay with a note of perpetual interrogative or suspended judgement about what these names signify, and how. Rather, we are confronted with a dependable invitation to enter growingly into their assured meaning through Christ. If we are right in inviting thoughtful Muslims into consideration of the common problems of thought which attach to the *Asma᾿ al-Husna* we may not stop there, as if abstraction was all.

No man is really "calling" God *Karim*, who is not experiencing his graciousness; nor *Rahim*, without a personal sense of being "mercied". It is idle to cry *Ya-Basir*, *Ya-ᶜAlim*, *Ya-Hayy al-Qayyum*, and not live in the light of his countenance. How shall we name him *Al-Wakil* and not depend upon his dependability? Can he truly be to us *Al-Hamid al-Majid*, unless we live, as St Paul has it, "to the praise of his glory"? It is surely on the *Subhah* of life in its rich fullness that we must "count" his names.

There is, in Doughty's *Arabia Deserta*, an intriguing passage about how place-names are always different according to whether the users dwell or merely pass.

> Here a word of the camping grounds of Moses: all their names we may never find again in these countries. And wherefore? Because they were a good part passengers' names, and without land right they could not remain in the desert, in the room of the old herdsmen's names. There is yet another kind of names, not rightly of the country, not known to the Beduins, which are caravaners' names. The caravaners, passing in haste, with fear of the nomads, know not the wide wilderness without their landmarks: nor even in the way have they a right knowledge of the land names. What wonder if we find not again some which are certainly caravaners' names in the old itineraries?

And he adds further on: "It were idle to ask these land names of the caravaners!"[1]

The *Asma al-Husna* are common to all users. But for some they have "land-right" as belonging to the God whose mercy is for them a native land. And they are much spoken also in the caravans of the casual.

QUESTIONS FOR STUDY AND DISCUSSION

1. The divine names are "counted" on the *Subhah*: what do they "count for" in life and experience? As you have been able to ascertain it, what do Muslims actually mean by saying: "God, he is *Karim*", or "God, he is *Rahman* and *Rahim*"? (Here any of the names may be substituted, the point of the inquiry being the living sense of their use.)

2. The very mention of the names of God can mean, by implication, very rich and inclusive petition, in that God, in being invoked, is being asked to be what he is. Could it then be said that what Christians

[1] C. M. Doughty, *Arabia Deserta*, vol. 1, p. 49.

believe about Christ is that, in Christ, God is being what he is? Does this offer any chance to break free of the futility of merely argumentative debates about terms? For just as any of the names have to be in human vocabulary if they are to make sense to us humans, so God's being to us all that in fact he is means his earthly coming, his suffering, and his active compassion.

3. Many of the names relate to God as Lawgiver, to God as Creator, to God as Sustainer and Provider and Ordainer. But can these names—and the patterns of relationship they describe—be complete unless he is also Saviour and Redeemer? Test any of the names by this idea of their meaning being incomplete short of what is found in Christ and you may open rich doors of spiritual discovery.

4. "God experienced", said Thomas Kelly, "is a vast surprise." Is there, then, a danger that the familiarity of these names makes men's ideas of God conventional and unexpectant? If so, what can be done to recover the sense of wonder?

5. The divine names witness to the reality of the business God has with men and the dependence men have on God. Each has business with the other. How far, according to Muslim concepts, and according to Christian, does this business reach?

6. In men's actual religious experience, imagination plays a much greater part than abstract terminology. How, in your view, do Muslims "feel" about God under and with these titles? What "pictures" go with the names? What is the Christian relation to the answer?

7. What is meant by saying that the *possibility* of the use of these names involves also the *possibility* of God's enterprise of incarnation? (In knowing God we involve him in our meanings: in making himself known he involves himself in our world.) How may we translate this truth into deep actual witness to users of the *Asma' al-Husna*?

9

The Mention of God

What happens to words is sometimes a parable. The English word "mention" now means an incidental notice, a casual reference or remark in the course of a discussion. But the original sense denotes much more than this. For "mention" comes from the Latin and means a constant bearing in mind, a thoughtful consideration. Since it now suggests not what is constantly in mind, but what came momentarily there and was dismissed, there has been quite an impoverishment in the sense.

Likewise the *dhikr* of God in Islam (sometimes *zikr* in the older books). It means, essentially, the mention of God's name in perpetual mindfulness of his presence and his nature. But it may become, degenerately, a mere mouthing of the word *Allah*, in starting a car or spurring a donkey. In concept, the acknowledging of the eternal in the present or the practice of the presence of God, it may in fact be no more than the idle pronouncing of God's name.

Life in Muslim lands is characterized by this frequent reference to the name of God. There is hardly a conversational exchange or an ordinary situation without such invocation. *Allah* would certainly be far and away the leading term in any word count. Greetings, commands, directives, congratulations, commiserations, hopes and fears, chances and changes, are all expressed to the accompaniment of divine invocation. The Muslim habit of God-reference is not of course *dhikr* in the technical sense. But it is the first, and constant, form under which the student encounters a basic feature of the Islamic way of things. Before taking up its quranic and devotional character in Islam, it may be well to take stock of its biblical antecedents.

DHIKR: A BIBLICAL RETROSPECT

We need not either presume or imply in detail *how* the biblical affected the quranic. Recollecting the divine name is deeply Semitic. The name (whether of men or of God) denotes the acknowledged nature: it is the very soul or quality of the bearer. It is in no sense just a label about which one could say: "What's in a name?", implying that any other would serve as well. On the contrary, the name is the expression and guarantee of nature and character. As such it is irreplaceable. The passing out of a man's name (e.g. by lack of sons), or deliberate "putting out" of his memory, meant extinction for the Old Testament people and was to be avoided at all costs. When Ps. 6.5 says that in Sheol there is no remembrance of God, it does not mean that there no one thinks to mention him, but that in Sheol God is not present. He does not act, his realm (as the psalmist believed) does not extend there.

Hence, throughout the Law, the Psalms, and the Prophets, the remembrance of God's names is the acknowledgement of his nature. It means a putting of oneself under the protection of the fact of him. It is an active relation of the soul to God as God, as his being God is known in his repute in history, nature, and law. When Moses visualized the people asking him in Egypt, "What is his name?" he rightly surmised that they would seek some assurance before committing themselves to any risky summons. They were not merely asking, for curiosity's sake, how he was denoted: their question, to use a modern phrase, was existential (Ex. 3.13).

So throughout the Old Testament. "The Lord is his memorial", says Hos. 12.5 of Judah. What can it mean save that the mentioned Name, the consciously-trusted character in his reliance, is the Lord. So in Ps. 71.16: "I will make mention of thy righteousness only", meaning that what I call to mind (and so call to aid) will be nothing but the right-dealing of God. The psalmist is not defining the extent of his conversation but the grounds of his trust.

Hence also the refusal to "mention" strange gods (cf. Ex. 22.13; Josh. 23.7, etc.). In Isa. 26.13, the writer protests that though the people have passed under the political hegemony of pagan rulers, they will not swerve from the sole "mention" of the Lord, by invoking the deities of heathen overlords. In the same sense is the thought that, by the conscious invocation of God, the believer forestalls the possible intrusion, into his mind or into his affairs, of other deities. The name of God cannot co-exist with other "names". Thus the Muslim will sometimes think of the *dhikr* as ensuring that he is not left alone with the demons or the jinns. The one true invocation is a sort of antiseptic against all false ones.

In the same context is set the tremendous Old Testament sense of history. God's name is part of experience through the corporate reality of his acts in history. The name, there disclosed and authenticated, remains "a strong tower" into which the righteous may run. What God has been not only reveals what he is but pledges what he will be. All three gather in the meaning of his name. So there is repeatedly in the Old Testament the thought of God's fidelity to his nature. "For my own name's sake" becomes an assurance and an indication of his relationships. God is self-consistent and is willing to be pledged. The sacred history, being the disclosure of his name, is a sure index to his ways.

Not all these meanings of the "mention" of God are rightly to be carried over into Islam. Important differences and contrasts must be elucidated by what the Quran does and does not say. But there is enough general affinity to make the parallels valid and suggestive, leaving aside all critical and historical questions as to how the common tradition survives and recurs. Certain New Testament bearings on the same theme will come in a final section.

DHIKR: THE QURANIC PICTURE

"Remember your Lord in your soul with humility and reverence and without ostentation: remember him morning and evening and do not be negligent." So Surah 7.205. There are repeated quranic exhortations to the same *dhikr*. Surah 33.41–2 runs: "Believers, be ever mindful of God: praise him morning and evening. He and his angels bless you" (cf. Surah 76.25). Surah 4.103 links the *dhikr* with the period after *Salat*: "When your prayers are ended, remember God, standing, sitting, or lying down. . . .", and 2.152 says: "Make mention of me and I will remember you; be grateful unto me and be not among the graceless unthankful."

Tradition, perhaps based on this last verse, declares that "there sits not a company remembering God but the angels surround them and divine mercy covers them and God most high glorifies them among those who are with him". This mention of God may be either *dhikr khafi*, or *dhikr jali*, inward or outward, of the heart and of the lips. It involves, of course, the use of the Beautiful Names of God, earlier studied, and is implied on every occasion of saying: *Allahu akbar*. All circumstantial things are to be set in the context of God's power and eternity. Thus Surah 18.23–4: "Do not say of anything: 'I will do it tomorrow' without adding: 'If God wills' and should you forget this, make mention of your Lord and say: 'May God guide me and bring me unto truth.'"

The way in which the personal experience of the Prophet is gathered into the meaning of *dhikr* is a large element in the Quranic thing, but may be more readily noted in the next section (cf. especially Surah 73, "The Enmantled One"). Equally important is the fact that all *dhikr*, or mention of God on the part of men, is reciprocal. God is mindful of man and from this mindfulness, or divine relation to man, comes the very possibility of man's responsive acknowledgement of God. Thus the Quran itself, as a whole, is described as the *dhikr*. Whose *dhikr*? God's. Several significant passages express this idea.

Surah 38.1 swears by the Quran as *dhi-al-dhikr*. Dawood prefers the more obvious translation "renowned" (i.e. "owner of repute").[1] But the more likely sense is that the Quran constitutes, or contains definitively, the divine reminder. "Warning" is sometimes made the translation of *dhikr* here: but this concentrates on only one of its functions. The Quran's view of itself is that it is the sum of what God intimates, or says in address, to man. Thus Surah 38.8 has the unbelievers asking: "Has the reminder been sent down to him?" and in 15.6 is their accusation that he upon whom the reminder is sent down is jinn-possessed (cf. 68.51). Surah 16.44 has God reassuring Muhammad that he has indeed sent down the *dhikr*, i.e. the Quran, upon him to give men to know clearly the revelation to them and in the hope they may take it seriously (cf. also 15.9: 36.10), and 41.41 states plainly that "the reminder . . . verily is the Book sublime". It is this fact which makes the rejection, or gainsaying, of the opposition to the Prophet so heinous in his eyes. In Surah 21.36 their denying the "mention of the merciful" (*Al-Rahman*) is linked with their accusation that Muhammad has made an evil mention of their gods—thus bearing out the thought, noted above, that the name, as the very being of its bearer, is incompatible with the "naming" of any other.

The Muslim view that the whole Quran is God's *dhikr* to man is reflected in the further fact of the *hifz* of the Book. The ambition of

[1] N. J. Dawood, *The Koran* (English text), 1956, p. 277.

every devout young Muslim is to be a *hafiz* or memorizer of the Quran, an achievement which has always been the indispensable condition of Islamic theology. Why do the faithful want to memorize by heart the whole Book, except that by doing so they are ensuring in the most inclusive way that they remember what it reminds? If the Quran is the point and place of the divine communication to man, memorizing takes that revelation to, and into, the *hafiz*. He makes it personal to himself in that he has absorbed it, verbatim. He is thus equipped for the most ready and comprehensive *dhikr* of God. His memory is promptly reproductive of the divine reminder.

It is not without significance that the same word *hafiz* is one of the descriptives of God—*Allahu Hafiz*. God keeps or preserves man, as man keeps or memorizes his word. The *hifz* in other words, is reciprocal, as the *dhikr* is. God's revelation to man, and man's acknowledgement of God, belong together. The same point is implicit in the association made in Surah 2.198, 203 between *dhikr* and pilgrimage. The pilgrim is, of course, at a divine rendezvous. "So remember God at the sacred monument, remember him who has guided you . . . and when you have performed your rites remember him as you remember your fathers or more intensely . . . remember him during the stipulated days." In 22.36–9 *dhikr* of God is enjoined at the time of animal sacrifice.

It remains to add that *dhikr* in the Quran is understood to lead to a most characteristic Islamic trait, namely, *itmiʾnan*. Surah 13.28: "Those who have believed it is whose hearts find rest (*tatmaʾinnu*) in the remembrance of God. Is it not in the remembrance of God that hearts are set at rest?" The root word here, "rest" or "tranquillity", sometimes denotes a general security (which can be misplaced, as in Surah 16.113). But its more inclusive meaning has to do with spiritual peace of mind, deriving, it may be, from confidence in the signs of God and his provision. It is what the disciples of Jesus sought in requesting to eat of the table from heaven (Surah 5.113) and what Abraham desired in seeking from God corroboration of his word (2.262). In *itmiʾnan* we are drawing near to the dimension of peace in the recollection of God. The name defends, secures, satisfies, and quietens.

All the foregoing, and not least the experience of *itmiʾnan*, receives a particular interpretation and intensity in the patterns of Sufism, and the mystical Orders, in Islam. The variety of Sufi adaptations of the ruling quranic principle of the recollection of God is a fascinating study. Its bearing on a practical Christian relation to Muslims depends upon the degree to which genuine Sufism exists in the context and this must be a matter of local concern and discovery.

The discipline of the Orders, and corporate participation in the zawiya, or circle, of initiates, shape the Sufi sense of divine awareness, the goal of which is the experience of ecstasy, and of *fana*ʾ, or passing away of the self in oneness with the divine. In such a context the Sufis came to their own characteristic understanding of *itmiʾnan*. It was for them a state of desirelessness, or utter contentment, induced by the deliberate abeyance of all will and longing. The soul's satisfaction with God meant what it also presupposed, namely its complete repudiation of all other loves.

A similar sense is denoted for mystical Islam by the term *tawakkul*—the Sufi's "In thee have I trusted". This "trust" means for him a studied disinterest in all normal wants and activities. It is exemplified in the story of a man down a well, without a ladder or a rope, who rebuffed a would-be rescuer and on being asked what he wanted replied: "The will of God." This utter quietism of *tawakkul* and *itmiʾnan* was the form in which such Sufis demonstrated that their only "mention", their sole reliance, was the fact of God. One can dispute their exegesis without mistaking the way in which even this caricature indicates the inner sense of what *dhikr* means, as a state in which the consciousness of the divine is the dominant reality.

A major textual source of this development was the quranic picture of Muhammad, with its implication that he could be described as a practising mystic. Surah 73 bears the title: "The Man in the Mantle." The Prophet, shrouded in his cloak, sought that abeyance of sense-awareness which became the technical goal of later Sufi *dhikr*. In this state of abstraction he is summoned to "remember his Lord's name with full devotion". The night watches are the ideal time for this, since in the day-time work presses distractingly. If the Prophet himself received under these conditions the intimations of the Quran's early contents, a true loyalty to that revelation lay in a conscious imitation of the conditions of its own descent. So the Sufis argued. Muhammad was, they implied, the first Sufi. In their technique of *dhikr* they were submitting themselves to the *ways* of knowledge—a proceeding that must offer the surest means of receiving its significance. In responding to the Quran, they took not only what it said but how it came. Their *dhikr* was modelled on Muhammad's.

DHIKR: THE POPULAR SITUATION

An instinctive outside reaction to Sufism is that it does not represent normal, ordinary people. Yet it is remarkable how many simple, artisan-type, manual workers have been involved in the Sufi Orders, which are far from being some monastic *élite* or intelligentsia. In any event, what is a Christian relation to *dhikr* in Islam, as it exists for people in general? Clearly, Christians must think out their duty towards the reiterated Muslim reference of daily things to God.

Perhaps the point of most urgency is the sheer difficulty of the real thing. One evident implication of the whole system of Sufism, however we may assess it, is just this fact that the practice of the presence of God does not happen easily or readily. *Dhikr* cannot be had merely by enjoining or assuming it. The true "mention" of God can only be by discipline, by deliberateness, by sincerity.

"The world is so much with us." Life is everywhere becoming more distracting in its demands and needs and pressures. Surah 73 may commend the Prophet to the watches of the night. But what average contemporary Muslim finds any retreat there, with the increasing competition of radio, of television, of the cinema, and all the wearying intrusions of the world by day? The situation, of course, is one which all religions and cultures face, now that western technology has become well-nigh universal. Here is something in which we are all akin. But what is to be done? That *dhikr* is impeded by *ghaflah* or "negligence" is a frequent quranic warning (e.g. 10.7, 92; 30.7). "Those who care only for the life of this world" are noted in 53.23 as being the people who ignore God's reminder. *Ghaflah* is, throughout, the antithesis of *dhikr*. Yet this indifference is precisely the thing that is so easy: it is what the generality of men practise.

It has to be admitted that habits of divine invocation and customary ejaculations of *Ya Allah* do not of themselves save men from *ghaflah*. Indeed, they may often minister to this very negligence, in that the outward word, the habit of expression, takes over for the meaning. God is then remembered in forgetfulness, as it were. When we have entrusted our recollection to a form of words we are by that very fact forgetting it. This impression is often deepened by the manner in which *Allah* recurs in Muslim conversation and mentality. Can the Christian, sharing as he does in much of this situation, do anything to bring a more alert sensitivity, a more conscious significance, into our endless "If God wills", "By God's leave", "God's be the praise"?

But this need to be real in our invoking and "mentioning" of God merges into a deeper question. *Dhikr* of God ought, truly, to be sincere and sincerely meant. But do we not all, even when sincere, "mention" God with glibness? Is our God-awareness not altogether too complacent? Have we not a ministry here with which to break through into *all* the areas of our human life, whatever their religious culture?

"I remember God", says the psalmist (Ps. 77.3), "and I am ill at ease." "I recollect in *dhikr*" he says, and in consequence "my whole soul is disquieted." This seems to be the opposite of *itmiʾnan*. The thought of God is far from tranquillizing. Such disquiet is a necessary prelude to the only right tranquillity. Have men really remembered God—his majesty, his lowliness, his mercy, his holiness, his purpose? Do we remember him as a psychological exercise, or in personal yearning? Is his name a syllable to pronounce or a reality to adore?

We can, of course, only face these deepest questions out of the resources of our Christian understanding of his grace. There, our remembrance of him is only enabled and validated in our response to what he is in Christ. The tokens which must guide our acknowledgement of his name are found in the active disclosure of what his name expresses. When, as noted earlier, Moses sensed that his people would demand an authentication of the call to exodus in terms of an inquiry as to the name of the God who sent him to them, he received from God the strange and moving reassurance: "I will be there, as he whom I there will be" (Ex. 3.14). The people's requirement of an antecedent guarantee about him was not to be met. Only in the event would they know what his name was: only in the concrete experience of his deliverance would they know him for the deliverer he was. This was the gist of God's reply to Moses. The knowledge of God is always an experimental knowledge. It is in the experience of exodus that the God of the Exodus is known. The event declares him.

Here lies the ultimate significance of the New Testament for all *dhikr*. The event declares him. God says to us in the history of the incarnation and the cross: "I am what here I am." "I have been there as he who I there have been." This active, actual, self-expression of God is the significance of the Gospel history. Truly to "mention" him is to recognize his name, his defined nature, his active grace, in this history.

So the Christian believes. He has to commend this conviction by the quality of his own awareness of God and the reality of his own walking in this light. Realizing the divine name in this sense may well begin with disquiet. But it ends in peace. It starts by rebuking our easy familiarity: it compels us to recognize that the very possibility of God's being truly "named" by us in the relationship of recognition derives only from the infinite condescension that has brought this knowledge, by "the Word made flesh", into the range of our forgiven and responding spirits.

Can we translate the "mention" of God, shaped by that Word in Christ, into the great world of Muslim *dhikr*? In Surah 16.43 comes the intriguing directive: "If you do not know, inquire of the people of the reminder." Are we the people of that reminder which is the Gospel?

QUESTIONS FOR STUDY AND DISCUSSION

1. What does *Ya Allah* actually mean as commonly reiterated among your Muslim fellow-men? Is it a term of resignation? of patience? of fear? a vague comment for lack of a definite one? a mere form of words? a serious invocation? What does God-consciousness amount to in choices of will, in ways of thought, in attitudes of heart?

2. Is there, in respect of question (1), any real difference between the average Christian and his Muslim fellow?

3. The Prayer Book version of Ps. 77.3 says: "When I am in heaviness I will think upon God." What the Hebrew text says is: "I am in heaviness because I think upon God." Most people expect thought about God to be "comforting" when things go hard. How can this attitude be educated into a right relation that has to do with the whole of life and with the true and awesome reality of God in holiness and grace?

4. "Let not your heart be troubled . . . believe in God . . ." (John 14.1). This would seem to agree that faith in God should lead to tranquillity of spirit. But what, in this connection, is the point of what follows—"believe also in me"?

5. While it is quite wrong to speak of *dhikr*, as some writers do, as wholly a Sufi thing, the Sufi *dhikr* has much to teach about Islam. Have you any direct acquaintance with it, or its literature and effect in personal life?

6. What would you learn about Islam from the assumption that one's first duty to the Quran is to know it by heart? Can we say that what the memory has readily, the mind has habitually? What of the Christian counterpart—"Christ dwelling in our hearts by faith" (Eph. 3.17)?

7. In Christian *dhikr*, or mention of God, in the words of Luther: "We run straight to the manger: we begin with the wounds of Jesus." Why? How do we draw others the same way?

8. What are the main modern sources of negligence of God (*ghaflah*) and how can they be faced?

10

The Meaning of Iman

WHAT IS MUSLIM FAITH?

Much the most characteristic distinction within the Quran and in the thought of Islam is that between the believer and the unbeliever, the insider and the outsider, in respect of *Iman*. But what, precisely, does *Iman*, or faith, mean and include? As a term, it is the name of the action from the root of which the name of the doer is *muʾmin*, or believer. A question so basic as the nature of the *Iman* by which the Muslim is "muslim" is clearly a vital theme for study.

To the question: What is *Iman*? a variety of answers might suitably be given. There is the formal answer of Surah 4.136 which lists the traditional items of faith to be taken up below. The architectural answer might well be the form and artistic expression of the mosque, with its eloquent patterns and meanings. The historical answer would be the campaigns and expansion of the seventh and succeeding centuries when Muslim *Iman* impressed itself on the shape of world affairs. A personal, even mystical, answer might be given in the words of a recent paper at a Muslim-Christian study meeting at Toumliline, Morocco: "... the sense of the divine presence, momentarily renewed in the heart of the believer and having its source in Truth and Love."[1]

All these answers—and many others—would have their particular validity. Pursuing the question in our own immediate relationships and friendships we would gather a variety of answers, all having their personal honesty, even if they are formally partial or even false. Indeed, part of our very alongsidedness is just this open-hearted effort to know by what truths and thoughts men ultimately live, move, and

[1] ʿUthman Yahya. See *The Muslim World*, vol. 49.1, Jan. 1959, translated by the author from the French of Dr ʿUthman Yahya, in *Toumliline, I, Principes d'Education*, Rabat, 1957, pp. 41–56.

have their being, political, social, and individual, in the world where we are in trust with Christ.

For purposes of present study and assessment, however, we had better return to Surah 4.136. *Iman* is the counterpart of *Din*, and the two definitively, make up Islam: the thing believed and the thing performed. *Din* stands on its famous Five Pillars (*Arkan al-Din al-Khamsa*) *Tashahhud*, *Salat*, *Zakat*, *Saum*, and *Hajj*: that is, confession, worship, alms, fasting, and pilgrimage. *Iman*, on which all these acts are based, articulates and amplifies the content of the first, namely confession.

CREDENCE: OR THE FORMAL MEANING

Without falling foul of long etymological and theological discussions of the matter, we may say that, in general, *Iman* in Islam has three broad senses belonging to the verb *amana* and as used with its prepositions. There is *amana* and *amana bihi* in the sense of credence or acknowledgement, and trust unto security or safety, and *amana lahu* meaning submission and obedience. These we may loosely call the formal, the emotional, and the moral connotations of the word.

The first is almost synonymous with *saddaqa*: "he believed in that he took to be true what was said", with the sense, perhaps, that in so doing the believer "secured" or "exempted" the source from the charge or suspicion of being untrue. The believer accepts as true, propositionally and actually, the items or elements which constitute the faith. As listed, according to traditional understanding, in Surah 4.136, these are: God and his apostle, the Book and the books, God's angels and other messengers, and the Last Day. Some also add the *Qadar* or decree of God as *de fide* in this technical sense.

It is at once clear that actual Muslim faith includes many more elements than these, such as the obligations of worship and the authority of tradition, the sources of the *Shari^cah*, the patterns of statehood, the corollaries of *Dar al-Islam*, the duty of *Jihad*, and many other basic concepts and sanctions of life. But these are all to be seen and understood as derivative from, and undergirded by, these five (or six) items of credal Islam.

The ground, so defined, on which the religious structure stands, is theological. There is no need to argue this. It is axiomatic. That sublime dogma of the divine Unity was the very prophet-creed which took Muslims to the four corners of the earth. There follows that crucial "and" which in the Muslim *Shahadah*, or witness, and in the "creed" of Surah 4.136 always follows the divine name and links Muhammad with it. Then there is revelation, cumulative and final, providence, and eschatological reckoning. These are of course the books, the angels, and the judgement.

The most adequate, single definition of Islam would be that it means, "Let God be God". Historically, the Prophet's mission was a drastic expulsion of the idols and a unification of human worship. The host of intervening deities and celestial powers or demons was negated in the passionate preaching of primitive Islam.

Its burden was that God's prerogative as God must never be alienated to another. Its anathema was the sin of *Shirk*, whereby men make trespass, in emotion, or creed, or reliance, or opinion, upon the sole Godness of God. *Tauhid*, or Unity, is thus a powerful, intense, and imperious thing. It does not merely state oneness, it requires it. In its great and strong negation it proclaims the non-entity of all the idols. That the latter, in the subtlety of their emotional hold on wistful men, defy this veto, Muslim superstition admits. But the credal witness to a sole sovereignty in heaven is unmistakable.

Angels, as presented in the Quran, have their great rôle in the mediation, or *Tanzil*, of the Holy Book (Surah 2.97, 98 and 66.4), but they have also protective functions in relation to men and take the soul at death (Surah 6.61). They are exempt from the dignities of man as a creature of moral freedom and responsibility—a status probably betokened in their being called upon to prostrate themselves before the creature Adam (Surah 7.11, *et al.*). The Devil, or *Iblis*, in refusal to do so indicates his disapproval of the divine "risk" in confiding so high a rôle to so fickle a creature. Thus the very "fallenness" of the Devil consists in his quarrel with the dignity of man—a most significant bit of anthropology. Because they are above men in their exemption from carnal desire and moral creaturehood, the angels are instruments of God's reckoning with man (e.g. Surah 82.11, 12) and bear witness against men at the judgement (Surah 50.16 f).

Death ushers into the next world, just as birth ushers into this one. The judgement is referred to repeatedly as the Day, the Day of separation, on which no soul can help another soul, the Day of reckoning when the scales will determine (Surah 101). It is *Yaum al muhit*, the day of the inescapable and all pressing "assize". It is the day of the final bankruptcy of all idolatrous trust, the catastrophe of the *mushrikin*, the total destruction of the works and claims of unbelief. The last of the items of faith is also the climax of its vindication.[1]

Eschatology in Islam is a theme in itself into which we cannot here venture if we are to keep our thread of *Iman*. These are the points of the Muslim's acknowledgement of truth. It is with these realms that his dogmatic faith has to do. God's will and man's will in their relation must be outlined separately elsewhere.[2] Central to the affirmations of *Iman* are God, revelation, providence, and moral accountability. Faith means and asserts the eternal Reality, the past of law and prophecy, and the future of destiny, and between these stretches our finite present, the place of decision and transit.

SECURITY: OR THE EMOTIONAL MEANING

There is a striking phrase in Surah 9.12: *La imana lahum*, to which Lane draws attention, meaning literally: "they (the people in question) have no faith", but where the sense is "they lack the power of granting protection". The promises they make being hollow, credence that is reposed in them is disappointed. There is here an interesting transference of sense from "faith" as a trust made to "faith" as a trust deserved. Nor is this merely a verbal matter. Faith in God is not simply a credence placed in him but a security held in or from him. The root concept behind the term is to render safe and secure. Just as the believer in a sense "vindicates" what he believes of God, so God "vindicates" the believer. In this context, we may understand *Al-Muʾmin* (59.23) as a name of God meaning "the guarantor", the one who is cognisant of man's reliance and ready to "justify" it in protective reciprocation. There is some ground for thinking that faith in the Prophet has the same implication in that by virtue of it the "believers" found a mutual relation in which the apostle of God and they were bonded in a single solidarity of community, leader and led, with mutual obligations of fidelity expressed in "defence" and loyalty. Certainly this was the pattern of Medinan development. It is reinforced by contrast in the meaning of the *Baraʾah*, by which the Prophet retorted to unbelief by repudiating obligations of protection. The obstinate and recalcitrant rejectors were rejected: the "outfaiths" were "outlaws" (Surah 9.1–28). Earlier "treaties" based on expediency or policy were now to be terminated after notice, so that faith alone could be the sole principle

[1] See below, ch. 19, "Death and the Muslim". [2] Ch. 15.

of immunity from molestation. Peace and religious allegiance were to belong together, with warfare and unfaith likewise indivisible.

With this communal security may be linked the Quran's frequent phrase, which first occurs in Surah 2.2, about its quality as "a book, *la raiba fihi*"—the volume about which there is no dubiety—not simply in the sense that people do not doubt it, but that it does not merit doubt, inasmuch as it secures or gives a total guarantee to those who give it the acknowledgement of their belief. It is clear, on reflection, that this situation goes very deep into the whole texture of Islam and may well be regarded as the heart of the emotional meaning of *Iman*. It is true that Islam has no doctrine of assurance such as Christianity proclaims, because it has no comparable doctrine of grace. But there is undoubtedly among Muslims an emotional sense of being right and being "secured", at the centre of the meaning of *Iman*.

This situation is to some degree characteristic of all faiths and it has very much to be kept in mind in all inter-religious relationship. Creeds are not abstract systems that can be argumentatively changed at will. They are homes of the spirit, havens, sanctuaries, refuges, that, by their very familiarity and the at-homeness of the generations in them, constitute a sort of motherland of the spirit, where a man finds confidence just in belonging.

This may be the best point to consider an underlying contrast in Islamic and in Christian *Iman*. It has often been very rightly said that the Christian faith cannot really be expressed without the use of the personal pronoun. One does not merely say, "Christ died". That is true. But Julius Caesar also died. One says, "Christ died for me". The involvement, in the very texture of what happened, of the believer who confesses it, is central to the whole meaning of faith in Christ. It is not merely that "he came down from heaven", but that "for us men and for our salvation" he did so. St Paul's comprehensive "confession" of the meaning of the cross was sharply personal: "The Son of God loved me and gave himself for me." And the same apostle affirmed the resurrection in the words, "He was seen of me".

In Muslim faith, the personal pronoun is involved only in the form of *Ashhadu*: "I bear witness. . . ." It is not used objectively in the statement of the significant things. *Iman* has to do with the reality, the fact, the truth, of revelation, judgement, providence, and scriptures. But, in actually witnessing *that* these are, one is not personally articulating *what* they are to oneself.

The distinction, of course, must not be overdone. No faith *that* so and so is can be altogether apart from *what* it is. In Sufi and in Shi[c]ah patterns of Islam, too, there are deep and moving expressions of personal apprehending and participating. Also, and not least in recent writing about Muhammad, there is frequently the language of devotional involvement and "existential" meaning. Our point throughout is that the significance of Islam for even the least sensitive is a soul-security in which he is communally and personally a part. So we are not saying, and must not say, that Muslim confession is externalized and "academic", except in the case of the sort of "nominalism" which afflicts all religious creeds.

Nevertheless, when these considerations have full justice done to them the essential contrast remains. Christianity offers to the volunteer for faith the acceptance of a personal judgement already upon himself, a way of life that must begin and continue in the recognition that he is what the cross mirrors him, that something has happened on his behalf which is not only a fact *in* his creed but a fact *of* himself. "We beseech you . . . be ye reconciled to God." This is offer as well as dogma: it is about things that not only *are* true without but *come* true within. This is the heart of the difference between Gospel and law, between the implications for us of the divine self-giving and humiliation, and of the divine giving of books, angels, prophets, and law.

Some further consequences of this situation follow us when we turn to:

OBEDIENCE: THE MORAL MEANING

There is the verb *amana lahu*, "to surrender to". Sometimes, it would appear, *amana bihi* has the same sense. In any event, faith has its corollary of obedience. It means the act and state of submission to God. The realm of *Din* must not be separated from the realm of *Iman*. To believe must be to do. In one passage in Surah 2.143, where the context has to do with the *Qiblah*, the Muslims are assured that God will not let prayers towards Jerusalem be lost and the word used for prayers is *Imanakum*.

There were, it is true, long controversies between the Khawarij and the Murjites on the question of the necessity or otherwise of good works to faith. Other sects also entered the controversy on these themes in a way that is more than a little abstruse to us to-day. We may conjecture that the main difficulty arose when the Khawarij in their puritan zeal wished to devalidate the Islam of those whose works, habits, or attitudes displeased them. The Murjites wished to postpone such drastic judgements with all their divisive and disruptive consequences, and allow that he was a Muslim who claimed to be so.

But if, for purposes of definition, he must be held a Muslim who confesses the faith with lip and heart, for purposes of adequacy there is no doubt that the works proper to a Muslim should also characterize him. It is true there is a problem in the reverse direction of one who goes through the outward performance of Muslim works but has no real faith in his mind and heart. Such *munafiqin*, or hypocrites, were an issue in the Quran (e.g. Surah 63.1 f) but need not detain us here. The true faith is a faith that does the works, even if it is well not to press the negative form of the same proposition. This problem of course is endemic in all faiths.

Positively, the theme of faith as obedience is best exemplified in the quranic Ibrahim, the biblical Abraham, the foremost type of the true Muslim, for whom belief is action. It is he who rejects the creature-worship and the ancestral idols (6.74–82; 43.25–6) and who takes the idolaters sharply to task (21.52–70; 37.81–96). So he is declared the true *Hanif* (3.58–61) and the "friend of God" (4.124). The Quran affirms that the "religion of Abraham" and that of Muhammad are one (2.124 and 6.162).

In a relationship of truth and love in Christ with Muslims our most constructive duty lies in two realms belonging to this theme of obedience within faith. The first has to do with the range of the obedience, the second with its possibility. Abraham may be our mentor in both.

A CHRISTIAN RELATION TO A MUSLIM'S IMAN

1. *The range of obedience.* To what areas of their faith are men surrendered? Islam has at its heart the tremendous thought of submission to divine patterns of life. Leave aside for the moment the fact that our concepts of these patterns differ. The idea is vast and awesome. What does it really mean? Can it be that none of us have really wrestled with what *Islam* demands? This business of no-idolatry is so inclusive and exacting. Have we admitted any false absolutism in the place of God? Surely indeed we have and sometimes it has been done even in the name or for the sake of empirical Islam.

Or this fearful conviction of the judgement? Is it entirely eschatological, a distant, posthumous affair? How far is our daily life conscious of and responsive to the reality that God reigns in righteousness? In Rom. 12.19 there is a striking phrase on this very point: "Avenge not yourselves but rather leave room for the judgement of God." It is not "give place unto wrath" in the sense of "don't be angry". It means "conduct your affairs and bemean yourselves as those who believe in the presidency in history of a sovereign divine authority". What might this mean for men's strident nationalisms and racialisms if they believed it? *Yaum al-Din*, or the Last Day, is something more than merely balances in the hereafter: it means criteria of behaviour in the here and now.

Or ponder those books and angels, God's communicability and his communication. For what are guardian, or other, angels but the truth that God's will, loving and righteous, presses relevantly upon our every situation? Was not the angel of the Church in Revelation 2 and 3 essentially the capacity of that Church to apprehend the voice of God? What then of our obedience to the intimations of heaven's rule and right? Perhaps the trouble is that we do not help the Muslim to be sufficiently alive to the obedience he proposes—a course that might well be a bigger duty of ours than beginning by the substitution of alternative items of belief. Or better, let these other items come in the context of each man's awakening to the dimensions of his own. This leads to the next point.

2. *The feasibility of obedience.* When we deepen our criteria we also deepen our categories. Most scholars know of the reluctance of many a classical theologian to say, *Ana Muslim* or *Ana Muʾmin*—"I am a Muslim: I am a believer." For this was a long theme of debate in the Muslim Middle Ages. God might not have willed for him to be one. Despite all that we have rightly said above about security in belonging, there was always the necessary reservation of not presuming upon the unpledgeable will of God, even in so central a matter as one's status as Muslim. So they would carefully say: "I am a Muslim if God has so willed."

Perhaps there are deeper reasons even than these why Muslims should question whether they are Muslim. If, as we have argued we must, we deepen our ideas of what submission to God means and involves, men may well pause before saying glibly, "I am surrendered". For how shall I be? Am I able for submission in any pattern pleasing to God?

How am I to obey? What ought belief in his judgement to mean now as well as then? "How shall a man be just with God?" was the agonizing question of a man very much exercised about the business of *islam* (see Job 9.2).

Likewise Abraham's rejection of the idols is one with his active acknowledgement of God's call and will. In denying his people's gods he affirmed their sole true Lord, and his. In this positive obedience he becomes the symbol in the New Testament of a loyal, even filial, relationship with God which antedated the whole system of Mosaic law, and experienced a righteousness which that law—for all its "goodness"—failed to bring about. In these terms Abraham, in Romans and Galatians, becomes the archetype of God's grace and of the life that fulfils and enjoys the divine promise.

This New Testament sense of the law as failing to deliver the goods of righteousness is a dimension which, normally, Islam fails to register. The Islamic assumption is that "life is by the law", that man can hear and heed, of himself, the demands of God's purpose, embodied in the law. Man's vocation in faith, is, for Muslim concepts of man, a perfectly feasible vocation. Man simply needs to see and do. Islam, for the most part takes all too little, if any, measure of the human capacity to say No! to this high destiny.

The Christian understanding of man, however, holds the radical nature of sin and believes that his being of the "community of Abraham" means more than simply an "education" into divine commands (which is the task of prophecy). It requires a work of recreating grace within, which man must freely receive as a self-transforming power. Without this, his very will to conformity to the divine law becomes a matter of merit and of pride, and these quite disqualify its real acceptability to God. "So then, they that are in the flesh cannot please God" (Rom. 8.8).

If we truly care about the Christian understanding of man, as not perfectible by law but blessedly redeemable by grace, how can we miss our deep and stirring "business" with Islam as a widespread system of "rightness" by law? Our Christian, biblical "radicalism" about man and his remaking gives us criteria by which to look at the positive concern of Islam for a human order of things that is rightly under God.

Consider the central conviction of Islam that there is a succession of prophets. They come confirming and reiterating each other—some of course to limited people or areas. Where are they finalized? Islam says:

"In one of their number." He is, admittedly, as Islam insists, the last, but still, for all that, belonging to the succession. The Gospel says they are finalized in something different from them all—not in "prophecy" at all, however "crowning", but in a saviour, in an act of redemption which confirms the prophetic claims, but realizes them as teaching alone never did or could. Is there not a real sense in which the very successiveness of the prophets proves their inconclusiveness? (Jer. 25.5; 29.19; etc., and 2 Chron. 36.15.) Would they need to be repeatedly sent, unless there was a claim perpetually to be made, and *repeatedly being refused*?

Does the like thing (i.e. prophecy), however superlatively seen, end the series? Or do we not rather end in something, literally, crucial, which brings to a climax, as the cross does, this entail of rejection and wrong, and through that climax masters by suffering the evil thus focused into one? (Cf. Luke 20.9–18, the parable of the Vineyard.) Is it not in this way that the whole quranic belief in a succession of divine spokesmen sent to men, claiming their submission to God's order, points beyond itself to a divine action which completes the prophetic purpose as prophecy never did?

Is it not here that we see our Christian "business" both with and in what Islam believes, and yet also beyond it? If we say that the Gospel supersedes prophecy (both biblical and otherwise), it is a superseding that also fulfils. We cannot have the negative relation without the positive: our witness must be to both. Or in other words, we must hold to Abraham as both our patriarch and theirs. We must share, if ever we are to discriminate.

To get men to pause with such thoughts is so important in a setting where they seem easily to think that once the mind is taught the will is right, that to know is of itself to do. Are we really in submission, we who believe in books that describe it, messengers that enjoin it, the providence that watches over it, and the judgement that assesses it? Surely that is the question we must press upon all such believers. In what sense essentially can a Muslim say: "I am *muslim*"? Perhaps our reservations about truly being so ought to be concerned, not (as in the classic days) about God's will to have it so, but about ours, and about our capacity "to will and do of his good pleasure".

For then we may awake to the real relevance of Christ to submission, and of right believing to right being. The heart of the Christian Gospel has always been that man's submission is not, first, an attempt at conformity to the pattern of goodness, but an entering into the peace of reconciliation. Our surrender is, first, that of rebels received in pardon, as the prerequisite to obedience in righteousness. It has to do with our being made into his likeness before our behaving after his will. Faith is more than a series of propositions by which to act: it is a power by which to become. Of the availability and the reality of those inward transactions of grace there is no doubt, and need be no reservation. To be truly conformed to God's law we must first be transformed by his grace (Rom. 12.2).

To represent these Christian truths in their bearing on the items of Muslim faith we must penetrate ourselves, and try to help Muslims to penetrate, into the widest reaches of what books, angels, and judgement divinely mean. The books, of course, include the Bible (though not, Islam believes, in its present form nor with all its New Testament parts). The average Muslim is well content that all the other divine writings should no longer be extant. Such is his confidence that the Quran does wholly in lieu of them. But in some quarters in contemporary Islam, there is an interest in the books of the Book of Christian faith. We must encourage the view that neglect of pre-quranic "oracles" of God is hardly consistent with faith in the Quran.

Then there are the angels. Nathaniel, in John 1.47–51, was assured that the final import of the ascending and descending angels of Jacob's ladder was the Son of Man—the inclusive and ultimate sphere of God's communication to man. In inseparable association with the same divine initiative of grace the biblical judgement is seen. For there we are concerned, not simply with the balances of human deeds and merits, but with the consummation of history, both cosmic and personal, in the setting of God in Christ. Again we find, as always, that lively penetration of sympathy into Muslim *Iman* brings us back responsibly to our own.

QUESTIONS FOR STUDY AND DISCUSSION

1. It is clear that *Iman*, just like Islam (or Christianity), may mean at least three different things: the personal living convictions of the individual; the items of a formal adherence; the historical entity within which these convictions or these items belong. In view of this what would you say *Iman* really means and holds for different Muslims of your acquaintance?

2. When searching, through friendship, for the real personal meaning of *Iman* to the Muslim *mu'min* it is well to think honestly into what, precisely, Christian faith means to us, not merely as a formal credence but an inward reliance.

3. What is the essential difference between the believer's relation to the day of judgement as it is understood in Islam and in Christianity?

4. Or, putting (3) in other terms, the New Testament makes "the day" synonymous with "the day of Christ" (cf. Phil. 1.6, 10; 2 Cor. 1.14; 1 Cor. 1.8, etc.). How does the phrase "of Christ" affect the whole concept of the ultimate reckoning of God?

5. Have the New Testament occasions of angelic commissions and ministries any light to throw on the nature and purposes of that communicativeness, on God's part, of which angels and messengers (in both our faiths) are the poetical symbol and for our imaginations the means? Think especially of what the angels rejoice over in heaven (Luke 15.7 and 10) and what they rejoiced about on earth (Luke 2.13 and 14).

6. "This is the work of God that ye believe on him whom God hath sent" (John 6.29). What is the precise meaning of this statement that *the* work is faith? What does the Christian belief (that faith in Christ is the condition of God's work within us and of his working through us) imply for the Muslim faith-works equation? How might this meaning of something we must first become, before something we ought to do, be expressed?

7. What experience have you of spiritual fellowship with Muslims in the genuinely shared items of belief? How far can or should these be expressed in common prayer or worship?

11

Islam and the Natural Order

There is in Muslim tradition a rather plaintive story of a weeping mountain to which the attention of Jesus was called by neighbouring villagers. They told him how they had heard the wailing of the hill from the time they had settled in the village. When Jesus sought the reason for its sorrows God gave the mountain the power of speech, and it said: "O Jesus, I am the hill from which the idols were hewn which men worship instead of God."

The hill's distress was allayed by Jesus who assured it that the quranic passages (2.24 and 66.6), about "stones" as well as men being the fuel of hell, did not apply in its case. But the story has a moral, for the perceptive reader, much more telling and immediate than a mountain's reprieve from the Fire. For it expresses the involvement of the natural order in the perversities and evils of human choice and human action. Men in their mastery over material things use them to shape and assert false absolutisms of their own and thus compel the resources of the natural world to be unwitting partners in idolatry.

The implications of this tradition, to which we will return, suggest, however, only one of several reasons for the urgency and promise of the topic, ISLAM AND THE NATURAL ORDER, as very proper to our studies. "Nature", wrote the seventeenth-century master of curious lore, Sir Thomas Browne, "is the art of God." It is "that universal and public manuscript that lies expansed unto the eyes of all". As such, the natural order is the biggest single common denominator among men, unifying them in their context even when they differ radically in their cultures and their creeds. In these days, when we have inherited so far-reaching a situation of mutual alienation and controversy between Islam and ourselves, is it not imperative to explore every possible chance of common experience? May it not be that nature, the shared arena of our life and of our science, affords us just such an occasion?

There are also, in the very dimensions of current technology, grounds for spiritual communication which, while urgent in themselves, are unencumbered with the polemic and estrangement of the past. If the very mountains can be apprehensive about our idolatries, they have much more awesome reason when they yield strontium for scientists than when they are quarried for pagan idolaters.

THE QURAN AND THE WONDER OF NATURE

"The old legend that Islam was born of the desert", wrote Professor Gibb in the first sentence of his *Mohammedanism*, "is taking a long time to die."[1] His remark is true enough as a protest against the familiar idea that Islamic monotheism reflects the all-embracing vault of heaven under the desert sun and an emphasis on the urban and commercial framework of quranic ideas. But his words do not disqualify the immense awareness of nature evident in the origin of Muhammad's mission or deny that, by and large, it had to do with a nature grim and awesome.

This is not the place to speculate on the influence of natural setting upon racial character. Not for the Arab in his peninsula, certainly, the situation testily described by Horace Walpole in a letter of 1768: "It began here on Monday last and then rained near eight and forty hours without intermission. . . . Every summer one lives in a state of mutiny and murmur . . . because we will affect to have a summer and we have no title to any such thing." Rather, for the haunts whence the Quran, the imperious sun and none of that damp and green which western isles gather from the Atlantic swell.

The quranic sense of nature reflects its context with immediate eloquence. It is a world where the dark clouds of rare rain, the springing wells with their attendant palms, and the mysterious olive that gives oil for light, are all "signs" or intimations of a divine power and presence. The vocabulary of nature-description in the Quran is vigorous and vivid. Its "earliest portion", as Lane Poole wrote, "is one long blazonry of nature's beauty".[2] Together with the imminence of the judgement, this theme of nature in its attestation of the divine was the ruling topic of Muhammad's first impassioned deliverances. Its

[1] H. A. R. Gibb, *Mohammedanism*, Oxford University Press, 1949, p. 1. Quoted with permission.

[2] S. Lane Poole, *Studies in a Mosque*, 2nd edn, 1893, p. 129.

impetus, though gradually dwindling, continued to influence both the content and form of his utterances to the end.

"By the star when it setteth" was the form in Surah 53.1 of the Prophet's pledge of his vocation. The same sense of the planets in their majesty informs such a passage as 10.5–6 which moves into the human doxology of verse 10. Surah 55 is another of the "nature" lyrics of the Quran with its repeated question to the unbelievers: "Which of the benisons of your Lord will ye deny?" found 31 times in 78 verses and relating to such varied items as dates, corn, fodder, jinns, pearls, seas, and the gardens of heaven.

The invocatory setting of the nature passages may also be illustrated from 81.15–16 and 93.1–2. "The bright morn" and "the still night" are in their dependable return a fair pledge of veracity. Here is to be seen that quranic sense of a link between God in creation and God in moral law and revelation, one of the sharpest illustrations of which is the thought of Surahs 44.38 and 21.16, which represents God as protesting that he has not created the heavens and the earth, and all that is between, in jest. Al-Baidawi, commenting on the first of these two passages paraphrases: "Rather we created them freighted with all kinds of wonders to arrest the attention of the beholder, as a token to the intelligent and as a means whereby all that relates to the servants of God may be ordered in this life and the next."

Nature as the realm of the divine will has the dimension of wonder in the double sense that it sustains and humbles man. Consider 10.24: "This present life is like the golden robe with which the earth bedecks itself when watered by the rain. Crops—the sustenance of man and beast—grow luxuriantly: but as its hopeful tenants prepare themselves for the rich harvest down comes our scourge upon it, by night or in broad day, laying it waste as though it had not blossomed only yesterday."

Perhaps the best way for the student to "find" nature in the Quran is to read it steadily, concentrating on the earlier Meccan Surahs and noting the oft-recurrence of the concept of "signs" and the associations of the phrase *Rabb al-ʿAlamin* ("Lord of the worlds") and of the *Asmaʾ al-Husna* or Beautiful Names, with special reference to those like *Al-Razzaq*, *Al-Wahhab*, and *Al-Wafi* that have to do with God's goodness in the natural order. The emphasis throughout is on an immediacy of dependence and on nature as the arena of the divine power.

This is evident in the further fact that the Quran's concern with nature is no merely poetic or artistic thing. It is not an essay in aesthetic appreciation. Interesting it is to note, for example, how many general words for natural phenomena, many of them popular in pre-Islamic poetry, are entirely absent from the quranic concordance. "Winter" (*shita*ᵓ) is there only once (106.2): "spring", "summer", "autumn", (*rabi*ᶜ, *saif*, *kharif*) not at all. Nor do we find *thalj* (snow) (perhaps understandably), *sahra*ᵓ and *bariyyah* and other common words for "desert" (very surprisingly). Nor, it has been noted, do we have any words having to do with "order" *rattaba*, *nazama*, *nassaqa*, and *dabata*. Many of the normal words for agriculture are all absent, though there is much about hunger. In all these respects, vocabulary only corroborates the evident fact that the meaning of nature is to be sought in its moral and religious significance. It is just this moral import which comes into crucial urgency when science begins to respond to nature in its own inductive and pragmatic way. The Quran, however, like the Bible, insists on the religious clue.

There is one other aspect of the Quran's wonder at nature, namely its firm participation in the prevailing Arabian belief in the reality of jinns. It firmly disqualifies (as in 34.41) the pagan instinct to worship these creatures, whom popular belief associated with natural phenomena, housing them in springs and winds and rocks. But it leaves them, though mere creatures and themselves hearers of the Quran (cf. 72.1), in full being in the popular imagination. The consequences of this are still evident in popular Islam all over the Muslim world. With a dogmatic monotheism goes a practical reliance on personified forces or factors in nature, in which men are confirmed by the quranic account of the jinn. There is, as it were, an emotional compromise of true *Tauhid*, or unity, as long as one's trust or credence is given to other than God. Only when nature is emptied of such personified powers is it really filled with God: only then are our acts of gratitude truly directed where they belong. Idolatry is as much, or more, the work of men's hearts and minds as it is of their hands. As long as, with the jinn, nature is "feared" pluralistically, the oneness of its creator and Lord is not fully recognized within it.

ISLAM AND THE WEALTH OF NATURE

Man's response to nature in its wonder leads to man's trusteeship of nature in its wealth. Both are central to the meaning of worship, which is both reverent gratitude for what is and grateful reverence in the use of it. In its accounts of the creation of Adam, the Quran sees him as accepting the trust of authority over nature on behalf of God (see 2.30–9). Surah 16 has a detailed and striking picture of nature's amenability to man's needs and of his enjoyment of her wealth—a wealth that is yielded up on condition of labour and intelligence.

The term *islam* is here applied in a double way. It has reference both to that automatic, or innate, conformity of external nature to the divine will, and to the chosen, voluntary obedience of men to the divine purpose. The former is the realm of natural law, the second of moral law. Law in nature happens necessarily, by virtue of the very constitution of things. The divine *amr* runs through the whole being of phenomena and gives them genesis and continuity. On the *amr* in nature see 32.4–5 and 41.12. With men, however, the *amr*, or command of revelatory behest, waits upon the proper submission of humanity. It is not in that sense "natural" or part of the constitution of things, as is nature's law-abiding: it is willed and chosen. Nature's cosmic *islam* provides the stage on which man's moral, religious *islam* is to take place, and by its dependabilities, which science harnesses, makes possible that empire of humanity in and over things which his submission concerns.

Here we return to the weeping mountain with which we began. Muslim and Christian understandings of both man and nature, and of the one within the other, come very close together at this point. Yet they also seriously and sometimes subtly diverge. Perhaps we can list a few considerations, keeping in mind that the pace of modern technology, as well as the common ground of faith about God, makes them rich and constant points of a Christian interpretation.

1. *Technicology and Wonder*. We live in a world where scientific ways of life are more and more pervasive. Works of technology are everywhere reshaping both the patterns of existence and the frames of mind. Electrification, as Muhammad Naguib points out in *Egypt's Destiny*, profoundly alters the way of thinking of an Indian village.[1] A universal danger—the more so because of the incredible speed with which these changes of mind have ensued in Asia and Africa—is that men lose the sense of wonder.

Old patterns of thought were too often and too much the victims of

[1] Muhammad Naguib, *Egypt's Destiny*, London, 1955, p. 161. He adds: ". . . and tends to reduce the rate of increase of their population".

"supernaturalism". Everything was directly credited to "spiritual" agencies—jinns, demons, evil eyes, etc. Superstition was, then, widespread and unquestioned. There are areas where this remains true, with the Quran's own permissive tolerance. But in general we are now increasingly faced with the opposite danger, namely that everything is merely "natural". Man's science undertakes to explain all and his technology to control all. Then the wonder, the gratitude, the awe, that underlie and inspire the sense of worship, fade and languish.

Not that phenomena we have scientifically explained are essentially any less mysterious and wonderful. But men in their new-found set of criteria think they are. There is the story of a scientist who, when confronted with a witness who said he had really seen ghosts, denied, but further remarked that even if it were true it would be "just another scientific fact". That is the mentality which turns awe into casual familiarity and supposes that when you have "explained" a thing it is no longer wonderful. We are living in a world where "our jaded, sated sense of fact is itself a fallacy". We confuse "science", for all its legitimacy, with meaning and behave as if "explaining" was "explaining away". The more we know about everything, in research, the less everything, in reverence, seems to concern us. We build scientifically on nature's *islam*, the dependable order of phenomena, without reference to our own. This proceeding is just as invalid as the perpetual "supernaturalism" which science had to begin by displacing.

And it is far more dangerous. Because nature is God's realm it is capable of being man's. The laws by which he has subordinated its ways to his will are what bring it into amenability with ours. Only, then, in our recognition in turn of his laws for us, the demands of his kingdom in spiritual force, is our sovereignty within nature's laws either right or secure. This is the underlying meaning of Islam which science has only now urgently corroborated.

2. *Worship and Will.* So far in the broad sense Muslim and Christian travel together—to the degree in which they are loyal to what their faiths affirm. Are we to have an equivocal, negligent, distorting attitude to "the favours of our Lord"—an attitude belying their real meaning and our status as recipients? This is the question of Surah 55 and the burden of that "controversy" with his people that God has in nature, biblically seen. We may compare Micah 1 and 6, "the Lord's

controversy", where nature, hills, and mountains are the witnesses and jury. Or will men bow in true worship?

But while Muslims and Christians together recognize man's God-ward accountability in and over nature, they part sharply in belief about the resulting situation. Granted this vocation of man, this obligation to worship, how does humanity in fact behave? What of our refusal of a true relation both to God and to his world? Islam sees man as readily capable of the right relation. When he errs from it he can be recovered for it by law and exhortation (coupled, no doubt, with sufficient political inducements). Islam in that sense is fundamentally sanguine about human responsiveness to God and about the "good" competence of the right Islamic state-hood. So sanguine is it in fact that redemption and regeneration have no place.

Yet, for all that, Islam is alert and vigilant and hostile enough about those idols! Somehow, in our spiritual and theological relation with our fellow men in Islam, we must move radically from the Islamic abhorrence of idolatry into the Christian diagnosis of human nature. For they belong potentially so close together. What, after all, is this chronic perversity of man, this inherent tendency to be idolatrous, if not, in another guise, the very thing Christianity is diagnosing when it talks about sin? Men, set in nature to exercise dominion and to bring due obedience to God, persist in preferring some other "absolute" to God. These "idols", of which nature improperly treated is the perpetual source, are equally "idolatrous" be they stones or races, rocks or Mammon, moons or ideologies. Islam is sure they can be disowned and dethroned merely by being identified and denounced.

Yet the problem of idols—or the problem of sin, identical as they are—requires a deeper solution, and one that proceeds upon a deeper diagnosis. If we propose the breaking of the idols, as Islam does, must we not realize that man's treatment of nature is immensely fertile in idolatrous invention? It matters little whether we have gods of wood and earth, or if we have turned gain by exploitation, blood and race by arrogance, economic systems by violence, or science itself by pretension, into actual usurpers of the recognition we owe to God. All is alike idolatry. Only these more contemporary forms of its expression are the more subtle and pernicious.

Taken with a proper diagnosis are they not quite evidently the expression of what Christian theology has always believed to be the sin of man? Being so, are they such as can be overcome simply in that they are identified? Is our rescue from their deceitfulness merely legal? Are we emancipated from their power merely by exhortation? The Christian does not think so. When we see that idolatry is synonymous with sin, we shall see, in turn, that a true worship, free and right and pure, comes only in the way of the cross.

The tears of the Prophet's mountain can only finally be dried by the power of that redemption. The Bible pictures nature as deeply involved, to the point of travail, in the iniquity of men (cf. Rom. 8.20–2). Its deliverance, in this tremendous New Testament analysis, hinges upon the "revelation of the sons of God", that is to say, upon the coming into being of a new quality of humanity, where nature is secure within the divine intention because men, its masters, are won to the divine obedience.

Is it not possible, in these days of man's awesome technological empire, to draw Muslims by a more radical understanding of their own repudiation of idols to a more hospitable reckoning with the meaning and necessity of the cross? Would that Muslim thinkers took their anti-idolatry seriously so that living theology might join it to the significance of the cross.

3. *Husbandry and Gratitude*. Finally, man the "eternal ploughman" keeping the creation alive.

> Only a man harrowing clods
> In a slow, silent walk
> With an old horse that stumbles and nods
> Half asleep as they stalk.

We know within us that this is the final pattern of man and nature—the partnership of husbandry. The horse is going of course, ousted by the tractor, and maybe one day technology will banish the cows also and give us milk from grass by laboratory action. But technology is not all. In any event most of humanity are still peasants with spades in their hands and the soil at their feet.

To make their agriculture more sure and more effective is the aim of all agricultural mission—a task close to the heart of the Gospel, with its deep emphasis on sowers and seed, husbandmen and harvest. But the final dimension of Christian faith as it relates to man's tenancy of his good earth is gratitude. And the Quran, with its insistence on reverence, would agree. "Thanks be into God" is the constant cry of farms and homesteads, of oases and folds, of soil and soul. If, across our religious barriers, we can learn and express in common this "natural" gratitude, we shall be nearer to the communication of our Christian gratitude at the grace that is beyond nature and in Christ. We shall be nearer to that worship in which alone the thoughts of men are saved, and all their doings sound and sure.

QUESTIONS FOR STUDY AND DISCUSSION

1. Have you been able to open any doors of common sympathy with Muslims by way of nature and its beauty, whether in the miracle of spring, the night sky, or growth after rain?

2. What is comparable between the quranic thought of nature and the biblical, whether in psalms, the prophets, or in the Gospels? What sort of nature parables do you find in the Quran?

3. How far do you think, in your region, the new "scientific" mentality (for which there is nothing more than positive "facts" of science) has displaced the old traditional and superstitious "supernaturalism"? Do you find, for example, a new attitude to medicine and surgery?

4. What, according to your knowledge, do literate and unlettered Muslims understand by the jinn of the Quran? Do some forms of belief in them compromise a true monotheism?

5. Why and how is man's vocation to submission to God different from that of general nature?

6. In what ways does the Islamic disavowal of idolatry involve Islam in the Christian doctrine of sin? How can we express this clue in our day-to-day evangelism?

7. Man is within nature by his body, in dominion over it by mind, and beyond it in his spirit. Each of these, which are necessary to a true worship, can contribute to a false one. Consider this in the light of the Muslim belief about rightness through law and the Christian faith in salvation through Christ crucified.

8. What are the potential idolatries in modern technology? How does Islam and how does the Church in fact face them?

12

Idolatry and the Arts: An Islamic Dilemma

WORDS WITHOUT PICTURES

Many are the posers of calligraphy for the non-Arab visitor who finds himself in a house of Muslim prayer. Whether it is in Cairo or Isfahan, Istanbul or Lahore, he will be at once fascinated and perplexed by the long "rivers" of quranic script that adorn the walls and domes and minarets. Letters and words superimposed upon each other defeat his desire to disentangle and translate them. But they express in the most characteristic form the devotion and the dogma of Islam.

This chapter cannot hope to handle the vast themes that belong with Islamic art. Its purpose is to investigate one central issue attaching to the relation between Islamic art and Muslim belief—that of idolatry and art. It not only has great interest in itself but also focuses certain deep questions of Christian understanding about God and man and nature. By exploring these we may be able to make Christian faith more plain and illuminate a problem attaching to all worship, which for Muslim reasons is acutest in Islam.

Words without pictures—such is the uncompromising law of Islam in the mosque. The central affirmation of Muslim dogma—*Tauhid*, or unity—lays its firm veto on representational art. The image, the ikon, the statue, the painting—these are banished. The new faith from Arabia was passionately iconoclastic. Expanding into lands with a rich Christian heritage of pictorial art and splendid iconography, Islam dismissed the whole as a dangerous temptation and rejected it contemptuously as a menace to the *la ilaha illa Allah* of its own mission.

The will to art could not, of course, be denied. Though arts other than poetry had been scanty or effete in original Arabia, the peoples of Islamic penetration, east and west, both Persian and Byzantine, were rich in artists. Nor could Islam, being solidly a human thing of living folk, seek, still less secure, a permanent or total abeyance of the will to art among its new adherents. But such was the strength of the veto that wherever the Islamic writ ran unchallenged the arts were left to palaces and homes. Or, within the mosque they were confined to minor arts of lamps and carpets, books and tiles, manuscripts and utensils, and to architecture and its contributory skills. Outside domesticity, where the puritan and the austere had less authority, the visual arts were firmly excluded. Calligraphy reigned supreme and entered everywhere, into niche and pulpit, *mihrab* and *minbar*, with geometric design as an ally, and without a rival. The pen dominated. The brush was only for the calligrapher. The chisel of the ikon-maker or the sculptor had neither part nor lot.

There was, of course, a positive reason why the pen should flourish. The divine revelation was, after all, a sacred text. Had not its first revelation extolled the gift of penmanship to man? "Recite: and thy Lord is most gracious, who taught by the pen, taught man what he knew not" (Surah 96.3–5). Was it not insistently "an Arabic Quran" (Surahs 12.2; 20.113; 41.3; 42.7; 43.3)? This Arabic quality, with all its grammatical features, was inseparable from the status of the book as "Quran". In this sacred language it had been vouchsafed to the Prophet; in this tongue he had heard and recited it; in this tongue it was in turn heard and recited by the faithful. Arabic had been chosen divinely as the condition if its true intelligibility. In any other translated language it was not authentically itself. All this was ample reason why the rich resources of Islamic creative art should go into calligraphy, why their cult of beauty should be an inscribing of texts—words as adornment and the adornment of words.

Yet this positive incentive to the pursuit of calligraphy could have well developed in harmony with other skills of the artist. Christian faith, too, being biblical, had loved its sacred text. The positive reasons are not enough to explain why it enjoyed so strong a monopoly. The veto on statuary and images is needed, not to explain the love of words but to require that they remain without pictures and representations. What we have to deal with is the fact that any image or visual symbol in religious worship is anathema to Muslims, making the mosque perhaps the most remarkable example of the power of dogma in religion over form and creation in art. It is well to explore the roots of this situation.

THE VETO AND THE UNITY

It is remarkable that the main Arabic words for idol, ikon, or representation, *asnam*, *ansab*, *suwar*, and *tamathil* (these being the plurals), occur very infrequently in the Quran itself. Modern exegesis, for reasons to be examined below, seems inclining to the view that the prohibition is not so absolute as for long it was thought to be. Certainly there is very little direct mention of these words in contexts forbidding idolatry. Surah 5.90 is the most important passage. It reads :"Wine, games of chance, idols (*ansab*) are an abomination, Satan's work; so avoid them that you may prosper." The other plural of the same word, *nusub*, occurs in 5.3, "... that which has been sacrificed to idols ... that is ungodliness".

The word *asnam* is mentioned in 6.74; 7.138; 14.35; 21.57, and 26.71, in all of which Abraham or the children of Israel either encounter or repudiate idolatry. The implication is clear but there is no precise prohibition as such in these verses. The word *suwar* is used only of God's fashioning the forms of men (Surah 40.64), though the word *taswir* (representation) is widely found outside the Quran in discussion of the rights and wrongs of image-making, painting, etc. As far as the Quran is concerned, God only is named as the *Musawwir* (59.24), the great fashioner. The word *tamathil* is used only in 21.52 and 34.13. In the first case Abraham rejects these "images": in the second Solomon is described as having them made for him, together with "places of worship", *maharib*, "porringers and cooking pots". The root *mathala* is in general more concerned with parable and allegory than physical image-ing.

Cursory examination of the quranic use of these nouns is interesting, if only for the somewhat meagre results it yields. But the anathema we are studying, fortified by the good example of such leaders as Abraham, rests squarely on the utter rejection of *Shirk*. The evil and folly of this "making of associates with God" are writ large in every section of the Quran. Those who are guilty of doing so are the *mushrikun*, and these are altogether contrasted with the *muslimun*. One aspect of *Shirk* (a many-sided enormity) is the veneration, or the invocation, of any but God. He and he alone is the sole, proper object of worship and prayer, and all that even by implication displaces him in the reliance, the expectation, or the adoration of men is an idol. So deep was this fear of alienating from God to another the worship due to him that representational art fled the precincts of Islamic religion.

It follows, of necessity, that the *Hadith* and the commentators corroborate and even intensify the prohibition of statuary and pictorial figures. The Prophet, for example, said that "angels will not enter a house in which there is either a picture (*surah*) or a dog". Al-Nawawi, commenting on this tradition, explains: "The making of such representations is tabu under all circumstances, whether or not it is applied to something that has a base use, since it contains a resemblance to the creation of God; it makes no difference whether it is on a garment, a carpet, a dirham, a dinar, or a fil, on a vessel, a wall, etc." This was a thoroughness of veto impossible of application (even when moderated by Al-Nawawi's allowance of representations of trees, mountains, and the like not reckoned as living creatures). But in mosques it was enforceable.

Another oft-quoted tradition declares: "Those who will be most severely tormented on the day of resurrection are those who make images (*al-musawwirin*)." Al-Tabari at once takes this *taswir* or imageing to be a conscious worship of what is not divine. There are other traditions about the Prophet destroying any garment in his house which had crosses on it. Without speculating as to how ᶜAʾishah (from whom this comes) had such garments, it suffices to note that the Prophet's action in this respect may have been directed against the cross as an emblem and not representations in particular.

There can thus be little doubt that the traditions and the ᶜulamaʾ, in commentary and fatwas, firmly and explicitly prohibit all painting or other depicting of living forms and that this disapproval was sustained and compelling enough seriously to curb, or deflect, Islamic artists from all religious expression in the arts that was inconsistent with it. Truly, caliphs in their palaces and the aristocracy in their patronage, as well as endless obscure craftsmen in Persia, India, and elsewhere, defied the ban and indulged their creative gifts or fancies undismayed. But, for the rest, the arts of pious and God-fearing Muslims were concentrated into forms and on to fabrics which tallied with the orthodox position, to the great enrichment of carpets, manuscripts, lamps, and tiles.

MODERN TIMES AND DIFFERENT VIEWS

That uneasy classical and medieval accommodation in Islam has been drastically affected by modern developments. The orthodox understanding, by which the artistic urge has to be suppressed to thwart an ever-present *Shirk*, falls foul of large and irresistible changes in the external world. Photography multiplies everywhere. The illustrated press grows apace in Muslim reading. Much photography is evidently beneficial: x-rays, for example, or aerial surveys of enemy territory (both examples have been cited in recent Muslim writing on this question). The representation of Islam, too, among non-Muslims may well be served by pictures.

On all these counts, practical and pious, photography has to be admitted, and, with it, why not painting and the other arts? After the manner of the bewildered or the dubious, conservatives fight a rear-guard action. When, in 1955, statues in New York of great legislators of history were being refurbished and it was found that one represented Muhammad, strong Muslim pressure dissuaded the authorities from re-erecting it. There have been similar incidents in which, for example, encyclopedias have been precluded by Muslim intervention from illustrating any of their articles on Islam. But these instances should be seen as substantiating by contrast a much stronger current running the other way. It is insisted increasingly in many quarters that artists and the arts should be liberated from theological vetoes and that creative painting should not be tarred with the brush of *Shirk*.

Even supposing, as the argument runs, the prohibitions in the Quran and the *Hadith* are as they have been interpreted, times obviously change; they change, indeed, because of the very success of Islam. A society like that in the Hijaz in the Prophet's day was so prone to idolatry that only the most ruthless prohibitions would suffice. With such *mushrikin* as Quraish were nothing would avail but a total and absolute veto. It would, however, be folly to treat a Muslim society to-day, after centuries of Islamic *Tauhid*, with the same stupid severity. Such a policy would be equivalent to saying that Islam had failed and that no Muslim could be trusted not to take a picture for an idol. A ban, once necessary, can surely be safely lifted: to dispute it would seem to disqualify Islam itself.

This interesting argument from time goes further and claims that quranic prohibitions (Surah 5.92, for example) do not forbid painting and statuary but only the idolatrous use of them. Early commentators were in error in hastily identifying art with idolatry, and failing to note that there was no inevitable *Shirk* in artistic reproduction. This exoneration of the artists from any presumption of guilt runs counter to centuries of fixed ideas. But it must be admitted that its case is very strong.

One recent writer to investigate the matter is Ahmad ᶜIsa in *Majallat al-Azhar.*[1] He urges that *asnab* and *nusub* were idolatrous because pagan Arabs set them up as stones or plinths and actually worshipped them in ritual sacrifices. Pictures etc. that were not the object of worship would be a quite different case. He cites the precedent of Solomon with his *tamathil* (34.13) and adds that the various traditions do not mean absolute prohibition, while the distinction between things that cast a shadow and things that do not (the latter not tabu) is foolish and untenable. He insists that the Prophet himself permitted figures on garments after the danger of a relapse into paganism had passed.

He continues: "Who knows but that if the problem of the making of representations had not been connected with the idols of the Kaᶜbah and the quarrel between the Muslims and the polytheists which arose over them, the Prophet might have given his explicit consent to the making of representations and statues, which in his law would have occupied a position like that which they have in the law of Solomon?"[2] This view is supported by citation from the opinion of Muhammad ᶜAbduh that art is a kind of "seen poetry". Pictorial art need in no way be involved in veneration and *Shirk*. The tongue, ᶜAbduh illustrates, is able to tell lies: but one does not for this reason deny it all speech. Art need not be for ever vetoed because some works of art have been implicated in the errors of the *mushrikin*.

The authorities of Al-Azhar demurred about ᶜAbduh's opinion and *Majallat al-Azhar* enters a note of reserve about Ahmad ᶜIsa's views, though it prints his articles. Nevertheless, there would seem to be eminent sense in his pleas and justice in his reminder that "the general law of life . . . sweeps aside those who do not go along with it".

IDOLS WITHOUT THE ARTS: THE VETO THAT CANNOT SUCCEED

It is important, however, to think further than this sane and practical conclusion. For much more is implicit here than simply agreeing that the arts do not deserve to be religiously vetoed because some have misguidedly worshipped the artistic form. The old view that artists make for idolaters is not only untenable in fact: it also proceeds upon a

[1] See *The Muslim World,* vol. 45.3, pp. 250–68, and *Majallat al-Azhar,* 1951, vol. 22, pp. 605–9, 730–5, 943–5, and vol. 23, pp. 147–51, 468–72.

[2] Ibid., pp. 267–8.

false materialization of idolatry and misses altogether the kindred truth that symbol is vital to true worship. To see that it is vital is much more than agreeing it may be innocuous. Since both these aspects are central to Christian worship, our witness and our relationships with Islam require a patient study of them. There is the added incentive that what is involved affects directly the relations of Islam with eastern Christian Orthodoxy, the most significant expression of Christianity among Muslim populations.

If anti-idolatry is the most magnificent thing about Islam, the limited senses in which idolatry is taken are the most unsatisfying. Through all discussions of the nature of *Shirk* runs the assumption that paganism is its most obvious haunt. The idols are literal, physical, tangible, material, destructible by axes, things to be pulverized by energetic zealots and burnt to ashes in fires. They are stocks and stones and pillars, or ikons and images. *Shirk* is something that is necessarily performed in temples or at prayers. To alienate from God is to ask protection from an angel, to venerate a saint or relic, to seek the intercession of an ancestor, to depend upon a charm or to invoke an image. *Shirk* happens when men pray, when they are fearful and want succour, or are misguided and lack wisdom.

Yet is it not more truly identified at its worst when happening outside temples and shrines, and when it springs not from apprehension but from pride, not from frailty but from defiance? Are the worst idols material at all? Is a final anti-idolatry properly equipped merely with hammers and brooms? Are there not more desperate disavowals of God in the heart when men, in self-will, defy the lordship of God in heaven? Is it only a sin in sanctuaries or also a disobedience in life, in politics, in commerce?

The long Islamic conviction that representation was idolatry is simply part of this preoccupation with the pious and the material when idols are considered. Now that time and change are helping Muslims to break loose from the idea that the idol is an image, that *Shirk* has to do with craftsmen, that the danger lies with things, may it not become plain also that there is and can be no veto on idolatry? Idolatry can be inwardly forsaken: it cannot be outwardly forbidden. It may be insisted with truth that "there is no god but God". But what matters is that men should "have no other gods but him". Men will invent idols of the state, of the market place, of the nation, of their own perversity, whether or not artists paint and chisellers carve. To veto these last in order to obviate the perverted use of their achievements is like proposing to curb drinking by taking away the signs from wine-stores. The signs, it is true, may attract indulgence but they do not generate it; nor does their absence terminate the will to drink. To remove a potential occasion is not to remedy an inner instinct.

In these days one of the most obvious and promising areas of Christian-Muslim encounter is just this issue of idolatry, bringing together the deepest concern in original Islamic mission with the central Christian diagnosis of man in sin.[1] If Muslim thinkers are seeing that idolatry is more than its possible occasions from the craftsmen, its real meaning, eluding all such veto power, may begin to engage their thoughts. But there is another side to the coin.

THE ARTS WITHOUT THE IDOLATRY: THE NEED THAT CANNOT BE DENIED

It is not simply that banning representation does not exclude the idolatrous: there is the other fact that the veto may disserve a true worship. There would seem to be in classical Islam an over-simplification on both counts. Words without pictures, faith without symbols, worship without arts may be an understandable objective in the setting of Islam's beginnings. But can it really be? Or does it really happen in this necessarily sacramental world? Are not the words, for the worshipper, a form of picture? Do they not "represent", visually and sensually, an intangible thing called "revelation"?

Is calligraphy not in the end a thing of the sense? No one, it is true, least of all a Muslim, is likely to count a script a thing to be worshipped. But may the same not equally properly be claimed for a right symbolism of statue and ikon, of crucifix and candle? Can we not break through Islam's supposed, but unreal, independence of the artistic to a deeper and more humble understanding of the glad Christian involvement in it? If we can, we may be nearer than we have ever been to penetrating Muslim thought with the meaning of the incarnation. This may seem a large claim. What follows is devoted to exploring it.

"Thou shalt not make to thyself any graven image" ran the old commandment. No Christian, loyal to this Old Testament heritage, will fail to see the negative point of the Islamic repudiation of all

[1] Some attempt was made in *Sandals at the Mosque*, London, 1959, to explore this fascinating theme.

representation. Early Christianity likewise was diffident about many of the arts which abounded, often idolatrously, in the Graeco-Roman world. Primitive Christianity was in fact the most widespread and the most effective eradication of idolatry known to history. As Athanasius writes in his *On the Incarnation*:

> In old times the whole world and every place in it was led astray by the worship of idols, and men thought that idols were the only gods that were. But now all over the world men are forsaking the fear of idols and taking refuge with Christ. The amazing thing, moreover, is this. The objects of worship formerly were varied and countless; each place had its own idol and the so called God of one place could not pass over to another to persuade the people there to worship him . . . but Christ has persuaded not only those close at hand but literally the entire world to worship one and the same Lord and Father through him.[1]

Yet for all that, as the catacombs so plainly show, the first Christians found sweet comfort in pictorial and symbolic art. They rarely, if ever, brooded on the sufferings of Christ, or their martyrs, in physical representation. But they rejoiced in the figure and the symbols of "the good shepherd". There was a spontaneous joy about their sense of the artistic in worship. Much of the anti-art in both Christian and Muslim history has origin in "puritan" concerns, in simplicity at war with luxury, wherein such as Tertullian could in this be compared with the Khawarij. But whatever may have been the disapproval of elaborate, or ostentatious, artistry the Church was too deeply rooted in the incarnation to stumble into prohibitions of the senses and their aids.

If "the Word became flesh" in Christ our Lord, then we can never doubt "the spiritual destiny of the visible" and its capacity to be the revelation of the spiritual. The Islamic warning of lurking idolatry, of man's chronic temptation to take the image for the substance, will never be unwanted. But to deny, in its name, the place of the image, the rôle of the visible, is to miss the sacramental meaning of the world and to invite a nemesis of unreality.

For all its proper caution, Islam does not escape the necessity to sacramentalize. Its postures at prayer, its *Qiblah* towards Mecca, its garb on pilgrimage, its very calligraphy, even the very absence of the pictorial—all proceed by enlisting the senses in the expression of divine-human things. Since the sacramental is necessarily there if there

[1] *De Incarnatione*, ch. 46.

is to be religion, it had better, and safer, be there consciously and theologically. Can Islamic thought not hold firmly to its fears of the perversities of art, without refusing and excluding its validities? Might it not learn to look, not merely with a new tolerance, but with a new eagerness, upon the symbols of Christian faith which, as concepts, it has so long controversially despised?

> Art may tell a truth
> Obliquely, do the thing shall breed the thought,
> Nor wrong the thought . . .
> Art was given for that:
> God uses us to help each other so,
> Lending our minds out.

For this very reason there is a deep likeness between what happens in a great work of art and what the Christian faith believes God is doing in Christ. Perhaps we have too much stated and commended the meaning of "God in Christ" (2 Cor. 5.19) in abstract, logical, and analytical terms, in theories about the two natures and one substance. Islamic rejection of that meaning has certainly based itself squarely on logical, even mathematical, argument.[1] May it not be more truly comprehended by likeness to a true art?

Great works of art in any form have always a double nature. There is the concrete event and the transcendent meaning, the material ground, be it paint or stone or other "base", yielded into the artistic genius, and the soul of the artist there self-expressed and self-fulfilled. What he is is inseparable from what he does: what he means is manifest in what he shapes. The tangible and visible are the home and residence of the spiritual and the eternal. Can we not see the incarnation in these terms as the self-revelation of God indwelling the fashion of the living and crucified Christ, who is "the express image of God's person, the out-shining of his glory" (Heb. 1.3), "the image of the invisible God" (Col. 1.15)? Is not this in truth what the Gospel means when it proclaims that "the Word became flesh"?

Perhaps, then, Islamic attitudes to art in worship may be seen as all

[1] One of the most recent examples of "mathematical" refutation of the Holy Trinity is that of Muhammad ᶜAbdul Baset, in *The Islamic Review*, vol. 50, nos. 10, 11, 12, 1962, p. 17. "One is part of three. How can the whole be equal to its part and vice versa? One is one-third of three. Now, if one and three are believed to be of equal dimension then it is tantamount to saying that the whole is equal to its one-third part."

of one piece with its misunderstanding of the incarnation. May it be that suspicions and misgivings in both spheres can be stayed by the same remedy? If there are, as we have urged, clues to theology from art, then there can, and must be, place for art in worship. The Muslim fear of idolatry is always sound. But the security against it is not in banning the artists, any more than God's unity is safeguarded by vetoing the incarnation: it is in a true recognition of him in undivided love. That love may include unashamedly the help and benediction of the senses and the arts. It is when men cease to offer adoration that they begin to practise idolatry. Their adoration of God will be not the less but the more true, for their delight in his creation. For the Christian that delight is all focused and completed in wonder at the marvel that our earthly context has seen and known and handled his incarnate presence.

QUESTIONS FOR STUDY AND DISCUSSION

1. What does Christian faith mean by declaring: "The Word became flesh" and that Christ is "the express image" of God's person?

2. Why did the Muslim lawyers and ʿulamaʾ prohibit painting, statuary, and other visual arts? Were they right? Does the Quran really sustain them? Does such a veto of itself prevent idolatry?

3. Do Islamic attitudes to art betray a limited idea of what idolatry is and means?

4. Protestant Christians have often taken a somewhat Islamic attitude to ikons in eastern Christian Orthodox practice. Have they been right?

5. What is meant by saying that calligraphy, too, is a visual (or at least a visible) representation of something spiritual, and that material symbol cannot be eliminated from the activity of worship?

6. What is your view of the claim that because times change Islam should change, or that the very past of Islam can make its present different? Could this be rightly applied to other issues beside that of art and representation?

7. In what senses, and with what provisos, can we say that the meaning of God being in Christ (2 Cor. 5.19) can be rightly illustrated from the way in which a great artist is in his art?

8. If (7) is a right line of thought, how is it preferable to purely logical ways of reasoning about "two natures" and "one Person"?

9. What is the difference between worship (due only to God) and hallowing or venerating places, objects, times, and symbols associated with such worship? Can there be worship without these? When they usurp worship instead of serving it they become idolatrous. How can men be saved from this?

10. "If your eyes are open . . . you will not suppose that idolatry is a strange, remote thing which cannot be found among 'Muslim' or 'Christian' peoples and presents no danger to us personally" (Vögel, *Iron Rations of a Christian*). How and why is this so?

PRECINCTS AND PEOPLE

13

Islam and Childhood

Half the population of the Sudan is under sixteen years of age and the figure is only a little less in such other lands with Muslim peoples as India, Pakistan, and Indonesia. In fact the world has more children in it, both in aggregate and in proportion, than ever before in history.

This exciting fact at once provokes far-reaching thoughts and certainly justifies the proposal of our present topic. It comes about not only from the phenomenal contemporary growth of world population. For that growth, in many countries, lies, not so much in increase in the number of births, as in a fall in the death rate, leading to steadily lengthening expectations of life (though these are still as low as twenty-eight years in the Sudan and thirty-six in India). This means that the adult population has a greater share, as well as children, in overall increase. But it has also to be remembered that improvement in child mortality is the most potent factor in lengthening the expectation of life, and thus high fertility rates are much more surely registered in actual child population than in the more precarious days, when womb and tomb were so much closer.

The villages and streets of Asia and Africa, then, are thronging more and more with a child population, surviving to adulthood better than any previous generation and with the ever bigger promise of the next. Ours is to that extent a children's world and a children's time. They are children, too, less prematurely old than their predecessors—at least wherever technical progress has begun to revise their habitat. Yet, for all that, it is a world of child-crisis.[1] Some of the largest decisions

[1] This, of course, in the ultimate sense, was always so. We may recall the poem:

In ancient shadows and twilights
Where childhood had strayed,
The world's greatest sorrows were born
And its heroes were made.
In the lost boyhood of Judas, Christ was betrayed.

of contemporary life are being shaped and made within the setting of childhood. Changes in the status of women; growing equality between sexes, altering the rôle and prospects of girls; changing standards of living and urbanization, tending to suggest family limitation by making the education of children more costly and more prolonged—these, and many other factors, are at work within the formative years of to-day's children. These bear within their own development the marks of a changing time and are involved in sharp inter-generation tensions in consequence. For all these reasons it seems appropriate to give thought and study to the Islamic patterns of childhood as holding and having a large stake in the present world of children.

There are, of course, several ways in which a study of Childhood in Islam might proceed. One might pursue the theme of laws relating to legitimacy, inheritance, wardship, adoption, and the like, of which there is a useful survey in Professor R. Levy's *The Social Structure of Islam.*[1] Or one might explore the standards and concepts of education with the aid of such a manual as R. Matthews and M. Akrawi, *Education in the Arab Countries of the Near East.*[2] Or again, there are several notable studies of a sociological kind and of descriptive "anthropology" which illustrate the patterns of family life, the customs, rites, ceremonies, and ideas associated with the young. E. W. Lane's celebrated *Manners and Customs of the Modern Egyptians* did this usefully for the Egyptians who were "modern" in the eighteen-thirties.[3] Dr Hilma Granquist, a Finnish scholar, has consecrated two large volumes to this kind of study with the titles: *Birth and Childhood among the Arabs* and *Child Problems among the Arabs,*[4] both of which depend upon data gathered in an Arab village in the vicinity of Bethlehem.

Yet another procedure would be to take the pulse of Muslim childhood in autobiography, of which, unhappily, there is all too little in Arabic literature. Taha Husain's *Al-Ayyam* exists in translation.[5] Or there are revealing pictures of a Cairo childhood at the end of last century in a book of which no English edition is yet published, Ahmad

[1] Cambridge, 1957, ch. 3, pp. 135–49, "The Status of the Child in Islam".

[2] American Council on Education, Washington, 1949.

[3] London, 1835, ch. 2.

[4] Soderstrom, Helsingfors, 1947 and 1950, respectively.

[5] *An Egyptian Childhood* and *A Student at the Azhar*, translated by E. H. Paxton, 1932 and H. Wayment, 1948, respectively.

Amin's *Hayati*.[1] Readers in other than Arab lands will perhaps be aware of autobiographical writing in their own languages. There is, in the more philosophic vein, A. K. Brohi's *An Adventure in Self-Expression*.[2] But part of our duty in sensitivity is to dig these out for ourselves.

Any one of these procedures, however, presents difficulties for an outline of this kind. Social studies have to be severely local if they are to be dependable. Time and date also are crucial factors. Change is constantly affecting both the psychology and the setting of childhood in the contemporary Muslim world. Perhaps it is possible none the less to attempt a few general considerations having to do with the "atmosphere" of childhood in Islam. All will need to be critically set in the reader's own context of time and place.

ENTERS THE BABE

In Muslim folklore there is a belief that if a grown-up person and a child die simultaneously the former enters the next world under the child's protection, for the latter has no sins to be requited. Entry to this world reverses the situation: parental sponsorship is far from being unencumbered here. The newcomer the world over is immediately involved in his parent's "accounts", not the least of which is how they see their progeny.

The underlying presuppositions of Islam and sex are studied in the succeeding chapter. Central to them is the status of marriage as a contract not an "estate", and the absence of the "one flesh" dimension which belongs to Christian marriage. One corollary of this situation, reinforced by other factors, economic, social, and religious, is the tendency of marriage to be seen, more entirely than it might be, in terms of procreation. "Enter the babe" is not only a fair heading in a scheme of exposition but the implicit theme of marriage itself.

Not that this overruling interest in procreation within marriage is distinctively Islamic, only the proportionate weight it has in the total meaning of marriage. The Quran itself is explicit about this: "Women are your fields: go then into your fields as you please" (Surah 2.223). The estimation of a wife thus depends to a great degree upon her

[1] Cairo, 1950. [2] Karachi, 1955.

fruitfulness. Barrenness is both a curse and a reproach, justifying divorce. This has often led to the practice of polygyny, or, where barrenness is due to a husband's impotence, to the practice of co-habitation outside marriage with a view to pregnancy. In that event, actual physical paternity is of less significance than family fertility.

These attitudes have, of course, antecedents far beyond Islam. And current social developments from outside it are also bringing noticeable changes. The increasing range and cost of education, and the sense of family "quality" of opportunity over against "quantity" of numbers, are tending in some quarters to the acceptance of the planned family. But the old order, if so it may be described, found security for marriage, and for the wife within marriage, in multiplied offspring. And given existing likelihoods of infant survival, pregnancies were often of necessity two or three times in excess of surviving progeny. Thus, for both material and spiritual reasons, the welfare of the on-coming generation tended to be subjected to the interests of the parent one. Children by the social and religious approach to procreation unconsciously forfeited a good deal, in the pattern of their parents' inter-relationship and the concepts of sex. In the end—though other factors may help immensely—the only final dimension in which children and marriage are in sound and blessed harmony is that of their parents' "one flesh". For there alone is an ultimate security of mutual self-giving in which, being utterly secure in one another, parents are able to bestow security upon their children rather than require it of them. Though it may be right to trace this difference that marriage as an estate can make for those born within it, compared with marriage as only contractual, it is also right to keep clearly in view the wondering reverence with which the Quran views the act of procreation. It is there in the first revelation (as Surah 96 is traditionally held to be). There are several intimately detailed passages which have to do with the miracle of sexual power. Take Surah 23.12–14, with a remarkable parallel in Surah 22.5, tracing the pre-natal mystery of human beginnings, with a constant insistence on the responsible setting of this power to beget. God's is the original creativity here entrusted to man. The only right attitude of soul in parenthood is: *Tabaraka Allah, ahsanu-l-khaliqin*, "Blessed be God the best of creators". Wherever else the *nutfah*, or seminal fluid, is mentioned, it is in a context of awe, divine knowledge, and human participation. The seed only fructifies when it is "lodged in its place", or "emitted in desire" as the translations of 53.46 run. (*Idha tumna* is the Arabic phrase.) Thus human sexuality is divinely constituted to be the locus of the creative act which derives from God. Hence, perhaps, the irony of 16.4 and 36.77. Who is man so mysteriously fashioned, to contend against the Most High?

Parents, this seems to say, should fulfil their ensuing rôle in the awe and dignity which cannot but be felt in their initiating act. Sex, in other words, should hold parenthood in its own sanctity. Is not this really why the "one flesh" fits, as no other pattern does, the essence of what marriage is and does? Muslim practice, under pressures of economic stress or sheer human perversity and passion, may have fallen away from these implications of sexuality as the Quran views it. And having an ideal is not of itself to achieve it, the more so when the actual law fails to reflect it. But, none the less, something of this parental situation as standing under a divinely ordered mystery permeates Muslim child-bearing.

We note elsewhere the implicit significance of the Quran's tenderness to orphans for a new view of marriage, since there is nothing that so "orphans" a child, aside from parents' death, as parents' divorce.[1] Here we need only emphasize again the way in which both quranic precept and Muslim practice care for wards and orphans as part of this underlying religious interpretation of child-birth.

Yet not orphans only. There is in *Qissat al-Raha* of Fatimah, a much-used devotional manual for Muslim women, the following passage:

> O Fatima, there is no woman who sets her hand to her spinning but for every thread thereof Allah writes in her record a good deed and blots out a hundred evil deeds . . . O Fatima, there is no woman who spins and then clothes her children and little ones but Allah will write in her record the merit of one who has fed a thousand hungry persons and clothed a thousand naked. O Fatima, there is no woman who has oiled the heads of her children, untangled their hair, washed their clothes and deloused them but Allah will for every hair write in her record a good deed and for every hair blot out an evil deed, and will make her resplendent in the eyes of all who behold.[2]

Surveys of domestic life, like those of Hilma Granqvist, indicate with

[1] See next chapter, "Islam and Sex".

[2] From *Islam: Muhammad and His Religion*, p. 219, ed. Arthur Jeffery, Copyright © 1958 by The Liberal Arts Press, Inc. By permission of The Liberal Arts Press Division of The Bobbs-Merrill Co., Inc.

abundant evidence the devotion and tenacity of Muslim mothers. "With every birth", says the proverb, "there falls a pillar of the mother", meaning she is weaker after every pregnancy. But in another sense every birth makes the pillar stouter since it carries more. "A mother cannot be recompensed", says the tradition, commenting on the story of how Moses told a man who had carried his mother seven times to Mecca on his back that he was in no way out of her debt.

Something of the Muslim instinct about birth and children must be sought in the most important birth festival in Islam, namely *Maulid al-Nabi*, or the Prophet's birthday, celebrated with some of the aspects of the Christian Christmas on the twelfth of *Rabiᶜa al-Awwal.*[1] Festivities, exchange of gifts and greetings, torchlight processions, and special mosque occasions all tend, despite Wahhabi disapproval, to focus attention on the young and on the ideal of the Prophet's biography. What the *Maulid* commemorates dominates the naming of children. Muhammad, Ahmad, Mahmud, and Mustafa—all names of the Prophet—are the most likely first names in the choice of Muslim parents. The *Maulid*, with the celebrations of the example and sanctity of Khadijah, first wife of Muhammad and Fatimah his daughter, serves to relate birth in general with that birth in particular by which Islam was shaped. The recent writings on the great feminine figures in the genesis of Islam and the *Sirah* of the Prophet, by Bint al-Shati, well-known Cairo authoress, embody an old tradition in modern form and mediate between the contemporary context of childhood and the Meccan exemplars.

GROWS THE CHILD

It was an ancient practice of Muslim piety to whisper the *Adhan*, or call to prayer, in the ear of the newborn babe soon after birth, so that it might be addressed by the summons, and the *Shahadah* within it, that should rule its life. It is also traditional that among the first phrases of the Quran to be taught are the two final Surahs known as the Refuge Seekers, from their initial cry: "I seek refuge with God." These two very early Surahs breathe the temper of age-long Muslim dependence and human finitude. Both belong with a context of wistful superstition and with the endless precariousness of the human condition.

[1] See below, ch. 18, "Round the Muslim Calendar".

In the name of the merciful Lord of mercy. Say: I seek refuge with the Lord of the daybreak, from the evil of what he has created, from the evil of the pouring dark, from the mischief of conjuring witches, and the evil of the envier in his envy.

In the name of the merciful Lord of mercy: Say: I seek refuge with the Lord of men, the King of men, the God of men, from the evil of the slinking prompter who whispers in the breasts of men, from jinn and men.

These are surely the evils of the child's world and the child's view of the adult's world, with its unpredictable dangers and its inarticulate fears. It is these, in their sensitive quality as the sheer business of being alive, with which religion, and education in religion, have to do. Thus in turn it is fair also to see in them the promise and the tasks of Muslim nurture.

It is fascinating, in any culture, to trace and consider the terms in which culture continuity is ensured through successive generations. How does the unconscious babe come to possess the world of the *Adhan* with which its communal setting greets its ear? How does "With God is my refuge" become an articulate experience in the growing child? Readers of this chapter who are teachers in schools will best know with what presuppositions, with what parental influences, their scholars reach them. Volumes, not paragraphs, are necessary to estimate Muslim education.

Where patterns have remained traditional there are mosque schools or *kuttabs* and quranic memoriter, which Ahmad Amin very graphically describes. Drab walls, threadbare mats, the turbaned master, and the long cane—these set the stage.

We went in the morning and sat cross-legged on the mat, herded together. Each of us took his board from the box. Since I was a new beginner mine was a new one . . . Each scholar read from his board according to his ability. One handled the *a b c* while another recited the opening Surah, the *Fatihah*, and another a Surah for invocation. When we had finished reciting the new lesson the previous one was heard, namely the one we had learned by heart from the Qur'an in the previous lessons. At lunch time, the master took a piastre, or half a piastre, or even a single mil, from each boy according to his resources and sent his assistant who returned with two green *majurs*. These contained either fresh or pickled beans and in either case broth. The scholars crowded round with their bread which they had brought from home.

They dipped their hands for a mouthful, now into one vessel, now into the other. Who bothered that they were a motley mixture of all sorts and conditions, sick and sound, dirty and clean, filthy and respectable. In God was their trust and *barakah* obviated any danger. When we recited we were supposed to rock to and fro and raise our voices. Any who failed to do so at once felt the stick descend on him . . . We continued in this fashion until nearly evening and then returned to our homes . . .

In this *kuttab* I mastered the alphabet in a very meaningless sort of way. The first lessons were *alif*, *lam*, *fa*ʾ. . . . I transferred to four schools of this kind and there was nothing to choose between them . . . the style of teaching was the same in all . . . During this time I memorized the Qurʾan and learned to read and write . . . What remains of all that nowadays for children of my social class? They go to kindergartens and sophisticated ladies or well-mannered young men teach them according to their latest pedagogic methods, leading them by stages from play to reading. . . . They impart knowledge stealthily by means of pictures, stories, and the like, thus transforming into sweetness the terrifying life we once knew . . . Teachers are concerned to have the explanation clear, not the body thrashed, and there are lots of other kindly changes. Yet even so I have a fear that we may have become over indulgent in these our children's days just as we were harsh in mine.[1]

Thus 1950 reflects on the eighteen-nineties. Not everywhere is the harshness, or at any rate the woodenness, obsolete. And mentalities change more slowly than the furniture. But everywhere, aided by State action, by oil revenues, by inner compulsion, are the vast transformations of the educational scene. Through them all it is well to remember what the same author says about his earlier and more abiding schools—the home, the suburb, the stories of grandmother, the street cries and the traders, the old characters who made up the local colour of the Cairo quarter that reared him. Though these, too, are in constant metamorphosis, we shall only learn Muslim childhood as we sense and sift them in our own vicinity. For there, before the dullness of adult familiarity descends, the child mind is seeing and discovering the elemental mysteries.

We had also a grandmother—my mother's mother, a goodhearted, strongly religious soul, with a radiant face . . . She had an inexhaustible fund of popular stories, from both the countryside and the town. We hung around and listened to these yarns until sleep overtook us. Some revolved around the power of fate and the force of chance, while others were about the artfulness of women and their shrewdness. There were tales of the *afarit* and their

[1] *Hayati*, *My Life*, Cairo, 1950, pp. 36–9, translation by the writer.

mischievousness, about kings and nobles, and how weak they were in the presence of fate, etc. Through these stories ran kindly popular proverbs and phrases embodying the moral. Sometimes my eldest brother would read to us from *The Thousand and One Nights* . . .

And, reflecting on the domestic changes of his later life, he concludes:

Our surprise and our wonder abate and little by little the strange becomes the familiar.[1]

Another feature of Muslim childhood worthy of observant study is the question of religious participation. The first occasion of such personal involvement in the *cultus* is circumcision (*khitan*). This takes place in a variety of circumstances in Arab, Asian, and African Islam, sometimes between the years of three and seven, but in cases later. Male circumcision seems often in history to have been attended with considerable ceremonial. In Indonesia it is often taken as an act of reception into Islam. Though the Quran itself does not refer to the practice, there is a tradition that the Prophet was born circumcised. Popular veneration holds it in high esteem, as embodying Islamic initiation and sometimes crowning attainment of the *hafiz* status in quranic recitation. In rural and undeveloped setting, a mass circumcision of numbers of boys makes for an indelible recollection.

It is evident also that the beginning of participation in the fast of Ramadan, from which the young are exempt, marks a significant religious stage. The age varies according to the practice and the piety of the region or family.

At ordinary times, children stand somewhat apart from the religious life: Islam is a religion for grown-ups. Children are not at the point of sufficient self-control to keep the rules of ritual purity. They must reach years of discretion before they can perform the ritual prayer. Until then they are satisfied to be onlookers. Grown-up example shapes and teaches them gradually what they have to do, what is allowed and what is forbidden. In some families, they are told religious stories within their reach. But they remain on the edge of things.

But by contrast, during Ramadan things are noticeably more alive. For then there is something out of the ordinary, especially where normally life is uneventful. For then nice things happen: there are dried fruits to eat in the evenings after sunset. One can stay up later: everything is lit up at night.

[1] Ibid., p. 11–12.

> But the fascination of Ramadan is certainly not limited to these material things, important as they are. Children wait for the time to come when they can fast, to do as their parents do of course, but also to demonstrate that they too can obey God and that they believe in Him. From the age of ten, there are children who ask to fast. At first their parents allow them to do so for a day or two. Then by degrees the habit forms and oftentimes children show themselves more zealous than their parents.[1]

One has also to keep in mind the vicarious experiences that result from returned pilgrims, bringing the water of Zamzam and tales of Mecca which, perhaps more than mosque discourse, serve to initiate the young into their corporate heritage.

These and a score of other factors in the endless inter-penetration of religion and society confirm the young in their Islam. But it is interesting that there is no single ceremony designed to mark a conscious, self-chosen adherence, in which a full, personal, convinced allegiance is confessed. This is not to say that the Islam of multitudes is not assured. But it is at the same time automatically assumed. Indeed the implicit *Islam* of all human born is affirmed by tradition. It is a child's parents that make it non-Muslim. In the case of Muslim children, then, being Muslim is automatic, unless deliberate apostasy is chosen.

The will to be Muslim is thus a will without a crisis, an assumption without an alternative. It is, in part, this fact which accounts for the varying religious qualities of Islam within an unquestioned Islamic standing. All culture communities, of course, in large measure assume a continuity between the generations. But there are some that make a sharp contrast with Islam in the degree to which their adherents really elect to become so, in an opted acceptance of their faith, or are able, specifically, to opt out of it in decisive rejection. When all are contained, without question as to conviction, faith is necessarily of a different texture. Baptism, with sponsors, and confirmation, have no parallel in the experience of Muslim youth. Their belonging is an assumed fact, even if their credence is tacitly an open question. If religious systems which do in fact attempt some watershed of membership dividing the implicit from the responsible discover that their ordinances are all too often less than "critical", then systems which omit the "critical" altogether must be understood as so much the more "taken for granted". Where forms are the less decisive they are liable to be the more neutral.

[1] *Mélanges*, op. cit., no. 3, Institut Dominicain, Cairo, 1956, p. 3.

This situation may be stated in other terms if one says that the faith's possessiveness over its people is not subject to their will. Though Islam is in fact wrestling, as, proportionately, are all faiths, with the fact of secularity and irreligion, it is not in essence doing so, because its theory is that by birth all its people are inalienably its own. Actuality plays havoc with the theory. But it remains a structure behind which life is not admitted to have unmade what birth made. Sooner or later, Islamic sincerity must come to terms with the whole meaning of secularity and with the fact that being prepared to let its people go is the first condition of holding them rightly.

Meanwhile, the rising generation is the focal point of this large issue. It would take us beyond the theme of childhood to pursue it. It bears, however, upon the whole question of our educational ministry. It means that any effort, however sincere, to penetrate into the deeper questions of human existence and of life's meaning must inevitably fall foul of communal suspicion and cultural prestige. What is intended for spiritual relationship is all too often seen as cultural subversion.

Yet the problems of existence in the world do not lose their sharpness or their urgency because the community insistently limits the range of spiritual territory from which the answers might be sought. No sane Christianity could, or would, seek to relate itself to childhood in Islamic mould save in the fullest humility at what it finds. "Take heed" was our Lord's injunction about "these little ones". Yet precisely in doing so it must see them in him.

We may conclude with the words of a former Law Minister of Pakistan, Professor A. K. Brohi:

> Ever since my childhood I have never been in doubt about the goal of my earthly existence. It is my destiny not merely to affirm as a matter of faith, but to realise as a matter of direct experience, that "I am from Him and unto Him is my return. . . ." Mine has been a life of longing—longing to get near to Him and perchance to have a glimpse of Him.[1]

If we take that as a symbol of Islamic childhood, articulate and serious, we cannot hesitate about the meaning for it of what we know in Christ. And if we remember how, for innumerable others, childhood is too mute, too deprived, too brief, too struggling, or too pampered

[1] A. K. Brohi, *An Adventure in Self-expression*, pp. 88–9.

for such a confession of its goal, shall our sense of Christian indebtedness be then the less?

QUESTIONS FOR STUDY AND DISCUSSION

1. What picture of Muslim childhood within Islam would you draw from your experience of homes or schools or families?

2. What legal, social, or religious changes have you observed in your environment affecting the size, pattern, and cohesion of the family?

3. How is your local mosque related to the child population around it? When do mosque attendance and Ramadan observance begin?

4. What should be the attitude of Christian schools to Muslim childhood, Muslim festivals, and Muslim rites?

5. What setting does the Islamic view of marriage provide for the children born within it? How would this be different if marriage were an estate rather than only a contract?

6. Have you encountered any special occasions of tension between the present parent and the present young generations, because of social changes, education, science, and secularism?

7. What does the Quran teach about parenthood? What should the due recognition and praise of God within it mean in the present-day situation?

8. How have modern educational curricula and methods affected the attitude of the young to the faith of their fathers? Are there any significant changes in mosque education?

9. To what extent, in your view, can faith be feasibly or rightly "inherited"? What is the meaning of the Christian doctrine of the new birth, hinging on personal faith, for the Islamic idea that parentage sufficiently determines allegiance?

14

Islam and Sex

"Who giveth this woman to be married to this man?" is the familiar question of Christian marriage liturgy. In some Eastern Churches a parallel question is put concerning the bridegroom: "Who giveth this man to be married to this woman?"—an equally fair inquiry. The traditional response links the families with the transaction, since it is out of the bosom of their history that the parties have come. Moreover, the contract being made has a public quality which society must know and register. But in the end the ultimate answer can only be that of the marrying persons themselves. Parents may preside over the nuptials and the congregation take note of them, but the mutual giving that is marriage is by its nature only within the competence of those it joins.

"Every wedding", wrote Bonhoeffer from prison, in a letter to a bride, "is an occasion of joy, that human beings can do such great things, that they have been given the freedom and power to take the rudder of their lives into their own hands." And marriage, properly seen, is the wedding in continuity, the steady sustaining of that "I do". "The proof of the lover is the married man." Was it in such conscious awe and trust that Robert Browning, whenever he returned to London, revisited the church where he and Elizabeth Barrett were married, and kissed the stones?

All this may seem a strange introduction to the exacting theme of "Islam and Sex". But it is deliberate. Our first business is to get straight what our study intends. The title means what it says. We are not, therefore, directly concerned with such topics as the Prophet's marriages, nor with purdah, the veil and the *harim* as such, nor with changes in the divorce laws, nor with contemporary feminist movements. All these of course stand in the background and have their bearings on the central theme. But it is just this last which receives all too little attention, though it conditions all else. There is, moreover, a wealth of literature on these legal and social topics.

It may be useful, though, to allow ourselves one illustration of how a related, but not here central, issue may divert attention from the heart question. The Prophet's marriages have been the subject of prolonged controversy and much has been written on the Christian side *con* and on the Muslim side *pro*. It is true, of course, that his practice bears inevitably on Muslim criteria and ideals. But in this realm the Quran explicitly states that his biography is not to be understood as exemplary for the ordinary believer. "This privilege is yours alone, being granted to no other believer" says Surah 33.49. For there were matters at stake which do not belong to the life of the day-to-day Muslim, such as the Prophet's heirlessness as a ruler (cf. Surah 33.40: "Muhammad is not the father of any man among you"). There was the policy of honouring widows of fallen heroes and dynastic considerations connected with accessions to Islam, and other factors. Moreover, the earlier more appropriate precedent of Muhammad's sole union with Khadijah deserves not to be obscured. Our task, without minimizing the impact of the Medinan marital situation in the *Sirah*, or prophetic biography, is to focus study on those realms which we most want the answers to concern. Only so can we keep a positive course through all the pitfalls of this subject.

SEX AND ITS MUTUAL MEANING IN ISLAM

Actual quranic passages that deal directly with the sex relationship are few. But it is well to study them, for they have some remarkable implications, whatever be the degree to which Muslim practice expresses or fulfils their sense in the institutions that belong with sex. The two most significant passages are Surahs 2.187 and 30.21. The former explains that sexual intercourse between husband and wife is quite legitimate during the nights of Ramadan when, as it appears, there had been abstinence under a misapprehension. After thus approving intercourse, incidentally forbidden in 2.197 during the Pilgrimage, the passage adds: "They (your wives) are a garment unto you and you for them." This literal translation deserves further scrutiny.

The word here "garment" is *libas*. What is this mutual *libas* which wife and husband are to each other? Is it the *masdar* of *labasa* which means: "he was in close and intimate connection with"? Lane's Lexicon indicates that it means simply, in this context, what a man's wife and a woman's husband are to each other, "because", it adds, "each embraces the other, each goes to the other for rest and consorts with the other . . . or because one conceals the state of the other". Every shade of sense here is meaningful. The word has of course to do with "covering" and occurs in 78.10: "We made the night a covering", and in 16.112, where, in construct with hunger, it means "the utmost degree of . . ." or something that is all-involving. The word also implies the covering of that which modesty bids one not expose. May it be, then, that this comes closest to the biblical expression for sexual experience, namely "knowledge"? ("Adam *knew* his wife. . . .") For here at once is the idea of mutuality, within a relationship that "justifies", or provides the seemly setting for, that which otherwise would be "uncovered", and so gross, and shameful. *Libas* means all the mutuality of marriage and the reciprocal completion of sex. The passage adds, after dispelling the misconception about Ramadan nights: "So go in unto them and enjoy what God has ordained for you", the subject pronoun being masculine and the objective feminine. The word *rafath* used in this verse is defined as "comprehending everything that a man desires of his wife". But the ultimate situation is mutual and in the phrase "what God has ordained for you" the pronoun may be understood as common.

Mutuality is the emphasis of the second passage in 30.21. It is prefaced by the most significant and frequent phrase: "One of his signs is that. . . ." Sex is here set, in a sense, among the sacraments. To call anything a sign quranically means that it must be an occasion of reverence, gratitude, and alertness of mind, as having within itself a secret that escapes the flippant or the casual. "He has created wives (or mates) for you from among yourselves that you might live in joy with them and he planted love and tenderness between you", adding: "Surely this holds signs for thoughtful folk." There is no more potential verse in the whole Quran on the sexual theme than this. It remains our largest ally in the quest for a Christian interpretation of the full equality, mutuality, and benediction of true sex and the divine institution of marriage.

Perhaps it is fair to hear an echo of this attitude, when it is hinted in Surah 4.21 that the marriage experience is something too sacred to allow of irreverent rupture. "How can ye take it back (the dowry) when you have lain with each other and entered into a firm covenant with your wives?" Perhaps there are other things more essential than mere dowries for which the same argument would apply? At least there is a gentle suggestion that exchange of sexual experience has so altered the relationship as properly to bespeak a permanent bond. (Or is this Christian exegesis?) The word *afda* used here is synonymous with *rafatha ila* in 2.187 and 197.

There is an actual echo of 30.21 in 7.189, which refers to God's creation of man in the words: "He it was who created you from a single being, and made therefrom his mate that he might find rest in her." What follows is also significant. After narrating how the pair came through the trials of pregnancy, in which they both prayed to God, it deplores how they returned back into polytheism once God had heard their desire. Is there here a suggestion that the wonder of sex and procreation should, properly seen, compel men to an undivided worship?

Mutual modesty and avoidance of temptation to lewdness are enjoined in Surah 24.30–1. The well-known passage in Surah 33.35 which describes, with sundry active participles, the true practising Muslim is careful to do so in both masculine and feminine, so that there is no doubt of the equal participation of male and female in the duties and meanings of Islam. The same equality between the sexes is asserted in 2.228, which reads: "Women have in equity rights like those exercised against them", adding rather enigmatically, "men have a status above women."

Though this is often interpreted in the sense of the general phrase, "the weaker sex", there can be no doubt that, in terms of the institutional framework of relationships of men and women, the Islamic pattern has proved in fact a man's world. This seems grounded in the words of Surah 2.223: "Women are your fields; go then into your fields as you please", but "keep in mind", it adds, "the fear due to God." It is imperative to have in view the potential implication of the verses cited so that our Christian attitude to sex in Islam may harness to the full the feasible quranic corroboration.

SEX AND ITS INSTITUTIONAL EXPRESSION IN ISLAM

It is clearly impossible here to attempt even the barest summary of Islamic law and practice relating to marriage, divorce, adultery, and dependent topics, in all the wide variety of the Muslim scene from Zanzibar to Tashkent, through nearly fourteen Hijri centuries.

The central fact is that with, or despite, the interpretation of sex in the verses just studied, marriage in Islam is purely a contractual affair, lacking the character of a "holy estate" such as to constitute "of twain one flesh". Though, necessarily, at the time of its initiation no marriage that deserves the name contemplates its own dissolution, no Muslim marriage includes a pledge that is abiding. The concept of "the one flesh" does not obtain. Marriage is not by its nature a single self-giving, accepting an estate that does not will retreat and cannot admit of duplication. On the contrary, marriage may be plural, both in the sense of concurrently double, or treble, or quadruple, and consecutively unlimited. One may, that is, be repeatedly husband, or repeatedly wife, within the present limit of four or the lifetime limits of feasibility.

Putting it this way serves to bring out how marriage in Islam, or the Islamic ordering of sex, means a contract, not an "estate". It can be illustrated in the recent exegetical discussions about the precise meaning of the pivotal passage in Surah 4.3. This passage was for centuries understood, at least in practice, as permitting plural marriage up to four (for men). It is now understood in widening circles as amounting to a virtual prohibition of more than one wife, since a condition is attached to the permission of plurality which is in fact unattainable, so that the permission lapses.

The significant point, from the Christian angle, is that the provision remains within the judgement of the individual. If a man cares to assume his competence to meet it, as generations of Muslim husbands have done, he is free to do so and then the plural marriages exist. In other words prohibition cannot properly be "virtual". It must be absolute, since the very notion of a concurrent marriage is an inner betrayal of the existing one. To imagine duplicating wives is already an essential injustice. That such a view is *not* held is the integral limitation of the status of "wife" in Islam.

The passage in question is set in a context relating to orphans and directs: "If you (men) fear you cannot do justly by them (i.e. the orphans) then marry other women who seem good to you; two, three, or four of them. But if you are afraid you cannot maintain an equality among them, marry only one or any slave girls you may own." Whether the setting about orphans, of whom there were many in early Islam through war or famine, means that circumstances can now be said to have changed, so changing the permission, is debatable. More urgent is the question as to what is meant by "equal treatment" or "justice". If it be financial and material provision for plural wives, it is readily feasible (as also is parity of sexual intercourse), and the permission stands (the old view). If it means sustained equality of emotional regard, it is manifestly impossible.

In the second event, the discovery of its impossibility is, in the nature of the case, a *post facto* discovery when the plurality exists. The "if" is left to the husband's discretion. In this connection, Surah 4.129 denies that impartiality is ever possible, so strengthening the second view, yet still assumes a plural marriage situation. "You will never be able to treat your wives impartially, however much you so desire, but do not go to extremes in one direction and leave her (i.e. the other wife) like a thing suspended." Other verses here (e.g. 23) seem to corroborate this concurrence in marriage. There is no point in forbidding two sisters together as wives, if a man is not to have two non-sisters. The pre-Islamic practice of marriage with two sisters would have needed no explicit prohibition if monogamy had been "virtual".

There can be no doubt that the newer exegesis is to be welcomed and that it may well develop further.[1] It represents the response of exegesis to external pressures, social, economic, and feminist. While rejoicing in those developments, our Christian duty is to witness winsomely to what they still lack.

If the contractual nature of Islamic marriage is clear in this study of its attitude to plurality of concurrent marriages, it is equally clear in the fact of plurality in consecutive marriage. For marriages in sequence are, by Christian criteria, in that sense also plural, since they involve repeatedness and revocability of self-giving—which can only be thought feasible on a lower concept of what self-giving is and how sex and personality are related.

Marriages in sequence are less frequent than they used to be in sophisticated Islamic circles, for reasons similar to those which have reduced concurrent marriages. Divorce, according to the familiar tradition, is the most hateful thing with God among things allowed. It is quranically available to the man for the sole sufficient reason that he wants it, or desires an alternative wife. The marital situation is thus entirely at the behest of the male partner and no bond has been entered into by him in which particular marriage has become an "estate", so hallowing and ordering his love that he has permanent

[1] The writer found it, though by no means unanimously accepted, in so remote a centre as Kaduna, Northern Nigeria.

responsibility to his wife, and with her to children, society, and God. The love that initiates and sustains marriage exists throughout under the condition of revocability, not the pledge of abidingness. The absence of such pledgedness makes a profound difference to its whole ontological status and to its personal dimensions in the spirit.

Nevertheless, the pattern of quranic divorce is wisely hedged about with provisions about restraint, fairness, and compassion. Surah 2.226–7, while stipulating no necessary grounds for divorce, lays down a waiting period of four months for the man and three menstrual periods for the woman, to avoid dubiety about possible paternity. In the meantime there is always the hope of reconciliation (2.228 and 65.1–8). When a man simply desires to take another wife he may do so, but the dowry must be retained by the earlier wife if the marriage has been consummated (4.20).

A divorce twice pronounced is revocable and only becomes absolute the third time. This also leaves room for checking hasty anger. Divorce by the thrice repeated formula means annulment and the wife can only be taken back after interim marriage to another (the *Muhallil*) which prevents an angry husband retaining, as it were, a divorced prisoner. Divorce ensures the right of the woman to go back into marriageability. She must be "dismissed with kindness" (2.228–9). Remarriage cannot be prevented and in the waiting interval divorced wives are to be maintained unless the marriage has not been consummated. Provision is also made quranically for the maintenance of pregnant or nursing wives through and beyond the interim period (2.233).

The intricacies of the Schools of Law on this theme of divorce cannot concern us here, nor the many far-reaching changes which are being made in current legal practice, whereby women have some scope in the initiation of divorce and male divorcing (and re-marriage) has many new conditions that circumscribe its quranic readiness. These are the product of changing times and concepts.

The corollary of the Islamic concept of marriage lies in the horror of *Zina*, or adultery. Sexual activity (aside from female slaves) must be strictly within the marriage tie. Though this tie is not the ontological thing it is in the Christian order, it remains in its contractual nature a most sacred thing. *Zina*, means, in effect, sexuality outside the marital relation. The subject may be studied in 4.15–16 and 24.2–26. Such is the situation that it can, in a sense, be said that Muslim men have a fiercer passion for their sisters' honour than they have for their wives' right to possess them wholly. One may readily read in the daily Muslim press of a brother who takes it into his hands to murder a sister whom he suspects of "immorality". Women are not considered the free and equal guardians of their own sexuality. A married man may find, by the path of divorce and re-marriage, the same fulfilment of urge involving a woman, which she for her part would be in utter social peril for offering, or even merely affording, to the same man outside marriage.

This is, in effect, the meaning of *Zina*. Only marriage legitimatizes sexual relations but in doing so it does not require them to be uniquely directed. A man is not in proper sexual relation to a woman unless she is in the legal sense his spouse: but the "spouse-necessity" (if the phrase be permitted) is no more than legal. It does not mean any incorporation into one. This is the paradox which lies within *Zina*. Or, phrasing it negatively, promiscuity is (or would be) a legal, not a personal, wrong. By "personal" here is meant that within Muslim marriage a pair, while legally a couple, are not spiritually a single flesh. Being spiritually a single flesh is the whole meaning of the Christian sacrament of marriage, where potential two-fleshness, i.e. the physical feasibility of divorce, is constantly transcended in the achievement, within mutual commitment, of married unity under God. Any marriage is, pragmatically, dissoluble; but not essentially one that God has joined together, since it is daily accomplishing the meaning of its perpetual nature. It is this which Islamic concepts do not allow.

These are the ultimates in the Muslim view of marriage. In many quarters the complete mutuality which is safeguarded spiritually in the Christian meaning of the "one flesh" is in fact approached within many Muslims homes at least in what relates to the sharing of interests, capacities, and responsibilities. If it is true that monogamy (and monogamy for the right reasons) is the only secure foundation of these equalities, they may be fostered by factors which do not either admit, or derive from, this source. This is happening widely, with the growth of female education, the sense of economic need for family limitation, and the abolition of the veil and the *harim* as incompatible with the dignities of womanhood and the self-respect of men.[1]

[1] On far-reaching contemporary changes in the laws relating to marriage and divorce, e.g. in Egypt, Syria, Tunisia and Morocco, see J. N. D. Anderson, "Significance of Islamic Law in the World Today," in *The American Journal of Comparative Law*, vol. 9, 2, Spring, 1960, pp. 187–98, and the articles there cited.

Yet the old patterns die hard. There was rearguard resistance in the Pakistan Government Commission on Marriage and the Family, in 1956, to attempts to secure a minimum age for marriage and compulsory registration, though the arguments for these were thoroughly deferential and founded on a wise claim of *qiyas*.[1] What, finally and in sum, are our Christian duties to all the foregoing?

FACTORS IN A CHRISTIAN ATTITUDE

We have in fact been answering that question in the whole analysis. All that has been said grows from the application of Christian criteria. If we are concerned for monogamy, and for the right reasons, what are our Christian obligations?

1. Clearly a deep penitence for the inroads from the west on Islamic traditions of behaviour in these fields. No alert person needs to be reminded of the inclusive, pervasive, deceptive influence of western films and magazines. There must be a strong sympathy for those forms of Muslim reaction that insist on the sanctions and patterns of conservatism.

2. Yet, with that lively sympathy for Islamic denunciation of western sex-expression must go a patient effort to disentangle the true Christian concepts of sex from these travesties. Christian doctrine here, as on many issues, is basically misunderstood by Muslims. Its ethic is not some ascetic disqualification of the body, nor some ideal but inaccessible notion beyond the range of common man, nor yet some rigidity turning, as the cynics say, wedlock into deadlock. "Receive ye one another to the glory of God" is its watchword. All God's gifts are to be received with worship and gratitude and in that context find their sanctity and fullness. Christian marriage is the freedom and power of love, ordered according to the divine will, where the act of a wedding in all its spontaneous mutuality is sustained in the constant attitude of marriedness, a state of wonder, love, and trust, hallowed by fidelity to love's meaning in a commensurate context. To communicate this demands both the loyal disclosure of its actuality in lives and homes, as well as the steady commending of its principles.

3. In such commending may we not both look for and redeem quranic insights? Some of these have been noted. What also of the

[1] See "Tests of Islamicity", in *Middle East Forum*, Beirut, Nov. 1957.

Islamic concern for orphans so notable in the Quran? Orphans are, as we have seen, the context of what it says about plurality. In a changed age, is it not evident that the claims of children are a first demand upon sexual loyalty? Is not the sundering of a marriage in some sense the orphaning of its offspring? If widows need husbands, as the Quran suggests, for justice to be done to their fatherless children, *a fortiori*, do not mothers need the husbands by whom they had the children, if justice is to be done them? Solicitude for children must be no less than that for orphans. Can you argue that children's loss in their father's death must be made good by a mother's re-marriage, and not allow they have at least an equal stake in a living father's remaining married to their mother?

There is an even deeper asset for the Christian view of marriage in the whole Islamic insistence on monotheism. A bond between plural marriage and plural worship may seem at first an odd notion. Yet it is real. We have seen a hint of it in Surah 7.189, where after the wonder of a pregnancy and birth a human pair are rebuked for falling back into idolatry. Is not idolatry really the attempt to take the part for the whole? Yet such also is the error of the setting of sexuality in any other context than a full self-giving. Must not the inner love of husband and wife be as securely undivided as their love of God? Pluralism in worship diversifies an allegiance that should be unique: so also do concurrent and consecutive marriages. A man's whole heart cannot be wholly in two places, either Godward or wifeward. Plural marriage is a sort of *Shirk* of the self. Uncompetitive and uncompeting, such is our obligation to our Creator, *la sharika lahu*.[1] Does he not will the sex in us, his creative and created gift, not to be divided against itself?

There, is, further, an interesting word used to describe in the Quran a married woman: *muhsanah* (in some authorities *muhsinah*), i.e. a woman of continence, one whose sexuality is wholly within marriage. The association of thought is very significant, for it underlines all the analysis above. Surah 21.91 has *Al-lati ahsanat farajaha*: "She who preserves herself from the sexually unlawful" by finding sex only within marriage (cf. 66.12). The word and its derivatives are used almost wholly of women (4.24,25; 5.5; 24.4,33). May we not also think of the same necessary association in the masculine—that a man's true sexuality is in his fidelity to marriage (as Islam teaches) and

[1] "For whom there are no associates to 'duplicate' him."

that his fidelity to marriage properly understood is fidelity to the wife of an undivided covenant, which is the Christian claim? For, in the end, as Surah 33.4 so pointedly reminds us, "God has not given to any man two hearts in one breast".

QUESTIONS FOR STUDY AND DISCUSSION

1. "Every creation of God is good and nothing to be refused, if it be received with thanksgiving, for then it is consecrated ..." (1 Tim. 4.4–5). Thanksgiving consecrates the gift, we may say, in the consecration of the receiver. What bearing does this gratitude or worship (which the Quran, of course, enjoins) for the gift of sex have upon the way we should think of its expression?

2. "In a true family children learn that there is one God" (Lambeth Report, 1958, 2. 151). In what senses does a stable marriage reflect and acknowledge the divine Unity?

3. How far is it true to say that Islam has been, characteristically, a man's world? What Christian, and what Islamic, considerations are there to militate against the fact?

4. Muslim marriage gives a strict legal context to the sex relationship. Does it give an adequate spiritual context?

5. How could you explain to a Muslim that the Christian ideal of "indissolubility" is not imprisonment within a legal formula but a spiritual truth translated into act. What does it mean for sex, society, and spirit?

6. There is no lock, for the man, in Muslim wedlock. How does its absence affect the weddedness?

7. What have you found locally and personally on the questions of exegesis and of woman's status raised in this outline?

8. Muslim law in this field insists that consent to sex-acts between two free parties should mean consent to marriage. Christianity agrees (for only this recognizes the full personal nature of both). But, in the light of the same fact, what should consent to marriage mean? And what truly is consenting marriage for both partners?

9. What bearing do population pressures have, or should they have, upon Muslim thought and practice in sex and family life?

15

The Divine and the Human Will

When Admiral Nelson was dying aboard his flagship at the Battle of Trafalgar in 1805 it is generally reputed that he said to his friend Captain Hardy: "Kiss me, Hardy." But what in fact, with more likelihood, he said was: "Qismet, Hardy", "Hardy, it is so fated."

Qismet (or *Kismet*), the Arabic word for "the portion", or "lot", and so "fate", is traditionally associated in western thought with Islamic and eastern attitudes. These, it is often alleged, are incurably fatalistic and apathetic. To western activism, contemplating Islamic history or a Muslim oriental market, there may seem much to justify the charge. But the whole matter calls for more patient study and discrimination.

Sooner or later, this topic is bound to confront us in any adequate reckoning with Islam. Predestination, destiny, fate—these are terms which popularly belong with and to Islam. To a subject with so many tangles and turnings we certainly cannot do even academic justice in a few pages. Our purpose, as always, is relational, and thus our first duty is to take the measure of the general psychological situation before we turn to the scientific revolution which has been spiritually so widespread in this field. We will then study the quranic evidence and finally take up—as we must if we are to be constructive—the personal crux or core of the whole issue in the freedom under law of the person and of humanity. In all these we shall be close to a vital as well as a rewarding area of potential ministry in mind and life to Muslims.

THE POPULAR TRADITION

Inshallah ("if God wills"), *Mashallah* ("what God wills")—the one said usually in prospect of events, the other in retrospect—are perpetual and recurrent phrases on Muslim lips. The literature, folklore, and terminology of Islam deeply reflects this overriding sense of an all-disposing presidency of the divine will. The sudden changes of fortune in stories like *The Arabian Nights*, bizarre situations oddly surmounted or unquestioned doom equally bizarrely descending, the unpredictability of events, the passive acceptance of even preventable delays and trials, and a score of other attitudes in the very warp and woof of Muslim life, witness to this dominant mentality. Fate is the shadow of an inscrutable Providence brooding over all.

This is, we may say, the pressure of the fact of God, as popularly felt in Muslim consciousness, where *Allahu Yaᶜlam*, "God knows", is the common explanation of what otherwise is inexplicable. It is generally related, with what validity we must assess later, to the terms *Qadar* and *Qada*. The former belongs to the particular disposition of events and character by God: it means individual destiny both here and hereafter. The latter has to do with a general ordering of divine sovereignty within which *Qadar* occurs. Even the theologians of the classic age of Islamic philosophy clung by a strange compromise to a view which, in effect, explained human freedom only as an illusion.

The famed Al-Ashᶜari, who was great at least in repute and "quotability", "resolved" for posterity the mystery of divine sovereignty and human freewill by the ingenious concept of *Kasb*, or *Iktisab*. God decreed what happened since he was the sole creator. But he decreed it within the will of the human doer. The latter in turn *acquired* (hence *Kasb*) the deed and this was regarded as saving his moral responsibility and accountability. The intellectual "solution" really hands back the problem in the form of an answer—a device to which philosophers are liable to resort. Since God willed the deed in the will of the doer, he was undividedly sovereign and man was still accountable. But the core of the issue, namely whether or not man could will otherwise than God willed in him, was left unfaced. The explanation of freedom in any event leaves it illusory.

What matters for our present purposes is not the evasive quality of Islamic thought at this point but the permeation of this instinct throughout Muslim life and attitudes. Man is not really in genuine possession of his own freedom. Superstition, lethargy, even climatic conditions and economic deprivations, with many other intangible factors, have all gone to reinforce attitudes of apathy in face of natural evils and of listlessness in the face of moral or social ones. Sometimes even the very root notion of *Islam*, or submission, has been perverted to signify a blind tolerance of every kind of event, both in time and in character, as if it were irretrievably "written down" and irreversibly decreed, so that there is nothing more appropriately human than gestures of exoneration, torpor, acquiescence, and indolence.

THE SCIENTIFIC "REVOLUTION"

The art of caricature is to sharpen truth by the device of disproportion. One gets things, so to speak, into focus by pulling them out of it. If there is something of that, deliberately, in the foregoing, the picture is certainly recognizable and authentic for any who have known popular Islam, as it mirrors itself, for example, in hospital patients, school children, illiterates, merchants, and travellers. But in this fourteenth of the Hijrah centuries it has to be borne in mind that external factors have done much to compel a difference of attitude.

Science obviously does not proceed by acquiescence, unless we use the term in relation to that acceptance of what nature discloses and of how nature submits to your experimentation which is the heart of the scientific mind. Science is the will to know and to use, to change, to adapt, to harness and to conquer. All the contemporary works of science proclaim a wide empire of the will of man. On the surface of society, as shaped by technology, we see ever more impressive evidence of the mastery and authority of man. In one sense the deepest fact about our time is just this recession in the immediacy of God to events. In some particulars God apparently becomes a dispensable hypothesis. Is it a question of drought, plague, disease, famine, or a host of other ills? Man now has recourse, less to temple or mosque or to gestures of *Mashallah* resignation, but to the drug, the artesian well, the aerial survey, the hospital, inoculation, or some other device deriving from the endless inventiveness of science. Technology confronts us with the seemingly limitless omnicompetence of man.

It needs no arguing that the evidences of this empire of the human will are being ever extended and multiplied before the simple mind. It almost seems in some respects as if man only has to say, "Be and it is", at least in what has to do with applied science. Thus, ever new lengths and reaches of human competence are thrust upon a bewildered tradition of divine sovereignty.

The human empire is not, of course, complete and much of its appearance is illusory. And in any event it is still achieved only by submission to the given-ness of matter, nature, space, time, reality, and their laws. Thus, fundamentally, science is no disproof but rather an immense corroboration of *Islam*, understood in the cosmic or natural sense of obedience to law. Since the law to which science bows is part of a given datum, the scientist remains at his greatest still a creature, still a servant, still a man. Only as he stoops does he conquer. The necessity for his moral submission is not less but a thousand times more urgent and crucial.

But these truths are not always immediately evident in the intoxications of technology. The man whose father was a shepherd or a pearl diver uses his Hi-Fi, or takes his coloured movies, and is immunized by inoculation from the ills that cursed his countless forbears. Islam in the popular sense is bound to become for him, either nothing, or something else. He must find a new realism about the human will and the divine, unless he is to miss his way and pass under new tyrannies of idolatry in the worship of his own hands.

Of course, this scientific "revolution" is not total. There remain wide areas of humanity, especially of the older generation, immune from it by the setness of their ideas and reactions. Moreover, even science does not remove the arbitrariness of events. To know that bacteria cause disease, and not devils or the evil eye, does not of itself solve the mystery of why the bacteria succeed with me and apparently ignore my neighbour. The cause may be explained where the incidence is not. I may know "Why", without knowing "Why *me*?" And it was just that which always lay behind fatalism and superstition.

In any case no spiritual emancipation can be scientifically achieved. If men are to be set free from the tyranny of a crude determinism it cannot be merely by the accumulation of scientific proof of man's mastery. Evil events in the natural order still remain. And as for the evil in the heart, evil of which man, not nature, is the source—this remains as real, as menacing, and as mysterious as ever. Yet, when we keep in mind all these facts, the scientific "revolution" now spreading throughout the Muslim world compels new dimensions in this perennial problem of the inter-will character of our human situation. The enlargement of the range of our own capacity to do and to determine means a yet more serious and discerning obligation to the will and authority of God.

THE QURANIC SITUATION

What may we understand about how the divine will and the human will are seen to be related in the Quran? First let it be clear that the modern technological "empire" of man belongs in that quranic concept of man as the *Khalifah*, or viceregent of God. It stands in the "dominion" which both the Bible and the Quran assign to man as being over things and under God. This in itself must mean that man has a real freedom. For without such how can he receive such a commission from God the Creator? God is certainly not replaced by deputies who are automata.

For the rest, it has to be admitted that there is a certain ambiguity in the Quran, which in any event does not purport to be a technical treatise in theology. It is a document of burning conviction and ardent preaching. Hence it does not believe that consistency is necessarily the first criterion of truth. We have to allow that there are areas within it of different emphasis. But what is clear is that much of what is popularly taken to justify a thoroughgoing determinism is far in fact from doing so. The classical commentators are, to put it crudely, much worse on this theme than the Quran itself. If they read into it their own concepts it now has to be liberated from the incubus of their *Taqlid* and their authority.

Take the very frequent phrase: *Wa Huwa ʿala kulli shaiʾin qadir*, "God is almighty, able for all". It has been held to teach that everything that happens, God does it. Whereas, studied contextually, it proclaims God's indubitable capacity for certain, apparently incredible, things there referred to. Its most recurrent context has to do with the resurrection of the dead—a theme about which Muhammad's Quraishi hearers were utterly incredulous. "Do not doubt the revivification of corpses", he urges them, "for all things are possible with God." The meaning is very comparable to the New Testament: "With God all things are possible." It does not mean that everything that is done, is done by God, but rather that he is competent for the thing at issue.

The word *Qismet* in the traditional sense is not in the Quran. Here the situation is the reverse of that at Trafalgar. It is thought to say what is traditionally in this word, when in fact it says something else. The word *Qadar*, too, basically means to measure or evaluate, not to predestine or predetermine. Take, for example, the important statement about the unbelievers: "They did not truly estimate God" (Surah 6.91), where the verb is *qadara*. There are many passages where the use of the word *qadara* applies to "measure" (e.g. Surah 23.18, rain from heaven; 17.30, food for his servants). A very profitable, if painstaking, study can be made with a concordance of the Quran, which will show that in most cases this root and its derivatives do not sustain the later theological implications of predestination.

Similarly, the word *Qada* means, primarily, not to issue an arbitrary decree but to accomplish or perform. Passages that may be cited are Surah 2.200, "And when you have performed your rites"; Surah 4.103, "When you have fulfilled your prayer"; Surah 17.4, "We decisively revealed (not decreed) unto the children of Israel", *et al.* Take a significant verse which might have been better heeded by commentators: "Do not be in a hurry over the Quran before its inspiration (*yuqda ilaika*) is finally achieved for thee" (Surah 20.114). The Prophet is warned against anticipating the deliverances of a yet unfinished thing. A concordance is also necessary patiently to assess this terminological evidence. But it is not difficult to see how overtones of inevitability came to attach to a term which basically means fulfilling, or bringing to the full, an action, or a revelation, or a judgement.

It is not here suggested of course that there are no quranic sources of the popular or classical tradition on this theme. Even Surah 13.12, often quoted as the sheet-anchor of freedom, contains when fully quoted a drastic proviso: "God does not change the condition of a people until *they* change what is in their hearts . . ." for when this seems to leave the onus with men the verse immediately adds: ". . . but if God has willed evil for a people there is none can (answer him back or) avert it." This verse epitomizes the ambiguity we have noted. Among the items the Quran mentions as things which could have been different had God elected, we find human disunity (5.48), human ignorance (6.35), idolatry (6.137), unbelief itself (10.99), and *Shirk* (16.35). In other words God in a sense has willed there should be discord, ignorance, idolatry, and unbelief. Yet in doing all these things for their part it is "their own selves men wrong" (cf. the reiterated phrase, *fa kana anfusahum yazlamun*). These things do not happen willy-nilly but by human choice. Perhaps we should argue that God does not explicitly will unbelief and idolatry, but that they happen within the setting of freedom which God has willed should be. But this is far from being the traditional understanding which is that God positively decrees the *Shirk* of x *mushrikin* and the *kufr* of x *kafirin*.

Yet we must also keep in mind the perpetual quranic insistence on responsibility. Man has the dignity of accountability. *La^cala*, the particle of choice, over one hundered times introduces quranic phrases about belief, worship, reverence, and obedience. Its "Perhaps ye may. . . ." throws the onus squarely on man and addresses him as responsible. Of like significance are the remonstrations and warnings of the Quran. It is a book addressed to people who, whether they are or not, are at least summoned as if they were, free agents. There is the clear option of faith; note, for example, Surah 18.28: "Let him who will, believe, and let him who will, disbelieve." On the idea of arbitrary "misleading" consider Surah 9.115: "God does not lead astray those whom he has guided except he first warn them", and Surah 8.33: "God did not punish them as long as they sought forgiveness" which seem to disqualify arbitrary concepts of man's error or perdition.

This whole study is only feebly sketched here to provide initial clues to our task in this field. But enough is clear to warrant the conclusion that the quranic situation on the theme of the inter-will quality of human-divine relation is far from being crudely arbitrary and determinist. It is impossible honestly to conclude from the Quran that human freedom is illusory.

THE PERSONAL EQUATION

In the last analysis what matters is not bare exegesis, still less formal theology, but living relatedness, "alive-ness unto God". How do we help deliver the victims of a crude predestinarian fatalism? How do we confront men who are intoxicated with scientific "freedoms" with the truth that they are all the while accountable under law? How do we find the true identity of wills between ourselves and God, if "our wills are ours to make them his"? These are the questions that matter religiously when we have silenced, dismissed, or awakened the theologians.

The issues belong in two realms: external, material, natural evil in our context, and moral, human, willed evil in our character. For the first we have the fact of a rational cosmos which precisely that it may be the arena of moral man is not morally discriminating. Only a world whose laws obtain indifferently to our feelings and willing can be the realm of the ethically responsible. Steel still behaves as steel, whether in the surgeon's scalpel or the murderer's dagger. Radio will still be radio, whether the substance is lying propaganda or the Gospel of peace. Nature is thus to be seen and understood as the sphere of our moral being and this is the necessity of its fixity of law within which our tragedies eventuate. The clue here is surely in the awareness of the character of the God whose presidency lies beyond it. "The Lord is my shepherd." To this theme of superstitious fatalism and its emancipation another chapter will be devoted.

As for our inward decisions of will that make our character, man's vocation is to will in freedom what God desires in law. But just as the divine law will address and never compel, so man's obedience, to be morally necessary, must also be essentially free. Both the dignity of God as Lord, and of man as servant, and of God's law as man's freedom, meet at the same point. In the Christian understanding of God and man, God exercises a sovereignty that is truly divine precisely because it relates to a humanity that is truly free. Freedom divine and human are not then exclusive of each other. To know and to make known this truth in the fullness of love, worship, and communion is the goal of all our obligations to men's fears, prejudices, and bondage.

These outward and inward relations of our human will to the evils of nature and the physical world in the one case, and of moral man and our human involvement in the other, are tangled by many emotions and fears. Emancipation from bondage does not come by thoughts alone even if these are rightly based. Deliverance has to come in terms of a new and living relationship with God in confidence and peace.

If we are looking round for a parable of the inter-will situation between God and man, as it is understood in the Christian faith, we might well borrow the analogy of education and the school. This happens, too, to fit certain lines of recent Muslim thought on the meaning of *Al-Rabb*, "the Lord", which, rightly or wrongly, argue that the term means "the Nurturer" who educates and nourishes his children and leads them on through experience and error into maturity and stature. Be this exegesis as it may—and it has several serious criticisms to encounter, despite its popularity in some quarters—human freedom, as understood in Christian faith, may be well compared to that which obtains in a well-ordered classroom, and such a comparison might invoke the notion of a divine "education" of man.

The teacher in school is the unquestioned ultimate authority: it is he on whom the order and the purpose depend. There can be no question that he, in theological terms, is "sovereign". But in the very meaning and purpose of his "sovereignty" is the objective of growing minds and guided wills. Accordingly, within this president authority of the teacher, which never abdicates, there is a modicum of freedom for the children, an area in which they are permitted to be truly free agents, even to the extent of being allowed to be in the wrong. For only so can their education proceed. Nobody learns anything, or becomes anything, in a state of total tyranny or dictated authority. The area of limited freedom, even to err, which the children enjoy, does not detract from the authority of the teacher. Since it is a self-willed limitation for his own end, it is precisely the form of his freedom and the condition of his ends. Muslim theology has all along instinctively feared that any seeming independence of God, which man was in theory allowed, somehow made God less sovereign. But no! His omnipotence is not to be so poorly thought of that he cannot allow us the grace of being free. So man has his realms of genuinely real freedom, and so of responsibility, meaningfulness, and sin, within and by the final sovereignty of God. In part, the fulfilment of the divine will, in those realms where it deliberately hinges on us, awaits what it never compels—namely the co-operation of man.

If we were not bedevilled by its own bogeys, this could be and would be the consensus of Muslim thought. For it is plainly the quranic situation. *Islam* itself, as submission, is not something capable of happening if God is all dominant. For in that event it is either unnecessary or impossible. There is a real sense in which to be genuinely *muslim*, man must be free.

Salvation from misunderstanding of the divine-human inter-will situation, however, does not arise merely from sound analogies or intellectual truths. It is the heart of Christian witness that in Christ and his cross we find a path of life in which our wills are more fully ours for being made over to him. The love of God within becomes the condition of the law of God without.

QUESTIONS FOR STUDY AND DISCUSSION

1. What impressions have you gathered, from experience, of Muslim attitudes which might be described as fatalist? Do they rest, in your view, on the general burden of adverse circumstances long sustained, or

on doctrinal conviction, or on customary belief? Have you found any efficacious way of countering such apathy?

2. How familiar do you find the Muslims of your acquaintance with the quranic emphases and texts which modify or rule out a rigid predestinarian view?

3. What is the precise meaning of the psalmist saying; "I will fear no evil"? How is such confidence in God generated in those who customarily and apprehensively anticipate evil?

4. Muslim thinkers and Muslim attitudes have usually believed it fitting that, in the interests of the divine power and majesty, human freedoms should be severely limited or totally denied. On fully Christian ground the case is very much the contrary. How and why is this so?

5. At the heart of the very meaning of *islam* (as something, namely surrender, that men do) is the necessity of freedom, since that is not submission which is inevitable. How, then, would you explain the long-standing idea of fixed destiny in Muslim religion?

6. What intellectual consequences of the new technology do you find among Muslims and how are their attitudes to belief and worship affected?

7. What would you say, from either Muslim or Christian viewpoints, to the person who assumed that science had made God a "dispensable hypothesis"?

8. What, in simple terms calculated to be clear to a Muslim, is the Christian account of the inter-will situation between God and man?

9. "To will and to do his good pleasure" (Phil. 2.13). "Men of God's good pleasure" (Luke 2.14). "The perfect law of liberty" (Jas. 1.25). How would you relate the meaning of these passages to the central problem of this study?

16

Muslims and Superstition

A mother was anxious to wean her small daughter from the need for a light in the bedroom when she went to sleep. The darkness, she wanted the child to learn, was as friendly as the light. But the small girl was loathe to believe it and cried for the candle. Whereupon the mother remonstrated and tried to reassure her, saying: "But my darling, God is here with you and there's nothing to be afraid of." "But Mummie", came the quick answer, "couldn't you take God and leave the candle?"

Like so many child-stories, this belongs to more than childhood and introduces usefully the whole question of human superstition, which here we study in its Muslim forms, with the attitudes of the Gospel in relation to it. "The candle", or be what it may, the rosary, the relic, the invocation, the *barakah*, the bead, the talisman—these are more comforting than God. And, conversely, only in the deep, intimate, personal sense of God, such as that which breathes for all time so wonderfully in Psalm 23, shall we find emancipation from the fears and follies that superstition holds.

Superstitious frames of mind are very diverse but very common. In considering the Muslim aspects of this topic we can be certain of the closest affinities with every other religious system, even though Islam be doctrinally the fiercest theoretical antagonist of all substitutes, emotional or otherwise, for God. Despite the intense rejection of *Shirk*, or letting anything be "God" to us save God, popular Islam has all kinds of cults and objects associated with the divine in protective, directive, or effective functions in life. The central categories of faith and the Quran itself are drawn into superstitious setting and become Muslim means to un-Islamic ends.

Yet there is nothing strange, except perhaps its irony, in this situation. It may be well, in an introductory way, to consider the inner nature and origins of the superstitious mind. As a preface to this, one may reflect on the different phrasing of contra-idolatry in the Muslim

Shahadah and in the first of the ten commandments. "There is no god except God" is a statement of metaphysical fact. But when we translate it into the actual realm of human behaviour it means also: "There ought not to be any god whom you trust and recognize except God." It is just this actuality the commandment has in mind: "*Thou shalt have* none other gods but me." This is a moral imperative which though certainly present in the *Shahadah* is in the form of a categorical command in the Decalogue. It is precisely the transition from the indicative: "There are no other gods" to the personal: "Thou shalt have none other gods" which is so vital. The distinction goes to the very heart of superstition. For when we substitute something for God at the heart of our trust and our devotion, we are "having other gods" irrespective of the denials of their existence which our creed makes. The unity of God has to be religiously recognized as well as credally stated. And that is precisely where the crux both of the problem and of our ministry lies. We will proceed by outlining: the superstitious mind, the means to superstition, and a ministry to the superstitious.

THE SUPERSTITIOUS MIND

A satisfactory definition is hard to come by. Often things can be best studied not by synonyms but by their antonyms. Faith is to be contrasted not simply with doubt, but with despair and with irresponsibility. Superstition is often pathetically trustful; but it is casual, self-centred, timid, partial, and prudent, and is in all these respects different from faith. While the latter is constant, total, and entire, involving the whole person, superstition is a kind of fragmentary relation to different aspects of existence, seeking, for the most part, protection and insurance, not obedience and surrender. It is a kind of protective reaction to experience, considered as unpredictable, precarious, fickle, and intimidating, whereas faith "knows whom it has believed" and commits the whole person, body, mind, and spirit.

The sources of superstition are many and complementary. The sheer precariousness of life is perhaps the greatest: "The sea is so wide and my boat is so small." Misery, as much as mystery, produces it. Poverty, disease, fear, wistfulness, danger, hardship, adversity, death, and sorrow, all play their part. "The hardness of the way", says Doughty of the wilderness in his great *Arabia Deserta*, "edges all men's spirits." This we may say is true of all human existence, wherever men by sickness, fear, and apprehension of the unknown feel themselves on the edge of things. It may be significant that the English word "superstition" has to do in origin with things that "stand over" us. Perhaps we may define it as men's reaction to circumstances they live under, to existence felt oppressively.

Nor does science of itself really liberate us from this oppressiveness, even if it does much to mitigate our plagues. At times it even develops new superstitions of its own, either by imposing new situations of stress, or by its remedies through dissociation from God being conceived as a new kind of magic. It is quite wrong to equate the superstitious mind only with ignorance, or to suppose the educated emancipated from having substitutes for God merely by the fact of education. Many a psychiatrist's consulting room, and even also his prescriptions, are witness to the contrary.

Another frequent source of superstition is the past. It is likely to be very potent where the generations are felt to be bound together in a retrospective duty. The rite of African libation, for example, reveres and invokes the ancestors so as to make the prosperity of the present actually hinge upon the veneration of the past. An African mother of the Didinga tribe sings to her first born about his father:

> You will tend his shrine when he is gone:
> With sacrifice and oblation you will recall his name
> Year by year:
> He will live in your prayers, my child.

The bundle of life anywhere is plainly more than contemporary. But this self-evident truth becomes the occasion of rooted superstition wherever this inter-involvement of the generations lies outside the sense of the eternal God as shepherd of our souls.

Piety itself is another prolific source of superstition. In the case of Islam, so much of it takes its rise within Sufism where the tenderest in Muslim devotion is also to be found. Its saints have sought a closer intimacy with God, a truer immediacy of communion than formal theology approves or fosters. And this in turn at second-hand produces a whole crop of attitudes resting superstitiously on Sufi sanctities. So the very Quran itself, for all its fierce intolerance of idolatry, becomes a means to the idolatrous mind. It is used for incantations or charms against beings which its verses affirm have no existence and certainly no right to be feared, invoked, appeased, or placated. Or the saint who taught and practised his own *Fana*ʾ, or transcendance of selfhood, in the mystical *Tauhid*, becomes in legend or devotion a powerful intermediary with God.

Finitude, the past, piety—the world around us, behind us, and beyond us—all shape the stage of the superstitious life. And sin too, the accusing instinct and the excusing (see Rom. 2.15), plays its part, impelling men to find some protective and effective means to obviate either human revenge, inward reproach, or divine retribution.

Yet when we reflect on these several sources of the superstitious mind we find at every point close affinities with what is validly religious. There are close ties and deep tensions between what is of faith and what is of superstition. The Sufi has a better attitude to mystery than the sophisticated. The pagan is in less danger than the secularist. His awe in the presence of nature, of time, and of death is a proper ingredient in true faith. Creatureliness and the confession of finitude, "laying help upon one that is mighty"—these are qualities of the true believer. To walk barefoot, as some Muslim saints have done, out of respect for the earth as the carpet of God, is better than to be soullessly soled. Within African libation, too, is a consciousness of "not living to oneself" which, rightly assured and proportioned, has its place in the kingdom of heaven. Before we overlook these things, as the disciples did in their understandable efforts to rid Jesus of the embarrassment of certain superstitious mothers who thought his touch would be a useful charm for their children, we must enter into the meaning of his own reaction in that "He forbade them not". This involves a patient effort to penetrate below the surface.

THE MEANS TO SUPERSTITION

Here we cannot hope to be comprehensive. For superstition is a vast field, reaching into the whole human situation on five continents and numerous planes. But a few general characteristics can be summarized, to be tested, corrected, amplified, and sifted by the sort of local observation and sensitivity which belong to a rightly Christian relation to men. The proverbs of the world are inexhaustibly varied in their idiom, their language, their metaphor. Yet, through all their variety, they betray certain common themes and types. So it is with the endless variety of Muslim superstitions.

One of the most deeply rooted ideas in superstition is that of association, physically established, or even tactually secured, by virtue of which blessedness accrues. The root idea here is *barakah*, a sort of vicarious benefit available in holy things, places, times, people, and rites, to be had by personal contact. It is this idea which has made Sufism so fruitful a source of superstition for the reason that it has produced so many saints and holy men, whose asceticisms and austerities have accumulated a sanctity far in excess of their own needs and so available for lesser folk. Hence the frequent veneration of relics, tombs, shrines, and memorials of such pirs, marabouts, or sayyids, on the part of a wide variety of suppliants, in sickness, barrenness, pregnancy, and perplexity. Association is established either by haunting the shadow of the tomb, hanging a votive offering on a grille, touching, kissing, or handling the holy thing.

Such *barakah* can sometimes be transferred to some other article and carried away, as, say, a handkerchief dipped in holy water. But the "virtue" is very easily lost or destroyed. A written charm, for example, may lose its effectiveness if dried at a fire, or a "beneficent" element shed its *barakah* if in contact with impurities of the body or shadowed by an unbeliever. Some manifestations of *barakah* are closely akin to "luck" in the western world and may have a relatively innocent quality. They may be relied on for a successful churning of butter or a making of dough. But it may have in it much physical menace (as when the water used in washing a corpse is drunk by a woman desiring pregnancy) or be the occasion of chronic spiritual fears. Many natural situations, like sterility, or problems that have an emotional explanation, like a loss of marital affection, are laid at the door of loss of *barakah*, perhaps maliciously occasioned.

It is the underlying notion of *barakah* which gives rise to the superstitious accretions of the Quran. For, obviously, all things associated with the sacred text, or with men of special sanctity in the faith, are a sure source of potential and vicarious holiness. So the Quran is drawn upon for charms and omens. Worn or carried on the person, it serves a protective purpose. Examples are legion. Thus Sir Ahmadu Bello, Sardauna of Sokoto, and Prime Minister of the Northern Region of Nigeria recollects:

> If any (of us) fell sick there was nothing that could be done about it, beyond the offering of prayers and drinking of water in which the correct charms had been washed.

He adds that some of the children died, "but though I was sick from time to time God's destiny lay before me and I was brought through it".[1] Kenneth Little, discussing the Mende people of Sierra Leone among whom there are numerous Muslims, observes:

> The Quran is regarded and used in much the same fashion as a native medicine. It is employed to manufacture a powerful charm by inscribing a Sura in Arabic writing upon a wooden board. The Arabic characters are washed off in water, which is bottled and then serves to endow its possessor with a commanding personality.[2]

Similarly, pilgrims returning from Mecca with the water of Zamzam, or from some other shrine like Meshed, Najaf, or Karbala', have in their persons—even in the crudest of ways—a potential blessedness that can be tapped by "association". The "virtue" of holy places and rites makes diverse occasions of *barakah*, the ramifications and minutiae of which are too miscellaneous to describe.

Quranic charms, whether used for protection, or divination, or accumulation of merit, raise some nice questions of Islamic theology which in turn reproduce the ambiguity of the Quran itself. For, despite its uncompromising monotheism, which should properly rule out all reliance on any agency other than God for those relationships in which only God is competent—such as mercy, guidance, providence, etc.—the Quran itself moves in a realm of jinn, sprites, and supernatural powers impinging on human life, to which the awe or worship or fear rightly reserved for God alone are in fact addressed. Or in other terms, monotheism, categorically so insistent in the Quran, was not emotionally secure or dominant. Muslims "had other gods" in the sense that they were conscious of beings to fear, placate, and implore, other than and apart from God himself.

Superstition in its recurrent and perpetual form merely reproduces this quranic situation. The faith and dogma firmly say *Aᶜudhu bi-Illahi*, "I seek refuge with God" (cf. Surahs 113 and 114); but emotion and fear tend too often to add, "I seek refuge with the charm and the *barakah*". The "rosary" or *subhah* in Muslim usage has a similar double rôle. It derives from the act of worship that recites the Names

[1] Al Haji Sir Ahmadu Bello, *My Life*, Cambridge University Press, 1962, p. 6. Quoted with permission.

[2] In "The Mende of Sierra Leone", *African Worlds*, Studies in the Cosmological Ideas and Social Values of African Peoples, edited by Daryll Forde, Oxford University Press, 1954, p. 113. Quoted with permission.

of God, the *Asma' al-Husna*, all of which in some way corroborate the sole sovereignty, unfailing knowledge, and exclusive reign of God. But the beads which tell off, and tell out, these names also serve as a means to superstition, in that they are utilized for divination, for charms, and for omens. The use of the divine names or of the *Bismillah* or of phrases like *Mashallah*, *Tawakkaltu ʿala Allah*, in conversation or inscription, may have a similar superstitious quality. Here also the line between a genuine spiritual trust, rightly focused in a material "sign", and an attitude that makes the phrase a mere charm may be hard to draw and there may well be a sort of oscillation between the two. But there is no doubt that the declension into culpable superstition occurs and that credal monotheism is all too often emotionally a chronic pluralism.

One of the most frequent pleas for these "means to superstition" is the prevalent belief in the "evil eye". In the last resort perhaps the real spelling should be "the evil I", the general menace of particular selfishness. Man's menacing jealousy and self-seeking threaten his neighbours, and the inquisitive glance, the lusty looking, are "the evil eye" which makes protective devices imperative. The idea derives also no doubt from that general precariousness already noted. The eye has to be symbolically blinded by charms or other means that ward it off or take up its malice, leaving the real object immune. These factors in the invisible warfare against envious or malicious jinns and men are as varied as *barakah*. Muslim art itself has been widely influenced by the fear of "the evil eye": hence the frequency of designs of the hand, the five-pointed star, triangles, and calligraphy, all calculated to "employ" "the evil eye" and so "buffer" or immunize the person himself.

Other practices include deliberate cultivating of dirt and poverty of appearance (for the spruce, the tidy, the evidently prosperous will naturally attract "the evil eye"). For the same reason boys are sometimes dressed as girls; people who express a great liking for something are pressed to take it before their envy grows more dangerous; objects like saucers, "brides of the corn", or an "eye" itself, are exhibited on houses or vehicles or rooms, to take up the surrounding or impending malevolence of life.[1]

A further potent source of superstitious inventiveness is belief in the

[1] For an excellent regional catalogue of such devices see Westermarck, *Ritual and Belief in Morocco*, 1926, vol. 1, ch. 8.

Qarin or *Qarinah*. The "double" of a person, always of the same sex, his mate in permanent attendance upon him, is frequently credited with being the cause of trouble, sudden temper, even sterility, sickness, and untoward event. The "double" is jealous, for example, of successful childbirth, since though a *Qarinah* marries when its human counterpart does so, it can only, in many cases, acquire children through infant mortality on earth. The fact that a *Qarin* or *Qarinah* is believed to testify at the judgement against its human mate gives them an intimidating power over earthly life. In some superstitious minds the *Dhikr* itself, or remembrance of the Name of God, is sometimes promoted by this very fear of the *Qarin*, for, apart from the remembrance of God, one would have no other companion but the malicious *Qarin*. Here once again we observe the close ties that superstition may assert with what is rightly religious. The foregoing are no more than random notes on the patterns of superstitious attitudes, which will be familiar enough to any sensitive person involved with ordinary folk, especially in the crises of life. But every one of them needs to be locally amplified, checked, and documented. It is time to turn to a constructive relation to people under superstition.

A MINISTRY TO THE SUPERSTITIOUS

Is it not all very much a case of "the smoking flax", this human superstition? The whole question is how, and through what relation of ministry, these attitudes can ripen into faith and a true worship. Negative and supercilious relationships will never win the superstitious. Fears must be felt for what they are. They cannot be got rid of by mere denial of their contents: they can only be expelled by a new confidence. We must see in superstition, as Jesus did on several occasions in the Gospels, the potential ground of a true faith.

The ultimate task is, of course, to *unify* the world of superstitious people. Worship, awe, reverence, mystery, dependence—all these are diversified and multiplied in superstition. What Islam in its first preaching aimed to achieve doctrinally has to be accomplished emotionally, until men know their direct dependence upon God alone. Only this unified trust can dislodge the complex fears and the manifold directions in which awe is rendered or "insurance" sought. Those who long for *barakah* must learn to go to the single source in the blesser himself. If the fear of the Lord is the beginning of wisdom, it is also the end of superstition. "Yea, I say unto you, fear him."

But the mere assertion of the single direction of all human need, unto God and under him, does not of itself emancipate. Indeed, as in the case of the Meccans, the depopulation of all the intervening realms of pagan deities may leave the fearful strangely friendless and forlorn. The comforting candle is not dislodged by argument. To learn that one has to do with God, and with God alone, is not of itself good news, unless one is reassured about his nature and his mercy. Indeed, the mere destruction of men's idols may only intensify their emotional polytheism unless they learn his trustworthiness. It takes love, as well as sovereignty, in God to drive out fear, and compassion, as well as dogma, to dethrone the idol-trusts.

It is not least in African Islam, with its inevitable absorption of African sensitivities, that this actual pluralism most readily co-exists with the allegation of divine unity. Much of African religion concedes the lordship of the supreme God, but believes him so splendidly enthroned that he is remote, either in low disdain or high dudgeon, from men's affairs. His neglect of humanity is thus reciprocated and mortals call upon him only, if ever, in the utmost extremity and as a desperate resort. It is into this meaninglessness of remoteness that assertions about *Allah* all too easily fall in the borderlands of Islam and the African world-view.

Thus it is that a true iconoclasm needs more than assertion. Men are only weaned from their instinctive reliance on the near, the intimate, the lesser, the adjacent deities, the pseudo gods, by the inward assurance that "the Most High who ruleth" is also "waiting to be inquired of. . . ." It is only by Emmanuel that lordship reigning in heaven reigns also in the lowly heart. The faith of the incarnation is the final liquidation of idolatry.

So our ministry has to *reconcile*, as well as to unify, men's world. We have to bring them to the point of being able to say, "The Lord is my shepherd" where the truth of his oneness, being implicit, is lost in the deeper truth that he is ours. This reality of God being "ours" is discovered and made good for the Christian in Christ. In him the oneness of God ceases to be a crucial dogma, for which we have to fight against an ever menacing danger of relapse into pluralism. It becomes instead a precious and abiding conviction of the loving One.

It is for this reason, of course—though the fact is often misunderstood among Muslims—that the New Testament is not perpetually reiterating the basic truth of the divine unity. He who truly knows God knows that there is only he. But this knowledge comes only fully in the sense of God's being loving. The answer to the superstitious minded is to call them to go to the fountain head. For the fountain head is accessible. When I know that God has come to men in Christ I have no need to go through charms and devices to deal with the divine. All the uncertainties of superstition are the uncertainties, about God, of the superstitious. They are met and conquered where we have come to know assuredly that God is love and make our way to him on that ground. This place is Christ, incarnate and crucified.

Such unifying and reconciling is the crux of the salvation of the superstitious. But there are certain other evident ministries of grace to the situation. For the interpreter there are parables everywhere. The evil eye "legend" has, in its crude way, fastened on a profound truth about sin, namely, that self-interest is the real blight of life, the deep menace of human relationships. There is a looking upon our fellows that does them ill (cf. Matt. 5.29 and passages dealing with the covetous). The way in which we "regard" things and people (to use deliberately an English word which is appropriately ambiguous) is what endangers them (cf. the quranic concept of *Zulm*).

A similar parable of spiritual truth may be said to attach to the idea of contact in *barakah*. The "virtue" or benison has to be had always by association, by touch, by adjacence. It cannot be had without a personal relation between the desire and the supply, between the need and the satisfaction. So it becomes a very right and feasible parable of the nature of faith. Was it not just this aspect of superstition which motivated our Lord in his welcome to the mothers, and the woman with the issue of blood? He saw in their simple-minded reliance on touch a token of the wistfulness of true faith. All that has to do with *barakah* has within it this rich lesson, "Come unto me". Salvation is never a second-hand affair: it must be had by the person personally. Given the Christian truth of the ever-accessible universal lover, the superstitious impulse to access has its true answer. The cross is the cost and the assurance of the blessed accessibility of the blesser of all. It is the form in the heart of God of his open invitation to mankind.

Superstition may also be to us a means to humility and a reminder of the need for vigilance. It is one of those factors that make all religions kin. One of our problems is just that many Muslims are more familiar with a Christianity that is superstitious than they are with one that is valid.

One final thought. Is not superstition everywhere a sort of doubt about whether life in general cares about life in particular, whether "what is" really has room for "I am"? It is an underlying fear of life's enmity to me. So then its one sure antidote is that love of our neighbour, the seeking of his good in all circumstances, which we learn in what is superstition's final solvent, namely, the assurance of the love of God. Therein every Christian's compassion is in turn a means to the redemption of his fellow's fears. When our environment is known as the arena of sure "philanthropy", this love of man for man banishes the bogeys of malevolence and blunts the ravages of unpredictable powers in nature and event.

QUESTIONS FOR STUDY AND DISCUSSION

1. What local and personal examples have you found of Muslim superstition? How far do they conform to the general pattern here described and what special features do you detect?

2. "Whom have I in heaven but thee: there is none upon earth that I desire beside thee" (Ps. 73.25). Here "Thou shalt have . . ." has become an unnecessary command. How does witness lead men to this point?

3. The fact of superstition within Islam shows that the recognition of *Tauhid*, or Unity, is more than a matter of dogma. The true Muslim is he who fears only God (cf. Surah 9.18). How, in fact, as well as in dogma, does the Gospel bring us to God "the true, the only" (cf. John 17.3)?

4. How are men freed from superstition within the New Testament? (Cf. Acts 19.19; Heb. 2.14–17; 1 John 4.15–19; Col. 2.14–20, etc.)

5. The woman in the New Testament story (Luke 8.43–8) sought only "the hem of his garment", but Jesus asked: "Who touched *me*?" How to-day are men to be brought beyond their own assessments of what they need into all that God is?

6. What is the meaning of the fact that all religions, if not equally, are, at least comparably, prone to superstition?

7. What potential parables and what actual snares do you find in popular notions of *barakah*, the evil eye, and other forms of superstition?

8. How far are we, in our lives and habits, expressing the reality of the love of God in and over the vicissitudes of life? Seeing it is only in the "light of his countenance" that our superstitious candles become needless.

17

Islam and the Political Order

> What man is more concerned about the Emperor than we are? Who loves him more honestly than we? For we pray incessantly for him that he may be granted long life and that he may rule the nations with a just sword and know an age of peace and plenty in his empire. Then we pray for the welfare of the army and for the blessing of mankind and of the world. But we cannot sacrifice to the Emperor in the temple. For who may pay divine honours to a man of flesh and blood?

Spoken around the year A.D. 250, on behalf of a Christian community by one of its leaders, these words state with typical forthrightness the attitude of the Church of the first three Christian centuries to the Empire. They embody the classic Christian concept of the relation of faith to citizenship, of Church to State, of the spiritual to the political—a ready obedience in all things lawful and honest, together with a fierce, uncompromising hostility to any state-demands which flouted the rights of God. The primitive Church had no desire either to subvert or disobey the imperial, civil power, even though identified, as that power was, with such monsters as Nero and Domitian. But with that docility and acknowledgement of citizen-duty went this quite heroic defiance in what had to do with faith and worship.

The parallel issue and the contrasted attitude are useful as an introduction to any study of Islam and the political order. There is in fact no clearer setting in which to assess the significance of Islamic beginnings than to set them alongside Christian origins. The sharp contrast develops in an initial similarity. It will be useful to review early Church history with an Islamic commentary, as a prelude to exploring Islamic political concepts.

AN ISLAMIC SITUATION IN CHRISTIAN FORM

When Islam began in Mecca, its rejection of idols brought it into steady conflict with an established political and civil order wedded by strong vested interests to the very idolatry Islam denied. Mecca exercised a powerful city authority, with a tribal hegemony devoted to the security of its Kaᶜbah (or pantheon) as the focal point of both its wealth and prestige. If Muhammad persisted in his anti-idolatry he would either have to break Mecca or be broken by it. He proclaimed a spiritual truth and ran into a political enmity. In affirming a faith, he had, as event made clear, in fact challenged a city.

Are there not elements in this situation suggesting a parallel with that in the New Testament? Jesus in a very different context and for only partially similar reasons, was regarded as a disturber of the *status quo*, as a menace to the Herodian compromise by which Jewish privileges subsisted under Roman rule. By his teaching he challenged the authority and traditions of the Scribes and Pharisees. His hearers who were in power judged that what he stood for could not coexist with their vital interests. Hence the "expediency" of his death.

To that degree, Mecca and Jerusalem present a comparable picture of irreconcilable issues between a new "Prophet" and an old order, between a message proclaimed and an antipathy entrenched. But what eventuates in the two cases makes a total contrast. The Muhammadan pattern in Mecca can be traced in the steady deterioration, or sharpening, of the situation, the uncertain "experiments" including the emigrations to Ethiopia, the crucial Hijrah by which the hostile city was evacuated and a new city-base secured, the inexorable build-up of power and influence through wise diplomacy and strong-handedness, and the final capitulation of Mecca to the faith-cum-army out of the Prophet's Medina.

The pattern in the Gospels hinges on the meaning of the triumphal entry with its unmistakable repudiation of a this-worldly messiahship. Its climax is the cross. The hostile city, under shrewd and resolute leadership, liquidates the Jesus danger, and therein, for his part, the prophet of Nazareth perfects the messianic loyalty chosen in the wilderness temptations and sustained through a patient devotion all the way from Galilee to Gethsemane. How sublime that pattern was. How different the finale might have been if Jesus, with all his strange authority over the populace, had elected to set himself squarely in the Maccabean tradition. Pilate would not then have washed his hands after a brief morning's embarrassment. The whole eastern empire had rather been set ablaze. But in no wise—that way—would the world have been redeemed. Jesus had no mind to overthrow the State, still less to displace it with another of his own, because he saw the salvation of the world in terms more ultimate than the political.

The disciples, little as they understood his way of messiahship before his death and resurrection, held closely to it afterwards. They went out into the world in the same terms. When in turn the Empire confronted them with a choice of insurrection or suffering, they consistently chose the second. Christianity spread for three centuries not with an empire but in spite of one, not in conquest but in catacombs. It denied to Caesar the throne of God. But it did not unseat him from the throne of his fathers. It was within the existent state as a new Gospel, not against it as a new Caesar.

The form of Islamic origins under the Caliphs is equally true to the initial and formative shape of the founder's decision. The Meccan submission became the pattern of rapid political and military subjugation and acceptance of a new régime when Islam welled out of the peninsula under Abu Bakr and ᶜUmar. What happened should not be crudely thought of as "expansion by the sword" but rather "expansion in the form of empire". What *Dar al-Harb* accepted when Islam rode into it was not merely a new creed but, as the name itself affirms, a new political and military master.

Nor should we miss the force of this contrast by supposing that the Roman situation confronting the infant Church was somehow less intractable than that which Islam faced in the Levant six centuries later. On the contrary. Had Islam tackled the Roman Empire in the full tide of its idolatrous strength from Nero to Diocletian it would surely have thought the Islamic procedures of anti-idolatry *a fortiori* imperative and indispensable. No reader of the New Testament and the apostolic history can fail to see how insidious, how dominant, how pervasive was the idolatry against which the Church was pitted. It was in the most deeply Islamic objective (*Tauhid*, the witness to divine unity) that Christianity chose the most un-Islamic means, and so doing perpetuated into history the contrast between the Hijrah and the cross.

It is important to explore this study in contrast quite patiently and temperately, with honesty but without acrimony. For polemic would lose its spiritual dimensions just as surely as would dishonesty. What matters now is the bearing of all the foregoing, both negatively and positively, upon the hopes and problems of contemporary politics. Our Christian duty of thought and relationship in this connection seems to suggest three themes.

THE RANGE OF COMPETENCE OF THE POLITICAL ORDER

It follows from all that has been said above that Islam has a basic confidence in the capacity of the State, as such, to bring about the right society. This is implicit in the inner decision that shaped its origins. The realm over which the Caliph ruled was by the same token the realm in which the divine will was done. The area submissive to the divine revelation could, it was believed, be extended coterminously with the extension of the empire of those who received it. This is the characteristic Islamic view. The State is the Kingdom. The will of God through the prophecy is actualized in the rule of its heirs and custodians. This is the whole sense of the traditional Caliphate.

Of course, it was recognised that the Islamic Empire did not in fact truly embody the kingdom of God. There are those who hold with the apologist, Sayyid Qutb, a noted Cairo author, that Islamic statehood suffered grievous distortion under the Ummayyads as early as A.D. 661.[1] But this should not obscure the general theory that the political order could of itself constitute the divine society. Moreover, when such delinquency or compromise was acknowledged, the corrective was usually thought of as still political. One should not argue, from these realistic considerations (so ran the philosophy) that the State, as such, was only relative and partial: rather one should ask what had gone wrong with it. The "discrepancy" between what was and what ought to have been lay, not in human nature or in spiritual rebellion, but in the weakness of the Caliph or the compromise of the law. There was no call for inward and total redemption of man as man, but only for political reformation of the institution of the State.

To clarify this underlying Islamic notion of the political order is not, of course, to suggest that Christianity thinks the State has no place at all, or is irrelevant to the doing of the divine will. On the contrary: things political have their part. But it is a relative one. What the

[1] *Al-ᶜAdalat al-Ijtimaᶜiyyah fi-l-Islam*, Cairo, n.d., pp. 195, 223.

State, however conceived, can accomplish is partial and belongs only to what is within its range. In the inner reaches of the human heart, where the divine kingdom must necessarily be, the State has neither writ nor competence. Nor are our human rebelliousnesses accessible either to its detection or its correction. The things that are Caesar's are far from being exempt from the concern of the things that are God's. But they are very far from being identical.

This inescapable contrast between the Christian and the Muslim concept of the State's competence in relation to the heavenly will underlies our whole Christian witness to Islam at the present juncture. For the Islamic view, implicit thus in its origins and whole tradition, has found a powerful emotional confirmation in the new nationalism of our own time.

CURRENT TASKS OF THE POLITICAL ORDER

Is it not true to say that almost the whole expectation of contemporary men in both Asia and Africa looks to, and turns on, the political order? Salvation by statehood is the dominant hope and driving inspiration of more than half the world. The Prime Minister of Ghana is not alone in assuming, and asserting: "Seek ye first the political kingdom and all else shall be added unto you." [1] This is the well-nigh universal "gospel" in the new nations.

The West, no doubt, bears large responsibility for the fact that this is so. Imperialism taught the world to idealize political salvation by making political action the only possible means to its termination. Only nationalism in full tide, and assertive, could oust and end the West's dominion. Thus, when the new nationalisms, strong and successful in their negative achievement of independence, proceeded to see their whole positive future, they saw it as lying within political competence to actualize and perfect. Thus, the innate Islamic instinct to expect all from the political was confirmed and encouraged by the necessary pattern of twentieth-century evolution.

It is this fact which explains the current preoccupation in the new nations of Islam with the political order. Both the logic of their long traditions and the circumstances of the recent past converge on the same results, namely the centrality of the State and the belief that all salvation is political.

[1] Kwame Nkrumah, *Autobiography*, 1957, p. ix.

These high hopes of statehood developed precisely at the moment when the problems confronting state authority were greatly intensified. There was the bewildering newness of the political situation itself. The old Caliphate had departed. It is now four decades extinct and shows no sign of being resuscitated. The sundered national entities which replaced it, or, as in Africa, east and west, have developed outside it, are launched upon their own careers, with all this high expectancy, when governing involves so much more than Caliphs ever knew.

In the vacuum left by the lapse of the Caliphate or by the recession of imperialism, the observer can trace the still inconclusive search for an answer to the problem of power. After the Treaty of Versailles there was in the Near East and elsewhere the ultimate ideal of parliamentary democracy. Whatever may be said of the abstract pros and cons about such a system that could be argued from both "egalitarianism" and "totalitarianism" in Islamic thought about law and society, the actualities of life seem to have necessitated its general abandonment.

This current suspension of democratic forms arises not only from the fact (evident everywhere in the world) that government, in these days of high dams, flooding populations, and industrialization, must be direct and efficient. It springs also from the fact that democratic processes, to be secure, require standards of general education and traditions of citizenship which often do not obtain, and for lack of which mere democratic processes play into the hands of exploiters and vested interests. Moreover, viable and valid democracy demands a vigorous party system and the concept of the dignity of opposition—elements still wanting, for a variety of reasons, in the structure of most Islamic communities. "Nowhere, except in India", writes K. M. Pannikar, "does there seem to be a serious effort to give meaning and substance to these conceptions."[1]

Thus, it is now patently clear that early hopes about democracy were premature, or at least that the substance, without which the forms are a dangerous façade, is still to come by. For this reason numbers of new régimes have replaced the earlier "constitutions" with patterns of power that correspond more realistically to the mood and need of the time. They aim to bring about the reform of economic and social

[1] K. M. Pannikar, *The Afro-Asian States and their Problems*, George Allen & Unwin, 1959, p. 27. Quoted with permission.

conditions which, they insist, is a prior necessity, and without which the governmental patterns that are in form correct are in effect vicious.

Realistic and often beneficial as these developments may be, they leave unfaced the ultimate problem of power and its relation to the good, and to the dignity of responsible community. If the effete "democracies" of past decades in this century took for granted, as either factual or feasible, ideal conditions that did not obtain, their efficient successors are in danger of likewise taking for granted assumptions it would be tragic to perpetuate, namely that power is not answerable to people, or that its being answerable need lie only in the ruler's judgement without the intrusion of necessary electoral processes.

This problem of power—power national, independent, and Islamic—is the heart of contemporary history in most of the areas of world Islam. It is a problem inherent in the filling of the vacuum left by a retreating political West. It searches the intellectual resources of Islam in a most radical manner. It lies behind the constant debates on constitutions and the successive acts of their suspension and replacement, whether in Lahore, Djakarta, Khartoum, Cairo, Damascus, or Ankara, these forty years. As an active experimentation in the form of the Islamic State, it provides a living contemporary commentary on that most Muslim of all issues—the rule of the Prophet's people.

As any observer can see, it is all accentuated by the vast, exacting questions that attach to modern society. If India has transformed the personal legal pattern of a society two and a half millenia old, Islam is almost everywhere revising the classical legal framework of its fourteen centuries. This has all kinds of attendant consequences. It brings a new type of lawyer to the fore and relegates many of the old niceties and their exponents to unimportance. It brings about a silent transformation in the whole idea of *Ijtihad*, or legal innovation, and of who is fitted to exercise it. It remodels the structure of courts and alters the mentality of litigants. It revises the concept of women and invades the innermost sanctuaries of personal status and the family.

Alongside it are the far-reaching economic transformations of daily life and commerce; the passing of barter economies; the emergence of the hitherto unknown phenomenon of leisure; the rise of collective bargaining and trade unions; the growth of mass media and thus of communal opinion; new attitudes to time, to wealth, to privilege; new criteria of status; new dimensions of citizenship; new vistas of opportunity; wide new problems of administration and public welfare.

All the time, alongside these demands upon the State, goes the subtle psychological and technical problem of the national development of scientific skills and projects. The new nations remember vividly that the scientific exploitation of their resources in their days of "backwardness" was a central factor in their subordination. Early oil and early railways in Iran, for example, are associated with imperialist pressures. Every country is anxious not to deepen technological dependence on the morrow of political statehood. Yet all too often lack of capital or technique requires them to admit some alien source of the technology they cannot forgo. The resulting dilemma is no small element in the tests of the contemporary Islamic State.

Thus, in what relates to a constant actual emergency as well as to deep essential theory, statehood in the Muslim world to-day is a central spiritual and practical issue. In all circumstances, primitive and contemporary, it is in no way surprising that the political is the form in which Islamic self-consciousness expresses itself. Detatchment from immediate pressures of external destiny is presently impossible. The lack of it precludes a more creative concentration on the intellectual and theological. Or perhaps we should rather say that the minds equipped for leadership are engrossed by what is absorbingly political, and are thus diverted from what vitally underlies it. These, at any rate, are the present concerns of that statehood which, as laid down in the Hijrah and perpetuated in the Hijri history, is the condition and shape of Islam.

CHRISTIAN THOUGHTS ON THE ISLAMIC SITUATION

Our study may conclude with some brief reflections on certain Christian obligations to, and in, all the foregoing, other than those immediate duties which attach to us as minorities within Muslim societies.[1]

There is, of course, a basic difference that obtains in the Christian assessment of the capacity of the State, as such, to inaugurate and accomplish a divine society. Christianity believes the state's competence to be limited and external, and its rôle partial. But this understanding leaves intact the practical aspects of state action and state obligation. It is important that we communicate the underlying reasons, in the

[1] See ch. 21.

biblical view of human nature, for the Christian critique of the State's rôle. And we must do so in lively recognition of actual problems.

Will it not be a right Christian instinct to see our first duty to the political order as lying in the region of our relationship to the persons who operate it? All that we have studied in the foregoing is a living, day-to-day, personal context, not some abstract analysis, for the numerous officials and servants of the public order. All that is political hinges in the end upon human quality and integrity, whether in the village postmaster or the cabinet minister. Both ʿAbd al-Nasir's study of his revolution, *Falsafat al-Thaurah*,[1] and Muhammad Naguib's *Egypt's Destiny*[2] emphasize this fact. Whether as civil servants themselves or, more likely, as witnessing custodians of the Gospel's recipe for personal newness of life, Christians are called to represent the meaning of Christ in the service of men.

This is the more true, since the State—and not only in Islam—can so easily become a sort of permanent excuse for our own delinquency. "Why doesn't the State do something about it?", we say. In these days of welfare government, not to speak of colossal technology such as only States can handle, the question makes a lot of sense. And, unless we have misunderstood the whole logic of Islamic history, it is a very Islamic question, too. The State is the entity that brings the good, and the goods. Yet, it is finally, whether for Muslims or Christians, an evasive and unworthy question, unless within its structures are the living cells of private fidelity and personal integrity.

In the end, is not *Islam* something which only *men* can do? This concept of an existence properly subordinated to the divine will—how, in spite of all that we have rightly discussed, can it be fulfilled other than in the wills of men? The political order is never on a prayer mat: it does not direct itself on a *Qiblah*. Nor is Medina, political capital, the focal point or *Qiblah*. Its own citizens have to look to Mecca. It is the religious city which holds the final direction of symbolic life. Behind the current Islamic wrestling, both traditional and realist, with the issue of the political order, is the final question of man, his nature as a subject of God, and his inward experience of the revolution of grace. And those are profoundly Christian concerns.

[1] Cairo, 1954, translated into English as *Egypt's Liberation*, Washington, 1955.
[2] London, 1955.

QUESTIONS FOR STUDY AND DISCUSSION

1. What would you say was comparable between the opposition of Mecca to Muhammad and that of Jerusalem to Jesus? Would there have been a Gospel if Jesus had handled Jerusalem in the Muhammadan way? How would Islam have been had the Prophet chosen the Jerusalem pattern?

2. How far is it true to say that the early Church in its Gentile Mission was engaged in an Islamic objective (i.e. the overcoming of idolatry). What were the distinctively Christian elements in the story?

3. "The Cross and the Crescent" is the usual, and barren, form of distinction between the two faiths. Study the truer and wiser point of contrast between "The Cross and the Hijrah".

4. From the point of view of Christian communication of the Gospel, what are the obstacles and what are the opportunities presented by the current assumption that statehood is the whole answer to human wrongness?

5. What are the duties of the Christian Churches within the new nationalisms?

6. Within the predominantly political form of Islamic expression in our time have you noted aspects which could, in the strict sense, be considered doctrinal and spiritual? In what form and in what strength?

7. Have you found any opportunities to discuss problems of a personal sort having to do with public welfare, either among administrative personnel or ordinary citizens?

8. Why is it right to say that Islamic vitality to-day is politically expressed and politically evident? Are Christian relationships, then, too "theological"?

18

Round the Muslim Calendar

Pereunt et imputantur. So runs a familiar Latin phrase, often found on sun-dials on cathedral walls. "The hours pass, and are laid to our charge." One of the ways of coping with this fleetingness is to lay meanings on time itself and enlist the moving calendar for particular significance. So we have lectionaries, festivals, red-letter days, and holy months. The idea is one that nature and time themselves afford. Life goes in seasons. Spring and autumn, summer and winter invite this association of distinctive meanings with appropriate occasions and require of us a rhythm in existence.

So in every religious tradition there is some place or other for the sacred calendar, the ordered sequence of recollection and celebration. Islam is no exception. The salient events of the Muslim year, the Pilgrimage and Ramadan, have already been explored with translations of the praying at these high days. There are, however, many byways and details of the Islamic use of the cycle of the year that deserve some further note.

One initial reflection is in order and applies to the whole issue of time and meaning, whatever the religious system. "To me", wrote William Morris, "*every* day begins and ends a year." His intense concern for every moment lest it be lost and vacant is true enough and can be said, without detracting from the thrill of Nuruz in Isfahan,[1] or of the New Year in the Scottish highlands. Such festivals of the new only focus the fact of incessant change. Any peculiar point and mark of time belongs with a continuity. So it is with the festivals of Christian liturgy. Christmas is not a truth only for 25 December, and after Easter it is always Easter. Each particular is the special present of the perpetual. It is always there; though we know that calendarwise it is to *come* again.

[1] See H. C. Paul, "The Nuruz in the Shahnama" in *The Islamic Review*, vol. 50, 1962, pp. 9–12.

We may draw here a parable from nature, which can be put in two quotations.

> Very old are the woods: and the buds that break
> Out of the brier's boughs when March winds wake
> So old with their beauty are—O no man knows
> Through what wild centuries roves back the rose.

And:

> This season's daffodil, she never hears
> What change, what chance, what chill,
> Cut down last year's.
> But with bold countenance and knowledge small,
> Esteems her seven days' continuance perpetual.

Each blossoming is, so to speak, as brief as a feast day. But it is the recurrence of something that endures. Piety finds something of the same relation between fleeting festival and abiding fact. They are as the time of the singing birds to the tireless music of nature. So the warm Christian would feel about Good Fridays in the calendar, and the cross once and for ever on Calvary.

We must keep this thought in view in going round the devout Muslim's year. And we must also have in mind that this cyclic use of time coincides with time's irreversible changes. The world that keeps returning Ramadans and greets the Prophet's birthdays is caught in a temporal flux that has no recurrence but carries away irrevocably what once has been. In no age has this been so total as to-day. Wilfred Thesiger, in his study of the vanishing nomadism of the Arabs, has caught this fact eloquently, on one symbolic front.

> I went to southern Arabia only just in time. Others will go there to study geology and archaeology . . . even the Arabs themselves, but they will move about in cars and will keep in touch with the outside world by wireless. They will bring back results more interesting than mine, but they will never know the spirit of the land nor the greatness of the Arabs. . . . Today the desert I travelled is scarred with the tracks of lorries and littered with discarded junk imported from Europe and America.[1]

And with that "litter" the demise of an old pattern gone for good. *The Last Migration* tells a similar story with its lament for a doomed

[1] Wilfred Thesiger, *Arabian Sands*, London, Longmans, Green & Co.; New York, E. P. Dutton & Co., 1959, p. 13. Quoted with permission.

order of things in the steppes of Persia.[1] Inexorably in cities as well as nomad camps, in beliefs as well as in barter, "times change". Whatever employs time as a cycle, be it liturgy or pilgrimage, must necessarily wrestle with time as a fast line onward.

THE MONTHS OF THE MUSLIM YEAR

1 Muharram—a sacred month, opening the year
2 Safar
3 Rabi[c]-al-Awwal—month of the Hijrah, i.e. 68 days after the A.H. era began: month of the Prophet's birth and death
4 Rabi[c]-al-Akhar
5 Jumadi-al-Awwal
6 Jumadi-al-Akhar
7 Rajab—a sacred month
8 Sha[c]ban
9 Ramadan: the month of Fasting
10 Shawwal (month most propitious for marriages)
11 Dhu-al-Qa[c]dah—a sacred month
12 Dhu-al-Hijjah: month of Pilgrimage

There are numerous problems of precise dating in early Islamic history, due to the question as to whether the Arab, pre-Islamic, and early post-Islamic calendars were lunar, or luni-solar.[2] For our present purposes, what matters is the popular celebrations and occasions, irrespective of the purely chronological issues they may raise. One has also to keep in mind that the first day of the Hijrah years was not in fact the Hijrah itself but the first day of the moon of Muharram preceding it.

The four sacred months were pre-Islamic and are noted (without names) in Surah 9.36. But elsewhere "*the* sacred month" is spoken of, in the singular (e.g. 2.194, 217; 5.2, 97). It is natural that the main concerns of Muslim memory as to dates relate to the Prophet himself and one can study the round of the year in its recollection of Muhammad's history. But first there is the opening month.

[1] Vincent Cronin, 1957.
[2] See H. Amir Ali in *The Muslim World*, 1954, vol. 44, no. 2, pp. 126–38.

MUHARRAM: THE SACRED BEGINNER

Mosque sermons at the beginning of Muharram usually deal with the fleetingness of time and the duty of its disciplined use.[1] For when *Dhu-al-Hijjah*, the month of the great Pilgrimage, has closed the old year, Muharram, "the sacred", opens the new. It is the month when according to tradition the original *Qiblah* of the Muslim community towards Jerusalem was laid down, and during it the interior of the Kaʿbah in Mecca's mosque is opened. Before the Islamic calendar became lunar and the months rotated round the seasons, Muharram fell in the autumn and thus resembled the Jewish new year month.

The Tenth of Muharram is of course its greatest day—for Sunnis the fast of *ʿAshura* and for Shiʿahs the remembrance of the tragedy of Karbalaʾ. The former belongs historically to the first two or so years after the Hijrah when the Muslim community was established in Medina. After the inauguration of Ramadan as the month of fasting, the day fast of the tenth of Muharram became an option of devotion. Its origins have generally been linked with Jewish influences. These are certainly apparent in its dating and its coincidence with atonement in the Jewish world. Al-Tabari's account of the inauguration of Ramadan links the *ʿAshura* with the deliverance of the Jews from Pharaoh and has Muhammad comment that, the Hijrah being an even greater deliverance, Muslims should likewise fast. There is also a tradition which associates the day with the release of the dove from Noah's ark.

It is difficult to assess, except by careful local observation, the precise meaning of the tenth of Muharram for the pious Sunni. The quranic precept (2.179) which underlies it is of the briefest and, giving no details, is at once followed by the displacing institution of Ramadan. Sunnis in Egypt have a local link with the Shiʿah Muharram in the Mosque of Hasanain where, during the Shiʿah Fatimid Caliphate, the head of Husain was brought. Lane (*Modern Egyptians*) describes the preparation of special sweetmeats for new year celebrations leading into the post-fast celebration that ends the first ten days of Muharram. But, short of personal acquaintance to the contrary, it would be fair to assume that it is the new year features which now dominate those days. In any event, the Sunni mind has little place for the earliest Jewish associations of *ʿAshura* unless it be in the sacrifices of the *ʿId al-Adha*, that ends Ramadan on the first of Shawwal.

[1] See the writer's *Sandals at the Mosque*, 1959, pp. 29–31 for an example.

Shiʿah keeping of the tenth of Muharram, however, is a very different story. There is perhaps no single event in Muslim existence where the essential distinctions between Sunni and Shiʿah are so manifest as in the memorial of Husain. The tenth of Muharram, more than any other time, releases the inner emotion of Shiʿah Islam, its cult of the suffering seed and its intense communal feeling.

The slaughter at Karbalaʾ on the tenth of Muharram, A.H. 61, when Husain was done to death with almost all his following, baptized the Shiʿah separatists with the sanction of vicarious sorrows and gave them a symbol of "passion" in which they found their identity. Thus, the yearly representation of the tragedy most graphically sacramentalizes their experience. Contemplation of Husain nourishes and expresses a religious sensitivity quite contrasted with the Sunni's world.

The *Taʿziyah*, or lamentation for Husain (and ʿAli and Hasan), is prefaced by the preliminaries from the first of Muharram. Garments of mourning are donned, black appears in the streets, and austerity takes over. Groups of men, their bodies dyed or stained with black and red, parade in the open, while mosque pulpits chant and bewail the innocence of Husain. A large procession brings the coffin of Husain, borne by eight bearers and accompanied by a long retinue of blood-smeared mourners and wailers beating in a doleful rhythm. A *tabut*, or replica, of Husain's tomb at Karbalaʾ is carried, with other emblems of the massacre.

The passion play itself follows on the stage to which the processions conduct the participants. The "tableau" varies in different localities, but sets the death of Husain in a long sequence of prophecy and symbol, going back to the patriarchs, while the women of the Quran (e.g. Eve and Mary) join in the griefs of Fatimah. Various other episodes are enacted, including the marriage and death of Husain's son, Al-Qasim, and the bringing of the martyr's head to Yazid at Damascus.

This ritual drama incorporates many features to which no justice can be done here. Its history may be idealized, and its emotions, by some criteria, wild and repellent, but it embodies in most telling manner the central dogma of Shiʿah Islam. All the resources of dramatic excitement are used to point the powerful moral of vicarious suffering. The Caliph Yazid, his general ʿUmar ibn Saʿd, and the actual murderer, Shimr, are depicted as the conscious, flagrant adversaries of the right. The last forswears all good and cries: "I care not about the day of judgement . . . and have no fear of God . . . I am he who has no share in Islam."

Worsted by these evil forces, Husain is seen as the apotheosis of innocent goodness, the rose untimely plucked from the garden of God, the victim of treachery, contempt, and cruel hatred. Muhammad, the Prophet-grandfather, looks on with dishevelled hair and finds comfort only in the assurance that with these stripes the people of Islam, within whose bosom this conflict of the ultimates occurs, will find pardon and peace. The family of ᶜAli, coming to its perfection of immolation in Husain, is "the phoenix of the universe" from whose slaughter comes the cosmic resurrection. Around the severed head of the martyr (itself a central speaker in the drama) the whole succession from Adam to Karbalaᵓ gathers to confess that here in this mystery of death are the keys of the kingdom. From this ritual-doctrine, this drama-mystery, of Shiᶜah Islam come the numerous pilgrimages that express their corporate memory, especially Mashad Husain at Karbalaᵓ, and Najaf.

What of a Christian relation? The intensity of the Shiᶜah preoccupation warns us of the immense obstacles. Here great Christian dimensions are, so to speak, precluded by being otherwise embodied. For here are the truths that there is power in the paradox of suffering, that a victim triumphs in defeat, that men kindle to the mystery of tragedy, and that evil overreaches itself and loses even where it wins.

Are not these, in measure, the truths of the cross? Yet how different the attendant circumstances. Calvary as the embodiment of human evil is a different world from Karbalaᵓ. It emerges from different antecedents. The encounter is not the idealized sequel to a forlorn bid for rebellion, the sad end of a dwindling expedition of dynastic aspiration. It is the climax of the rejection of a teacher, the studied response of enmity to a message of pure truth. It is the self-assertion of a whole people against the universal, compassionate interpretation (by Jesus) of their deepest insights. There is therefore a more elemental, a more representative, "sin of the world" on Good Friday, and a more ultimate encounter with its concentration of evil, than the history of Muharram's Tenth Day.

Yet it is doubtful if this sort of necessary comparison alone will penetrate the preoccupied territory of the Shiᶜah soul. It is actually Good Friday on which these paragraphs are written. Whenever they are read it will be Good Friday in our hearts. For no Christian can note 10 Muharram on the calendar and not be back on that morrow of "the night in which he was betrayed". Only in that "wisdom of God" which Christ crucified is, shall we of the community of the cross know how to confront both the sympathy and the antipathy that is in Shi^{c}ah Muharrams.

MAULID TIME

The Islamic calendar moves on to 12 Rabi^{c} al-Awwal, the traditional date of the Prophet's birth and death. The cult of the Prophet, the growth of which became strong in the twelfth century A.D., has always struggled with the disapproval and condemnation of the purists. It has found spontaneous popular favour and stern official veto. Sufis, for example, have rejoiced in its celebration and reproduced it in their own cult of saints, while Wahhabis, and other rigorists, have denounced all its ways.

The tension is, of course, implicit in the very form of the Islamic *Shahadah*, with its unbreakable link between God the sole worship and Muhammad *the* apostle. Always there is this "God and Muhammad" throughout the Quran—whether in claims to obedience, in warnings, in tests of loyalty, in activity. It was impossible for a human name to be so invariably and necessarily associated with God and not be regarded with superhuman veneration. The Quran, in a sense, here militates against its own dogma. It actually refers to the Prophet by his personal name, Muhammad, only four times (3.138; 33.40; 47.2 and 48.29). It is insistent that he is only human and no more than a messenger (cf. 3.138; 17.92, etc.). He disclaims any miracle save the Quran, and this is of his receiving not his making. Jesus is in fact given more titles and powers than the Prophet of Islam.

Yet, inevitably, devotion built around Muhammad an aura of more than human honour. Thus his birthday came to be celebrated with hymns of praise, recounting his virtues and extolling his person. The language of these panegyrics, often under Sufi influence, finds in the Prophet the emanation of heavenly light and the cosmic repository of all truth. These *Maulid* poems are an eloquent witness to the way in which religious devotion often runs away with theology.

It may be that they also owe something to the sense of need to offset the Christian status of Christ by moving in the direction of "incarnation". Some have also linked their tendencies to the strict Sunni isolation of God from the human with the resultant gulf calling for some divine-human mediatorship such as the *Maulid* Muhammad affords. He becomes therein the image of the invisible God, the copy of the Lord, and immune from sin and error. The fact that the day of the Prophet's death coincides, at least for calendar purposes, with his birth tends to make the single *Maulid* a festival of his total sojourn among men.

The actual patterns of the festival, which is very widespread in the dispersion of Islam, vary considerably. In modern days one may expect poems and editorials in newspapers and special occasions in mosques. Traditionally, processions with torches and chants, exchange of cards and presents, public reviews, and *dhikr* ceremonies mark the *Maulid*. Preparations may begin on the first of the month, giving a popular background to the crown of the celebrations on the twelfth day.

In the *Maulid* songs, the Christian student encounters deep problems of relation and ministry. For here, as in Muharram, is emotionally occupied territory. The Prophet is praised as the fairest rose in creation, the splendour of the sun in strength. In his hands is a fountain of waters: his body is radiant and his wonders continue to the end of time. His father, ᶜAbdallah, sought his bride, the Prophet's mother, with prayers and when he found her she shone in his eyes like a pearl. On the night of a Friday in Rajab when Muhammad was conceived, God ordered that Paradise should be opened and angelic voices announced the coming one.

Where shall this prepossession be penetrated by the meaning of Christ? Surely only as we can hold forth the proven character of Jesus in his active ministry, and as we can steadily press the ordered faith in the incarnation to the need of which, in their indirect way, these sentiments bear unintended witness while diverting elsewhere their expectations. We need also to think out patiently a Christian account of the Prophet of Islam that reckons fully and deeply with his entire rôle in Muslim history and in popular religion.

There are numerous lesser *Maulids* (though historically they may well have antedated the *Maulid* of Muhammad). These belong to the numerous Sufi Orders whose saints (or *awliya*) continue to be commemorated by tomb visitations and lyrics of devotion. Passages like Surah 56.11 and 10.62 suggested to Sufi piety that God had his chosen ones, eminent in grace and nearness to himself, whose influence and vicarious benediction might avail for lesser folk. Hence the cult of saints and the celebration of their virtues on their birthdays. Local shrines and sanctuaries have a marked, if often limited, impact upon the hopes and fears of simple people. They can only be effectively studied in the places of their honour.

THE TWO GREAT ᶜIDS

The greatest days of the Islamic year are those of the *ᶜId-al-Fitr*, with which Ramadan ends, and the *ᶜId al-Kabir* (*al-Adha*), coinciding with the end of Pilgrimage. The former is really the feast of the First of Shawwal (a month often considered most propitious for Muslim weddings). The latter is the Tenth of Dhu al-Hijjah. Both are extended occasions which provide Islam with its deepest sense of community and solidarity, kept as they are throughout the whole household of Muslims. Mosque prayers and sermons then have a focus of devotion that is climactic. Presents are exchanged; there are greetings, new clothes, new resolves, and upsurging goodwill.

The significance of Fasting and Pilgrimage as pillars of Islam has been studied in chapters 3 and 6. It remains here only to take stock of the popular aspects of their closing festivals. This is best done—like so much else—on the local level by imaginative and attentive observation. The feast with which Ramadan closes is a festival of accomplishment. It provides an occasion of hearty corporate release. It marks that return to the enjoyment of things which Islam has always inculcated and which its fast was designed, not to question, but only to discipline. There is relief not merely that Ramadan is once again achieved but that abstention has afresh corroborated the goodness of the world under God.

Changes in the incidence of Ramadan, such as those demanded by the President of Tunis and, in measure, compelled by new economic and social conditions, will doubtless impair this physical release of the *ᶜId-al-Fitr*. When the fast has been spiritualized its terminus will be the less dramatic. But as long as Ramadan keeps its literal shape, there will be no more unifying and confirmatory experience among Muslims than this *ᶜId* of its completion.

It is the synchronizing of the *ᶜId-al-Adha* with the animal sacrifice at Mina during the pilgrimage which serves to focus the whole participating dispersion of Islam with the pilgrims themselves. Contemporary scientific devices, like radio and television, for mediating a single experience of universal "moments" will sooner or later be applied to this also. The *ᶜId-al-Adha* in any event makes the daily *Qiblah* a sort of annual "awareness". It provides a rite in which the geography of Islam finds a single symbol of community.

There is no simple answer to the question as to what Muslims mean by this animal sacrifice. It is obligatory (*wajib*) and the *takbirs* and prayers made at the slaughter indicate that it is "offered" or at least "done" as their "worship". Surah 6.162 is sometimes quoted at this point. The animal, too, must be free of blemish and should be slain in a proper ritual manner. Poverty is no reason for omitting the action, since debts incurred to provide a sacrificial victim God will make good. While it is virtuous to offer one animal per person, families may act as one unit, or numbers (five? or seven?) combine for one camel, sheep, cow, or goat. It is proper to prepare the first meal after the sacrifice from that animal's flesh and to distribute the rest. "O God accept this for me" is the plea. But how one should understand its intention is difficult to make precise. The surest devotional clue to both great ᶜ*Ids* lies in the prayers earlier done into English.

A meticulous knowledge of the calendar would furnish many other points for discussion. There is the night of the twenty-seventh of Rajab, now linked with the Night Journey and Ascension of the Prophet (see Surah 17.1)—the events which give Jerusalem such sanctity in Muslim eyes. Or the night of the middle of Shaᶜban when, as some believe, the fate of every living man is determined for the ensuing year, by the shaking of the Sidr tree of Paradise whose leaves each bear the name of a soul. If they fall off at the shaking, the soul dies that year following, and sooner or later according to how more or less withered was the leaf that fell. Mosque prayers on that night echo the familiar Muslim petition for leave to die a Muslim and for the cancelling of evil deeds and for security in the things God only knows.

So we leave the recurrences of the Muslim's year. Our practical concern with fast and festival and celebration is with our fellow men and these channels of sequence that make the passage of their lives.

> For time is like a fashionable host
> That slightly shakes his parting guest by hand
> And with his arms outstretched as he would fly
> Grasps in the comer: welcome ever smiles,
> And farewell goes out sighing.

The greetings and speedings of time as Islam informs them are properly our study who are neighbours in place and present.

QUESTIONS FOR STUDY AND DISCUSSION

1. What is your local experience of the observance of the Muslim calendar? Are there special features significant in your area—local saints? particular occasions?

2. Because the months are lunar in Islam, the anniversaries are free of the seasons and rotate. What effect does this have on their content and meaning?

3. Do you note any changes which to-day's different times are causing in the recurrent times of Muslim feasts and ritual?

4. How would you relate the Christian fact of Good Friday with the tragedy at Karbalaʾ? What has the Gospel to say to keepers of 10 Muharram?

5. From any study that is possible to you of the language and feeling of the *Taʿziyah*, how would you analyse and interpret its significance for Shiʿah people?

6. What are the sources, popular or deep, of the ideas about Muhammad to which *Maulid* songs and ceremonies give expression? How do you explain their prevalence in the light of orthodox dogma about his status as "only a messenger"?

7. How would you attempt, and state, a Christian attitude to the person of Muhammad, in respect either of *Maulid* devotion or strict Islamic history?

8. In the cult of saints in many places there is much that is comparable in Muslim and Christian practice, though the saints themselves are different. How would you explain this fact and what duties does it set for our ministry?

9. What do the *ʿId-al-Fitr* and the *ʿId-al-Adha* mean for Muslims of your town or village?

10. It is in festivals that faiths are popularly felt and their solidarities experienced. What then should be our Christian attitude to Muslim occasions, belonging as we do with Christ, but living side by side?

19

Death and the Muslim

It comes equally to us all, and it makes us all equal when it comes. The ashes of the oak in the chimney are no epitaph of that oak to tell us how large it was. . . . The dust of great persons' graves is speechless too . . . and when a whirlwind hath blown the dust of the churchyard into the church, and the man sweeps the dust of the church out into the churchyard, who will undertake to sift those dusts again?

So John Donne writing in the seventeenth century on death the leveller—the surest common denominator of our existence. Mortality prevails on every continent and the grave oppresses the soul of every creed with its perplexities and hidden face. Men in every culture grow old and in the end "the milestones into headstones change", or there comes that little abode of which Emily Dickinson wrote:

> . . . a house that seemed
> A swelling in the ground,
> The roof was scarcely visible
> The cornice but a mound.

Yet all one as we are in the presence of this universal leveller and last enemy, men and faiths differ in their behaviour and posture when it comes. The Greeks, for example, sought in the main to ignore it, while their artists concentrated on the beauty of youth and glory of the living body, or they saw death as the casting off of the prison of matter by the soul. For the Christian faith, physical death in the context of the love of God becomes a kind of sacrament of the truth that life must be lost before it is fully won. And thus the cross of Jesus, his death in the body, becomes the central symbol and pledge of eternity.

The purpose of this outline is to study the Muslim in the incidence of the great leveller and to see what the Quran and tradition have to teach about the drama of the grave and the Muslim's state within it and beyond. Then it will be right to look at some of the thoughts and reactions of the living in Islam at the time of burial and mourning. Only the barest of outlines can be attempted. The whole subject, both quranic and popular, bristles with difficulties, and the range both of literature and custom is immense and manifold. We can venture no more than the merest sketch of death and the Muslim soul.

THE GRAVE AND THE SOJOURN OF THE DEPARTED

General summaries of the passages in the Quran dealing with heaven and hell and judgement can readily be found in several manuals. "Serve thy Lord until the certain comes to thee" runs the last verse of Surah 15. "The certain" is *Al-Yaqin*, a most eloquent synonym for death. Surah 74.47 uses the same word: "We were wont to deny the day of judgement until the certain came upon us." So "every soul must taste death" (Surah 3.185). If it be asked: "What of those who are alive when the last trump sounds?" it is said, on the ground of Surah 34.40, that all at that moment expire, except those whom God pleases to exempt, these, according to Al-Baidawi, being the greater angels.

The incidence of death is within the all-seeing competence of God. Surah 6.57–61 declares this divine omniscience which nothing escapes: "Not a leaf falleth but he knoweth it." Man's down-sitting in sleep and his rising to a new dawn and a new vigour are known before him. Then, when the appointed span of days in their sequence ends, there is the gathering unto God, who still scans and penetrates the secret of the day of life as of every day in life. (This analogy between death and nightfall may be compared to several biblical images in the same sense.) God's agents in this taking of the soul at the day's end (of life) are the angels who "neglect not". The precise hour of each man's death is ordained (Surah 16.61) so that it is, traditionally, improper to pray for death or to fear it.

God is he who brings to life at birth and he who brings to death: *Al-Muhyi* and *Al-Mumit*. Both events have something of a corresponding finality. Just as birth ushers man into this world, so death ushers him into the next, in the single particularity of his own being. Both are the crossing of a Rubicon—a decisive passage, the one into, the other out of, this mortal scene. It is here that the significant term *Barzakh* calls for study, since it has played so large a part in Muslim thought and word about what is beyond death.

The most relevant of its three occurrences in the Quran is in Surah

23.100. Here the unrighteous ask to be allowed to return to earth to do the good which in life they neglected. The wish is idle and futile, for "behind them there is a barrier (*Barzakh*) until the day when they will be raised up". The commentators have offered many detailed explanations of this term. It is found in Surahs 25.53 and 55.20 in the obviously physical sense of a material divide between two seas, i.e. a bar or isthmus (cf. 27.61 with a different word for this same idea). What then is the *Barzakh* between this life and the next intended by 23.100?

Some explain it in moral terms, as a divine prohibition of return to life, as a symbol of the irrevocability of death. Sufism, which has made much of it, takes it figuratively as expressing the earthly and the spiritual. But the general exegesis sees it as a literal "bar" closing the world of the grave from earth and the eternal future from the temporal past. It is where man lies, after death, beyond recall to this life and in the ante-chamber, so to speak, of eternal judgement. Before we proceed to the latter, it is right to take further the Muslim view of the grave and death as "the crossing of a bar".

That realm is necessarily shadowy and we cannot expect consistency in all that speaks, or hints, of it. One fact is clear, namely that it is within the divine domain. We never pass beyond the reach of divine power and authority. "Unto him is your returning" is the most characteristic quranic phrase about the after-death history of the soul (cf. 5.105), or the passive version: "Unto him shall ye be brought back" (cf. 10.56; 28.88; 32.11, etc.). So that beyond death is God and God's judgement and God's lordship.

To the departed that crossing over the *Barzakh*, or great divide beyond mortality, ushers in what seems a very brief interlude. So strong is the quranic emphasis on the Day, the Hour (i.e. of judgement), that it seems within the experience of dying to be almost instantaneous as a sequel. The closing verses of Surah 23 are apposite here. Life's end looks back over the briefest of spans and confronts the soul with the utter seriousness of terrestrial existence. "Did you think we created you in vain?" This sense of being confronted with the divine reckoning is only, in a sense, the extension into eschatology of the doctrine of unity (cf. 28.70). That there is none other than God is a truth of theology, but also of death's morrow.

But it must be, and is, supposed that this immediacy of judgement in fact leaves room for a long period of unconsciousness into which the soul sinks at death. Surah 18.9–25, with its account of the seven sleepers of Ephesus, belongs with this same realm of thought. The soul in the grave is awaiting the judgement in a state of dreamless sleep, until at the resurrection it is reunited with the body and the day of judgement opens.

There is one exception to this otherwise universal state, namely, the martyrs who fall in *Jihad*. According to 3.169–71, they are at once in Paradise, being somehow in their soul-body unity before the general resurrection. There is an inconsistency here into which it is perhaps right not to penetrate. Muhammad evidently preached the bliss of those who "fell in the way of God" without careful reconciliation with the doctrine of a disembodied sleep of men's souls between death and judgement. Believers, other than martyrs, who do undergo this sleep and interlude, somehow know on the resurrection awakening where and how they are. It is the unbelievers who, deceived by the sleep, think that they died only yesternight and are being haled from a scarcely entered grave to the awesome grand assize (10.45; 46.35, etc.).

The Quran and tradition explain the advent of the angels of death who seize the soul at the death-rattle and thrust it, the intervening sleep unsensed, into the presence of the Judge. Unless we take the passages in this way, they might seem to be by-passing resurrection and even the grave, in the very urgency of their hastening into requital. In fact, "the moment of death and judgement have become fused into a single event".[1]

Ragnar Eklund's careful study, *Life between Death and Resurrection according to Islam*,[2] examines very fully the Muslim beliefs and concepts about the intermediate state. Alone among the canonical traditionalists, Al-Tirmidhi writes of the famous Munkar and Nakir, angels of interrogation, who catechize the deceased as to his religion, his opinion of Muhammad, and his belief as to whether he can see God. Punishment, either by rods, or whips, or the pressure of earth on the grave, is associated with this questioning, though views diverge on whether both Muslims and unbelievers undergo it. The dead are shown foretastes of heaven and hell as what they have earned or missed. There are many variants and elaborations of these traditions.

[1] Tor Andrae, *Muhammad, the Man and His Faith*, New York, revised edn, 1955, translated by Theophil Menzel, p. 59.

[2] Upsala, 1941.

It is difficult to reconcile what they mean for popular mentality with the quranic doctrine of the intermediate sleep. It is noticeable that the word *Barzakh* (and the divide associated with it) seems not to occur at all in the traditions. These ideas stand apart from the notion of the intermediate state. Perhaps we may say they are the form in which popular imagery fills the void of pure abeyance which the imagination can feebly hold. Resulting questions as to what it is that really goes on, and, if it is the soul, how it suffers, from whips and unquiet soil, etc., are too difficult of access to avail us here. About punishment in the grave, where the grave is in relation to Paradise, and kindred questions, the Quran, too, is silent, though its silence may well be not that of disapproval, but simply of concentration on the prophetic theme of judgement.

THE GRAVE AND HUMAN DESTINY

Beyond the dying and burying, long and conscious, brief and void, as it may be, comes the judgement, that final reality of the Quran, second only to the reality of God himself. The language is stark and simple. The soul issues through the throat (Surah 56.83 and 75.26) and is haled by the angels beyond the point of no return (6.93). The dead are gathered into the realized eschatology of the Quran's vivid Domesday. The Day opens; the heavens are rolled back; the trump sounds; the throne of God appears to view, flanked by the heavenly hosts and before it the hosts of men called from their graves or from the mortal side of *Barzakh*. The books of deeds are opened. Men's very limbs and members testify against them. (Cf. Surahs 34, 73, 78, and 82.) The balances will decide (21.47; 101.6–8). Passages in 2.48; 26.99, and 82.19 state categorically that there will be no intercession or mediation: 2.255 qualifies this negation with the phrase "save by his leave". Commentators differ over whether this permission to mediate is ever given, or whether the impossibility is absolute. But popular belief is sure that the apostle of God has a singular authority in this respect. Certainly the deeds of the devout Muslim weigh heavily in the scales that acquit, while there can be no hope for those who have stubbornly refused the *Shahadah* and rejected the messengers of God. Any intercessorship the Prophet might have would naturally turn upon these criteria.

The Islamic concept of the judgement, then, belongs closely with the entire quranic scheme of a divine legislation, given through successive prophets, finalized in the Quran, and incumbent on man in its ceremonial and moral demands as the stuff of his obedience to the divine sovereignty which speaks through it. Since man is capable, given the right polity and upbringing, of a perfectible conformity to this divine blue-print for life, his falling short, as tested by the scales, must necessarily be perverse and damnable. Quranic eschatology is thus in full accord with Islamic doctrines of man and law and society.

Beyond the grand assize which determines the issue of eternity lie the contrasted abodes of heaven and hell. Highly embellished by a fertile tradition, the quranic description of these two states may be quickly summarized. The hell of the Quran has a variety of titles, or, where these are not equal, then aspects. The most frequent is *Al-Nar*, the Fire. *Al-Jahim* is used some twenty-five times and *Al-Jihannam* seventy-six times. *Al-Hawiyah*, "the Pit", also occurs, and there are four other names: *Al-Huzamah*, "the Burning One" (104.4); *Laza* ,"the Fire" (70.15); *Sair*, "the Fire" (4.55); and *Saqar*, "the burning" (74.26).

According to Surah 74.30–1, hell has seven gates, guarded by nineteen angels. Its fires are clearly visible from the place of judgement, blazing in intolerable flames, in which a death in life of perpetual torture is passed unendingly. Aside from the physical images of boiling waters, the bitter Zaqqum tree (56.52) whose fruit is a harsh thorn, and the loaded chains, the chief agony of hell would seem to be the sheer inability to escape. The undying frustration of this desolation is repeatedly rehearsed in numerous passages (cf. 40.49; 43.74–7; 78.21–30).

Much discussion ranged throughout Muslim tradition and eschatology as to the relation of the true Muslim to hell. The heart of the matter would seem to be the enigmatic verse in 19.71: "There is not one of you but shall approach it", which appears to include all humanity without exception. "Approach", however, is different from "enter". The next verse goes on to add that God knows who should burn therein. Perhaps the meaning is that true Muslims come only to the "bridge" along which tradition makes the judgement issue. It must also be remembered that, for many, "Muslim" is a denominator which only God can authenticate. We may say all Muslims will be saved, if we understand that our being Muslim is entirely God's decree. (Cf. the careful and frequent reservation in Muslim speech: "I am a Muslim, if God wills" noted in chapter 15.)

The heaven of the Quran is similarly depicted in sharp, sensuous terms. *Al-Jannah*, the Garden, is the most frequent term (like *Al-Nar*, it occupies four and a half columns of the concordance), and is often pluralized: *Al-Jannat*. *Firdaus*, Paradise, occurs only in 18.107 and 23.11. Many of the "hell" passages also describe the abode of bliss. Silken carpets, sweet wines, couches of delightsome ease, pleasant converse, refreshing fountains, beauty, and calm, combine in pictures of idyllic peace and content.

There has been much debate, within and without Islam, on the theme of the *Hurun ᶜAinun* pure-eyed maidens (sing., *Haura*), spoken of in 44.54; 55.22, 72; and 56.22. Though marriage with these is stated in 44.54 and 52.20, there seems no absolute need to interpret their meaning in only sensuous terms, as if heaven were a place of mainly male delectation. Tradition may have its imaginative anticipation of the physical attraction of heaven but theology, in its modern mood, tends to find in the pattern of quranic description a necessary form, in a society inured to hardships and given to concrete images, of spiritual teaching couched in vivid metaphor. Writers as old as Al-Farabi and Ibn Sina took these areas of the Quran as deliberately "slanted" to a mentality unequipped for philosophic abstraction and needing to be taught in literalist fashion.

Such spiritualizing both of heaven and hell may serve to obviate the potential crudity of exegesis. But it cannot of itself make good the silences. The beatific vision as the ultimate ground and meaning of heaven is not present. Nor is the thought of growth in service, nor yet of purgation in remorse. Rather, the picture is of a secure and static bliss and a pointless, hapless anguish. The stark literalism of this eschatology was of course the central quality of Muhammad's preaching. As with quranic teaching on man, idols, sovereignty, and law, it simplified all issues into the sharpest and most absolute form, leaving to subsequent theology tasks of penetration into mystery which its own sheer dogmatisms left it little leisure or temper to accomplish.

Here then is human destiny, the twin issue of the last assize, the making eternally definitive of the submission or the unbelief of men as these have issued from their own deeds and the ineluctable decree of God. "Once to die, and after this the judgement" (Heb. 9.27). But, absent from the experience of either, the dimension of Christ's own death wondrously transforming both.

THE GRAVE AND THE THOUGHTS OF THE LIVING

The patter of the feet of the departing mourners after a burial are heard, say the traditions, by the deceased in his grave. The retreating sound in his ears is soon lost in the dread interrogations of Munkar and Nakir. Whether they are heard again or not, the footsteps return frequently to the cemeteries. Visits to tombs and burying places are a noted feature of Islamic life in many parts, particularly among women.[1] Funeral practices and the forms of mourning are too wide a theme for more than the barest notes here, the aim of which is to serve a truly Christian relation to fellow men in Islam, in the presence of "the last enemy".

Its incidence is accompanied by a fairly consistent pattern of behaviour. The dying are turned to face the *Qiblah* of Mecca while the gathered relatives repeat the *Shahadah* and call upon the departing to greet those who have gone before. A difficult death is by some regarded as indicating ill-conduct in life. Angels disquiet the passing soul that has caused other men trouble on earth. Where the spirit is yielded in stillness, the angels are merciful. Death is accompanied by wailings and pious ejaculations, despite the traditions which forbid lamentation.

After death, the deceased is washed, the jaw is bound and the legs tied. Care must be taken with the disposal of the water used in bathing since it is tabu. This is the work of the professional washer and after ablution no one touches the corpse, the farewell kisses and greetings preceding it. After shrouding there may be ceremonies in which offerings are made and presented, in part, to the shaikh, then to others, to make good, or add to, the prayers of the deceased.

The soul is still thought to be in the body, within hearing, until burial, so that the ceremonies up to interment are understood by him. The corpse is sprinkled with perfume and carried on a bier with simple muslin, cotton, or silk grave-clothes. Funeral processions provide as it were a bosom of fellow humanity on which the dead are borne from house to cemetery. It is an act of merit to join the cortège and to give a hand as bearer. The deceased is thus borne of many and all to the accompaniment of recited *Ayahs* and chanting. The body is laid in the tomb on its right side with face Mecca-wards. The shrouds

[1] Cf. L. Massignon, *Cité des Morts* and E. W. Lane, *Manners and Customs of the Modern Egyptians*, ch. 28.

are loosened and a little earth sprinkled. The Surah of Unity may be recited, or: "Thereof we created you and thereunto we cause you to return and from thence we bring you forth anew" (Surah 20.55).

The grave and its occupant are not left in solitude until a *Fatihah* has been said for him and the other denizens of the cemetery, or before a shaikh has instructed him in the answers to the impending catechism of the angels. He is to say that God is his God, Muhammad his apostle, Islam his religion, the Quran his Book, and the Kaᶜbah his *Qiblah*. These responses will sustain the deceased in the night of desolation, his first in the grave.

A period of some forty days after the funeral sees weekly, or nightly, visits to the place of burial in which the larger part is played by women, for some of whom in traditional Islamic society, cemetery visitation was the major errand of their lives outside the house. The characteristic Muslim grave has upright stones at both head and feet, the former often carved with a surmounting turban. There is perhaps no more eloquent single exponent of the "feel" of Muslim grief than Mustafa Lutfi al-Manfaluti, whose essays, though now somewhat eclipsed, have for half a century echoed the Egyptian soul, in its experience of bereavement and sorrow.

There are many proverbial sayings on death.

> "It is written on his brow that he will die of this sickness."
>
> "God requires what he has given."
>
> "There is no more oil in the lamp."
>
> "What was remote has come close to hand."
>
> "Death must have its due and to flee it is shame."
>
> "A soul is never content except by a handful of earth."
>
> "Death is a chalice put to the lips of all."
>
> "God save us from the women mourners."

Maybe the deep pathos of our theme, the discovery of our common humanity across faith-frontiers, and the realism of the Muslim's thought beside the grave, are all caught in that gesture of casting the dust on the open face, with the words: "All thou hast from the world is this handful of dust."

QUESTIONS FOR STUDY AND DISCUSSION

1. How would your experience amplify, amend, or confirm the brief note in the last section on burial, or funeral, customs among Muslims?

2. What is uppermost in the thoughts and emotions of the average mourner? How would you minister to him in the love and Gospel of Christ?

3. How does the ordinary Muslim of your acquaintance view death? What are the chief differences as between Islam and Christianity in the prospect of death?

4. What meaning does cemetery visitation have in popular life, especially among women?

5. How is the Quran's teaching on heaven and hell to be understood? Is the literalism a device to aid simple minds? Are the details allegorical?

6. How does the fact of the cross and of divine grace in Christ crucified affect the whole Christian understanding of judgement and eternity? How would you explain to Muslim certainty that it was blasphemous, the Gospel confidence: "He that heareth . . . and believeth . . . is passed from death unto life" (John 5.24)?

7. What does Islam, orthodox or traditional, teach about the grave as the intermediate abode? What is *Barzakh*? Why is it an impassable barrier closing the way back to mortality?

8. The awe and dread of the last judgement were a tremendous element in original Islam. How is it seen by typical Muslims to-day?

9. A winding sheet and no coffin, a sea of bearing hands and no hearse—these characterize a Muslim's journey to the grave. It is simple, realist, communal. What inner witness do we intend, or do we attain, in our Christian practices at death?

10. On what answers do *we* depend in "the night of desolation"?

STREETS OF JERUSALEM

20

Believing and Belonging

How is it possible to be both a Muslim and an unbeliever? The two would seem to exclude each other. In the popular view, belonging is taken for believing: to be of the community is to be of the faith.

However, a significant quranic passage at an interesting juncture in the Prophet's story makes exactly this distinction between being Muslim and being a believer. It occurs in the Surah (49) that has the title "The Private Apartments", the quarters of Muhammad's *ménage* in Medina, which, as Surah 33.53 enjoins, were not accessible to the general public. Their privacy had been invaded by deputations of apparently ill-mannered people anxious to embrace Islam, who, if we can regard the whole short Surah as relating to one time, came even behind the "chambers" protesting their faith and allegiance.

The Prophet, according to the Surah, was directed to check them. But the important point is that he was not merely to reprove their lack of courtesy. More serious was their instinctive idea that in submitting to a new ruler they were also truly partaking in a new faith. The verse (14) runs: "The Arabs of the desert say: 'We have believed.' You (Muhammad) must tell them: 'Ye have not believed, ye must say rather: "We have submitted." Faith has not entered your hearts.'" The verb "We have submitted", *aslamna*, means also: "We have become Muslims" or "We have embraced Islam." There is a complete identity between the two meanings. Becoming Muslim was this political submission to the ruler of Medina. That is why the Bedouin tribes here referred to came to Medina to make it. Surrender and Islamization were identical.

Yet the Prophet is directed to distinguish between this civil, politic step and any genuine belief. It is not that their allegiance is being rejected. They must, however, realize that faith is another thing. Al-Baidawi says that the Bedouin in question were the Banu Asad who came to Muhammad for purely prudential reasons. But the passage speaks of tribes in general and the whole vivid setting of the Surah suggests a varied convergence of peoples intending acknowledgement of the sovereignty of Muhammad. For this reason it seems likely that the passage is very late, perhaps the ninth or tenth year of the Hijrah.

It may be argued that not too much should be made of this warning about an Islamizing that is not belief. These perhaps were impetuous and ignorant, as well as uncouth, folk. Caution was obviously required: there was need to guard against the superficial. Perhaps even treachery could not be left out of the reckoning. The passage goes on to urge a sustained obedience that does not doubt and gives of its substance in the cause. There is also in the final verse of the Surah the reminder that becoming Muslim is not a sort of favour bestowed on the Prophet, which evidently some were inclined to suppose. Clearly, Muhammad had to preserve himself from merely time-serving or hypocritical accessions from the desert tribes who had not been earlier involved in the actual history of the new creed in its twin cities.

Yet, when due allowance is made for all these immediate factors, which exegesis must recognize, there remains a much larger implication. Here is the Quran insisting that being Muslim may be different from having faith. A principle which can occur dangerously in origins can be reproduced with like peril in long-standing Islam. Tribes of the desert are not the only people capable of insincerity. Nor is the moment of accession the only time when belonging may be erroneously taken for believing. Indeed, the menace of merely external adherence may be all the greater when faith is traditionally supposed. The implication of Surah 49.14 is therefore very great. The Quran is on record here as requiring us to challenge any assumption that belonging is believing—precisely the assumption which the world of Islam to-day habitually makes.

We are suffering on all sides from unexamined but entrenched ideas of community and faith which inhibit real spiritual activity, obscure the whole concept of conversion, and stagnate theological relations. Religious community is inseparable from the situation throughout the contemporary Muslim world and yet constitutes the largest single deterrent to valid faith. The issues are vital to everything for which this book cares and works.

COMMUNITY AND THE ISOLATION OF TRUTH

Does that seem too harsh a heading? Yet it is a sober fact. Whole areas of doctrine and meaning are effectively immunized from men by the sheer fact of religious frontiers. To the average Muslim, for communal reasons which have no proper right to place it, there is a wide ban on the Gospel. Deep and significant implications of the Quran are unknown to the average Christian merely because he is Christian and they are quranic.

It is not only the damage this does which should appal us, but the fact that most people in both communities are quite content to have it so. Indeed, they take a complacent pride that it is entirely right and creditable. The Quran is thus a closed book to Christians because the Muslim community "possesses" it. Christian faith is a closed realm to the Muslim because it is the faith of Christians. "Nosism" rules everywhere—a *nahniyyah*, a "we-ness".[1] Not being "of us" means for all practical purposes exclusion from what is "ours".

There are long historical factors from which this situation has been inherited. First the long Islamic pattern of minority toleration.[2] *Dhimmis*, or tolerated non-Muslims, had virtually to retire into cultural and mental isolation as the price and condition of their communal survival. They could persist so long as they agreed as it were to do so surreptitiously. But this concept of "liberty" completed the isolation of Islam also. Nor is that central fact in any way altered by the obvious truth that Christians and other *dhimmis* played big parts in the administration, finances, and armies of Islamic Caliphates and Empires. The theological *apartheid*, or *separateness* (with certain shining exceptions), was complete. This legacy we have inherited.

Contemporary factors have sharpened it, precisely because of that current preoccupation of Islam with things politically inseparable from new independence and nationalism. Though nationhood for multi-religious populations might be thought to conduce to spiritual "meeting", it has for the most part tended to a near identification of Arabism with Islam, and a nervous, communal, defensiveness in the minorities.[3] The instinct of the latter has been to draw further into their communal shell, either prudentially, or because there is hardly any other option.

Thus the isolation of truth by community is almost total. There may

[1] The term is Arnold Toynbee's: see *A Historian's Approach to Religion*, 1956, pp. 265–267, *et al.*

[2] See next chapter.

[3] The note, "We are *all* Egyptians now", sounded for example in the early days of the new régime in 1952, has been less evident in more recent years.

be large realms in common. But they are not known and are not explored in common. There are no mutual theologies wrestling with them. What is quranic, irrespective of its content, is for that reason largely unknown territory to the generality of people in the Church. Likewise, the faith of Christ and the meaning of the cross are outside the pale for the usual Muslim, for the reason that they are what Christians believe. Community, which, as we shall see, is a proper consequence of belief, has somehow become also its imprisonment.

It becomes urgent to find some way to break out of this crippling confinement by community, however tolerable it may seem to the complacent. Otherwise we shall be faced with another and quite different sense to Plato's old saying: *Soma sema*—"the body (communal) a tomb". Both religious groupings suffer by the isolation of truth. Take, for example, William Cowper's great poem:

> . . . one Spirit—His
> Who wore the platted thorns with bleeding brows—
> Rules universal nature. Not a flower
> But shows some touch, in freckle, streak, or stain,
> Of His unrivalled pencil . . .
> Happy he who walks with Him, whom what he finds . . .
> In nature, from the broad majestic oak
> To the green blade that twinkles in the sun,
> Prompts with remembrance of a present God.

The last line, all unknown to Cowper, is one with the recurrent insistence of the Quran that nature summons us to the "mention" of its great Sustainer. The Quran reciter from the East would not likely talk of oaks and the green grass. But, for any soul alive to the quranic recognition of God and nature, the spiritual kinship is unmistakable.

This, of course, is not the last or the greatest realm of Muslim-Christian kinship. But how many within either community thrill and answer to it? How shall we transcend our insulations over harder themes unless we forswear them here? No Muslim, it is true, would see in nature's Lord him "Who wore the . . . thorns on bleeding brows". But need we make that truth still more remote by cherishing it behind walls of communal separation? Is not our duty to mediate and communicate made all the more imperative by the fact that the average Muslim dismisses the sort of plea we are making, on the ground that Islam already knows Jesus fully and truly? Yet how does it

—as long as it refuses to reckon with what he meant by ordaining a sacrament of remembrance in the meaning of his death?

Thus, it is not only the truths we share in common which community-consciousness precludes our serving, but also those truths which are only ours who are in Christ. Either way, whether it be what we need to learn with and from Islam, or what we offer to Islam in Christ and his cross, we remain silenced and silent as long as we stay within ourselves. Nor do ventures of expression need to wait until we have solved all the problems involved, such as a Christian theory about quranic status, or the like. Ventures beyond community will never begin if we have to wait for these more final decisions.

COMMUNITY AND THE EXTERNALIZATION OF FAITH

Isolation of truth, tragic as it is, is not the only consequence of the tradition of religious communalism. Another important result, evident in varying ways, among both Muslims and Christians, is that the fact of belonging leads to the unexamined assumption of believing. Here we are back at the sense of Surah 49.14. People are, or their ancestors became, Muslims: they are in, of, and under Islam, and therefore they believe. Faith is thus liable to be externalized and formal, a thing to take for granted, rather than a thing to question, to scrutinize, and to weigh.

Something of the same situation obtains in the Christian segment of the population. As long as believing has this corporate continuity of family and heredity, it will be in danger of being thought of as automatic. Or it will have a quite inadequate ground in personal character. Men will be "Christians" for the reason that their fathers were. The category of "Christian" in some quarters even comes to be taken synonymously with something racial. Being Christian is being Armenian, Greek, or Coptic.

It is not suggested here that multitudes do not combine genuine believing participation with such "accidents" of birth and blood. Nor is it meant to disqualify factors of corporate continuity in the things of faith. But the fact remains that these criteria tend to diminish and even to exclude the truth that faith demands a personal rediscovery in every generation. Nobody is validly either Christian or Muslim merely since his father was or because he was born into that community.

This issue, as might be expected, comes to a head, for Islam, in the domain of education. As noted in Chapter 13, *Dar al-Islam*, the household of Islam, is a concept which has no serious threshold for the adolescent. It is assumed that he is in it. It does not confront him with any decision, except the implied negative one that he does not contract out of it. He may, of course, be characterized by a wide variety, or lack, of devotional and intellectual conviction. But, though this may dismay the shaikhs, it does not de-Islamize him. Failing such a drastic and rare denunciatory step, which not even Communists for example generally take, he is still "there" within the allegiance. Yet in what quality of participation? This issue tends to make the whole concept of *Dar al-Islam* an anachronism in a world beset by secularism and irreligion.

Where education remains loyal, devout, pious, and traditional, it proposes quranic memoriter, the mastery of tradition and Shari^cah, and the discipleships of the Schools. It does not, generally speaking, create a theological or spiritual curiosity or even tolerate one that may be there. It assumes that the new generation is, by nature, participant and only needs to acquire the technical disciplines. Where education is modern, secular, scientific, professional, it leaves the religious realms almost entirely to silence and takes the easy line of supposing that Islam is there, without caring how it is, or whether it should be. Life is too competitive to take undue pains or care for religious dimensions. So many things are spiritually evaporated by being taken complacently for granted.

It cannot be thought that such a situation is good for the health of Islam, nor yet for the Christian communities in the same national and political life. Yet the latter can do little or nothing in spiritual relation to it, as long as the mentality prevailing keeps them sealed in to themselves. Nor do they escape the same dangers. In educating their own, the Christian minorities use this liberty, which is an important positive part of the Muslim pattern of toleration, as an expression of communal self-consciousness. This is right and inevitable. But does it then become a defensive, rather than a creative, education? Does it lead more to the mentality, "This is our orthodoxy, absorb it" than to the conviction, "This is truth, become its servant among all"? It is not suggested that the two need exclude each other, though the first can readily obviate the second.

Community, then, tends strongly towards an externalized concept of faith in which allegiance takes precedence over conviction, or belonging dominates believing.

FAITH, EXPERIENCE, AND COMMUNITY

All the foregoing, of course, sharply complicates the question, when it comes to what might be called experience beyond frontiers. Because of all we have outlined, awareness of truth outside one's own community all too rarely happens. But, when and as it does, community then asserts its imprisoning authority all the more tyrannically. It is loathe to let men go, even when it is the dominant community. Yet in the end, if believing, as Surah 49 affirms, is to be determinative of belonging, not belonging of believing, the right and obligation of "conversion" cannot be denied.

Much emotion and many deep passions are aroused by this word and we are in urgent need of working out its full theological and spiritual meaning and validity. The problem is sharpened by sheer bigotries, by mixtures of motives, by pressures of unworthy things. Its very mention often raises false notions of religious "imperialism" or cultural competition. But, when all these have been surmounted, the right to belong where one believes, abides, though law and custom insist to the contrary.

Since this issue is larger than any study, as such, can do more than state, it may be useful to reflect on certain other aspects of the interrelation of faith and group, which have an element of paradox about them. Muhammad, in the story in Surah 49, as we noted, did not exclude "the tribes of the desert" from the new community because "faith was not in their heart". This would stand for the general right and possibility of political, social group-existence without religious identity, though in the case of Surah 49 the religious identity was soon to follow. The status of *dhimmis* can be seen as an extension of this principle and it underlies a great deal of contemporary practice.

Political or national community is thus possible without immediate, or even ultimate, religious identity. Is it not feasible then to strive for at least some sense of "community" to-day, without requiring religious identity or doctrinal agreement? So often, transference of allegiance is made the big, practical element in conversion. Response to truth is then thought of exclusively in terms of communal change. As such, bitterness and passion tend to frustrate and distort it. Is it not possible to build some "community", some intercourse and fellowship of heart, on the foundation of mutual experience, prior to and aside from any communal transference? Is it not true that truth is only learned in participation and fellowship? Yet, so often, we only allow fellowship as a sequel to assent and acceptance. We put the cart before the horse. Little wonder that inter-religious expression, bedevilled by communal prestige and status, makes small headway.

Belief and community, it is clear, have a reciprocal relation. To believe is to belong and to belong is to believe. But in actual life this relation has been allowed, by long tradition and inertia, to become thoroughly static and hidebound. A Muslim cannot reckon with Christian thought and faith without being suspected of communal disloyalty. A Christian who takes any creative interest in Islamic studies tends in the East to be regarded as dubiously loyal to his own. Questions of belonging dominate: they loom over all spiritual life and inquiry. Can some way out of the impasse not be pioneered where Muslim and Christian meet in the day-to-day obligations of citizenship and commerce, or in the common setting of nation, the twentieth century, and being human?

It may be that the principles of such an expectant attitude on the Christian side could be stated as follows:

1. Be vitally Christian, in an outward looking way.

2. Disown and repudiate all communal exclusiveness, however orthodox. Loyalty does not require isolation from others. It may be difficult, the more so as the other party may prefer, perhaps even demand, that we stay within our own.

3. Strive after personal relationships beyond community. It is often possible to do in the personal realm what may be impossible on a more formal plane.

4. Put your own community, as far as lies within your power, in a posture of translation to people of another. We rarely realize how foreign we are, even to those who speak our tongue as native. What is familiar to us within the Church—liturgy, language, traditions, patterns of thought and being—is a largely, often wholly, unknown region to others. It must be in the forefront of our loyalty to what we believe that it should be available to the outsider. Do not demand capitulation before you will allow expression.

5. Discover, possess, and acknowledge to the utmost, all that, by your Christian criteria, is valid elsewhere. Be adventurous and

expectant in this enterprise: do not be deterred in it by feeble hopes or dull imagination. There is more for our discovery and recognition in the community over against us than most of us are ready or disposed to admit. Do not pretend to be looking when you have first closed your eyes. And do all this without waiting for a full assessment of the final and absolute claims of the other religion. One can move into a voyage of discovery through the Quran, for example, without waiting for a final verdict. Our Lord did not base his hospitality of soul towards the Samaritan woman on a full evaluation of the Samaritan dogmas. He was prepared to move within her mental world as it was to her and there make plain his own.

6. (Lest all the foregoing should seem too exacting, too presumptuous, or too bold.) Rely creatively and doggedly upon the living Holy Spirit in the breadth and depth of Christ.

There are sharp problems in each of these which another chapter must explore.

QUESTIONS FOR STUDY AND DISCUSSION

1. In Surah 11.28 there is an interesting comment on the lips of Noah, who says to his audience: "Think, my people, if my Lord has revealed to me his will and bestowed on me his grace, though it is hidden from you, can we compel you to accept it against your will?" This is in line with the basic ruling of Surah 2.256: "There is no compulsion in religion." Would it be right to say that the mere fact of community, when there is no option out of it, is a form of compulsion, and so invalid?

2. Is it possible to have community of spirit with others, across actual communal boundaries, and irrespective of full acceptance of new faith?

3. If you take an affirmative attitude to (2) what are the most likely themes of such "fellowship" in the case of Muslims and Christians? How might it be expressed? What obstacles would it meet?

4. People are all so made as to need to "belong". This is true racially, domestically, economically, culturally, and in other vital ways. When such indispensable "belonging" impedes or excludes any real reckoning with the Gospel, what can and should the Church do?

5. Are we, in our local situation, properly subjecting our community in Christ to the universality of Christ?

6. What are the factors which make us prone to turn in upon ourselves and acquiesce in Christian faith being a monopoly of our community? Some of these factors are beyond our control. Others are in our own mentality—how can we overcome them?

7. What do you believe the Holy Spirit is saying to the Church in the present situation, where religious community has so long complicated and strangled communication?

8. In the sequence of the generations, faith cannot rightly be assumed: it has to be decided, chosen, embraced. How far is our Christianity only a legacy? How far a life?

21

The Art of Being a Minority

Among travellers in Arabia from the western world, perhaps the two most remarkable were Richard Burton and Charles Doughty. There was at least one radical difference between them. The former, successfully impersonating an Afghani shaikh, went everywhere in disguise. Doughty, refusing to cloke for a moment his Christian status as a hated Nasrani, travelled the pilgrim road from Damascus as far as Wajd in a magnificent minority of one!

This contrasted attitude sets the ultimate problem of all minorities—namely, that of being *what* we are *where* we are. It is worth adding that, of the two explorers, Doughty had a much keener eye for common humanity. In never ceasing to be himself, he belonged to and with Arabia Deserta more intimately than Richard Burton. Commenting on this paradoxical fact, an observer wrote: "The instinct to imitate, to cloke your own convictions and follow alien and perhaps disliked conventions, is based on a deep distrust of human brotherhood." The man who sees differences of colour, race, creed, and language within the context of a common humanity is never afraid to admit the reality and significance of those distinctions.

Doughty refused to allow *where* he was to determine or decide *what* he was. His "whatness", so to say, mastered and controlled his "whereness", and, for that very reason, he was all the more vitally *where* he was. Admittedly, his solution only concerned a journey. For Christian minorities in the Islamic world the status is for life and all. Thus Burton's solution is not literally possible. But its attitudes, in the form of introversion, passivity, seclusion, certainly are. What then is the art of being Christianly different—since, in being Christian, we establish, or inherit, or incur, this burdensome relation of the *what* of our Christian being to the *where* of our Islamic setting? Outside the Dome and the Rock are the streets of Jerusalem, and mosques as well as Stations of the Cross belong on the Via Dolorosa.

CENSUS AND CONSENSUS

Minority status is the situation in which Christians find themselves almost everywhere in the Islamic world. The percentage may be almost nil, as in Saudi Arabia, or approximately equal as is supposedly the case in the Lebanon. Something between five and fifteen per cent is the general ratio of Christians to Muslims throughout the major Islamic countries, both of West Asia and further east, and in Muslim territories in Africa, such as the Sudan and Northern Nigeria. What matters is not the precise mathematical distribution but the general fact of Christian minority status.

The world of men's thoughts and emotions is so much governed by "census and consensus"—if the phrase may be permitted. Folk are counted according to their religious allegiance and they "count" by the same tests. *What* you are, census-wise, is as important as *that* you are. In numerous subtle ways a consensus of opinion is shaped by majority religion and by dominant creed. The life of Christian communities is passed in perpetual consciousness of not being what the many are, of not holding what the many hold. Where, unhappily, racial and language factors complicate the religious diversity—as Armenians and Greeks in Turkey, Yorubas, or Ibos among Hausa people, Syriac-speaking people among Arabs—the situation becomes the more potential of friction, suspicion, and "otherness" in a variety of forms.

The purpose here is merely to set the scene. Every alert observer knows its local ramifications better than could be here summarized. Two general aspects of "census and consensus", however, may be noted. The one is that the situation, numerically, tends to sharpen by the sheer growth of population, through which, naturally, minority ratios diminish. The larger the majority, the greater and the more rapid the growth of its majority status—quite aside from any particular factors, like marriage practices, divorce habits, or the patterns of the family which may further accentuate the situation. Minority status, therefore, in the present population "flood", is an intensifying thing. Christians are becoming, proportionately, fewer in the world.

It follows, secondly, that where economic pressures are sharpened by population growth they tend to fall more heavily upon minorities. In part, of course, this may be offset by other factors that operate, educationally or materially, in their favour. But, in the last analysis, the phenomenal and awesome growth of Asian population in our day must tend in the main to increase the precariousness of minority status, and what to do with precariousness, or the threat of it, is no small part of the burden of being a minority.

Leaving the reader to draw his factual picture as truly as he can within his own local area, let us move to the heart of the study.

PRECEDENTS AND THE PRESENT

Since so much of our present, in this respect, is our participation in the ongoing past, it is well to turn to the precedents, both Muslim and Christian, in this field.

The Muslim precedents take us back into the whole idea of toleration in Islam, and it is an idea which dies hard. "The people of the Book" had their right to persist in the exercise of their faith and became tolerated communities within Islam. Having the general sanction of empire and the prestige of conquest, Islam tended to attract the allegiance of those who wanted to belong with what succeeded. For internal reasons also, there were many Christian defections to Islam. But, except in isolated or exceptional circumstances, such Islamizing on the part of Christians was not due to the absence of a genuine alternative to remain Christian.

It was, however, only a liberty to remain, and this has always been its unsatisfactory quality, as a "freedom". It meant, merely that the Copt, the Armenian, the Jew, would not be required to become a Muslim. If he thought it prudential or profitable, he could join Islam. But there was no movement in the other direction. The Christian was not free to recruit disciples: his faith had to remain a family affair, a communal entity, a kin-continuity. The Muslim had, in fact, an option-less situation in which he could do nothing but remain. Freedom was not a freedom to become, but only a freedom to persist.

This concept of toleration, though superior to any notion of forced conversion, radically fails by any adequate test of what freedom should constitute. It continued through the centuries and the Christian communities slowly imbibed it as part of their mentality. Surrounded as they were by conditions that forbade their expansion and denied new church-building or enlargement, they approximated to the Muslim concept of their status and became introverted, self-preoccupied, non-welcoming entities sufficient unto themselves.

In modern times, there has been much more interpenetration of communities, commercially, politically, socially, culturally. But the old concept, religiously, seems as rigid as ever. Few modern Muslims have seriously questioned it. It is said that Islam is a freely-willed adherence. But the corollary of this, in a genuine ability to contract out of it for the Muslim who no longer feels he belongs, does not exist. The duty to press, in law and public opinion, for a true order of liberty, understood as liberty to become, should exercise all thinking men of integrity, whether Muslim or Christian, and irrespective of the directions in which it might be used. No self-respecting faith can be satisfied to be the virtual prison it is, if it retains its adherents only because these are in no legal position to be anything else.

Islam may be helped towards this objective by developments in the contemporary world. One is the fact that certain segments of Islam have themselves entered into permanent minority status. In independent India, for example, the full freedom of over forty million of them turns upon the continuity of the secular concept that has hitherto actuated the Indian Government. If there have been voices raised, demanding the identification of Indian nationalism with Hindu religion,[1] that fact introduces the same element of insecurity, the same exacting feeling of existing by the graces of others, that has for so long attached to non-Muslim existence within Islam. There is hope that mutuality of minority status may help to commend full freedom, to be and to become, to the mind of Islam. Nor need such genuine freedoms necessarily require complete secularity in the concept of the State. Some general association of the State with a majority faith, if disciplined, may co-exist with sound minority freedom.

As for the Christian precedents, they are of two sorts—those of the

[1] See for example Chandran and Thomas, *Political Outlook in India Today*, Bangalore, pp. 112–13 for a quotation from Maha Sabha sources: "In this country Hindus alone are the nationals and the Muslims and others, if not actually anti-national, are outside the body of the nation. . . . The non-Hindu peoples in Hindustan must either adopt Hindu culture and language, must learn to respect and hold in reverence the Hindu religion, must entertain no idea but the glorification of the Hindu race and culture, or may stay in the country wholly subordinate to the Hindu nation. . . ." It is clear that such sentiments and parallel concepts within Islam are a protest against a quite different view of the relation of majority religion to national unity. Yet the existence of such concepts reminds the minorities that their securities hinge upon an internal issue decided outside themselves.

introverted Christianity of Islamic hegemony already considered, and the splendid patterns of the New Testament. The former, as already indicated, tended to arise out of a Christian acquiescence in the kin-community concept of the Christian entity forced upon it by the circumstances attending the Islamic concept of toleration. For the historical factors, within this absorption of the Muslim notion of what a Church might be permitted to be, one can have the liveliest sympathy. But this should not involve one in approval. If such has been, because of Islam, the Christian pattern of survival, we must still ask: survival for what?

The question carries us back to the authentic precedents of the New Testament. There the meaning of conversion and the right to it were differently understood. Being converted to Christ meant refusing worship to the Emperor. When such worship was demanded the Church sealed its minority status in suffering. For the rest, the indifferentism of the Empire left the Christian minority free to grow. It might require it to be heroic: it never obliged it to be quiescent.

So the New Testament offers us a rich and stirring set of precedents for inferior status, a magnificent lesson in the art of being a minority. It held paramount loyalties to the truth of its Gospel. For the rest it was loyal to the State and open-hearted to humanity. In taking its stand with Christ it did not turn its back upon men. Precisely in being sure of its distinctive Word, it was also content to be in and with the world around it. In not allowing itself to be intimidated it did not allow itself to be insulated. There may well be for the contemporary Church, lessons of the most relevant kind in this quality of minority existence. How different were the two imperialisms—the Roman, with its brutal intolerance in one vital issue, and for the rest bemused, scornful, or wistful tolerance, and the Islamic—tolerant only on the condition of a perpetually quiescent community. The Islamic empire tolerated by disallowing all but survival. The Romans may have shown the greater ruthlessness, but they also took the greater risks.

DANGERS AND DEMANDS

But precedents, by definition, are in the past. What is to be said of the present? What may be done on the part of the contemporary Church to foster, and to deserve, full freedoms of becoming within Muslim societies? And how should the inward patterns of New Testament minority behaviour be understood and fulfilled to-day? Reflection on both questions seems to involve a series of dangers and demands that belong together and may be easier to analyse than to face.

Where situations are complex it is natural that people should have complexes. There is complexity to be faced and "complexity" to be rid of. An element in the latter is the sullenness, suspicion, and introversion to which all minorities are prone. A victim-mentality is an ever-present menace where insecurity attaches to status. The Christian communities need a deliberate attitude of suspecting their own suspicions and of cultivating the widest possible alertness to how the majority sees them.

This means a resolute attitude to the main factors that make for the precariousness of our situation. These are, among others:

1. *The sense of the past.* Fears and resentments die hard. When toleration has instilled into us that we are communities and survive as such, it cannot be a thing of wonder if we continue to see the past in communal terms. The remembrance, in the communal soul, of massacre or repression in the previous generation and beyond, inevitably lies oppressively upon us. Yet its entail only deepens in tragedy if it is not transcended.

2. *Dubiety about the temper of the majority.* In the last resort minorities have to exist with their ultimate securities outside their own direct power and control. A refusal to accept this state of affairs (on the part of Muslims) as tolerable in an undivided India (despite the same sort of assurances in equal faith that almost every majority in the modern world, including Pakistan, makes to its minorities) was the inner impulse to the creation of Pakistan at the price of a divided subcontinent. It is not to be wondered at if any minorities anywhere have a sort of "pakistan" complex about majority graces and attitudes. No doubt, being less numerous and not independently viable, they cannot opt for Christian, Hindu, Coptic, Syriac, or other "pakistans" —states of the "pure" self-responsible community. But, precisely because of that impossibility, the same fears remain. With such a great, and standing, example of their "justification", they cannot be discounted elsewhere.

For all that, the guarantees which Pakistani Islam distrusted when proffered by Hindu goodwill, and which she in turn has been at pains to assure to her own minorities, are sincerely offered in many parts of the world, Hindu and Muslim. While militant elements remain, in movements like the Maha Sabha or the Ikhwan al-Muslimun, such assurances can never be absolute and the security they offer never more than probable. Yet what other sort of security is there in this world? Great experiments are afoot in many quarters for the building up of national life on a basis of inter-religious equality. To these the Christian minorities have an obvious obligation. Too often religions have been an unlovely and divisive influence in society. Theologians and religious leaders of action have often given unhappy cause for the pleas of outright secularists that religion is an obstacle to unity and a bane of society. If there are dangers in resulting self-sufficient humanism, these must not blind us to the justice of the critics of self-assertion in religious guise.

There are more exacting issues in this whole field than can be adequately noted here. What is clear is that Christian minority status, if creatively taken, affords rich contemporary opportunities for constructive relations to both the ambition and the weakness of current "secular" nationalisms. Are we to be so preoccupied with communal survival, with defences against hypothetical eventualities damaging to us, that we do not see and seize occasions of large-hearted ministry in a changing world?

3. *Majority suspicions of the rôle of the minorities.* Here is another potent source of insecurity, in which, to some degree, is involved the principle: "With what measure ye mete, it shall be measured to you" (Matt. 7.2). Minorities need to recognize that some of their precariousness in fact arises from the means they took, or take, to protect themselves. Such are the paradoxes of religious life. There were the nineteenth-century patterns of Christian minority reliance upon European powers for protection. Doubtless, given the character and habits of the Ottoman Empire, this was inevitable. In the new day of Arab self-responsibility the memory of these patterns lingers—on the one side as a suspicion, on the other as a temptation—when their feasibility is past.

For good and ill, the Arab Christian minorities are now squarely set in the stream of Arab, and therefore Muslim, history. Their assimilation and its independence have, so to speak, coincided. Yet some of the old complications remain when, as now, Arabism as a whole lives in strained relations with the West, the erstwhile source of Christian "protection".

The situation may perhaps best be illustrated from the Lebanon. The crisis of events there in 1958 was in effect a development of Muslim weight in affairs, in the form of a struggle about relations with the West. The content and the form of the struggle certainly belong together historically. In earlier days of Lebanese independence, political as well as educational leadership tended to be in Christian hands. Christians were ahead in trade and education and they were, for the most part, the spokesmen and leaders of the national movement.[1]

More recently, however, the older Christian middle class has been challenged by a newer Muslim intelligentsia and middle class. Muslims, too, tend now to have the influence with the surrounding Arab states in their resurgent Arabism, which the Christians mostly held with foreign powers at an earlier stage. The vigour—perhaps, at times, the ebullience—of those states encourages the Muslim sense of importance and stature, and bewilders or dismays the Christian assessments. Moreover, in ceasing to be, insofar as they ever were, "tools of foreign powers" Christian elements are, from the Muslim point of view, "disarmed". When their potential menace diminishes, so does their potential part in affairs.

Though it is well to try the utmost to avoid the close identification of Lebanese issues with religious groupings, there is no doubt that events have in fact registered a shift, in which Arabism, even in its Lebanese form, has come closer to Muslim criteria of what it should be. That does not of itself menace the Christian elements: it simply makes their calling more exacting and more creative. There are powerful concepts in the Arab-Muslim realm, like the Ba'ath Party, that seek an Arabism in which there will be a clear distinction between religion and politics.[2] But, if it is to "secure" these concepts, as the stuff of its own security, the Christian minority has before it a long and patient task of reshaping past attitudes and patterns. Is it not to be expected that since these problems are mutual, they can only be faced in reciprocal confidence between communities? If such confidence is to be enjoyed, must it not also be merited?

The majority suspicion of the external links of minorities for their self-defence takes a quite different form in the sub-continent of India. If it may be said that Pakistan was created to "protect" more Muslims

[1] See George Antonius, *The Arab Awakening*, London, 1938.

[2] See A. H. Hourani, *Frontier*, vol. 1, Oct. 1958, pp. 265–70; and L. Binder, "Radical-Reform Nationalism in Syria and Egypt", *The Muslim World*, vol. 49, no. 2, April 1959.

than it could include (by a perpetuation of the old concept of "hostage" communities), it is little wonder that the potential Pakistani escape, or reliance, of Indian Muslims queers the pitch in their relations with the Hindu majority. That this factor is far from merely hypothetical is seen from the aftermath of particular Indian Muslim defections across the border.[1] The relevance of all this to Christian minorities anywhere is only that it provides an instructive parallel. What issues from it all is the plain fact that minority "survival and welfare depend squarely on the secularity of the state". What Professor Smith adds for Islam is equally true for any Christianity of Muslim context: "The full theological implications of this are as yet far from worked out."[2] New situations can only be confronted when we transcend the emotions that went with those that history has now left behind.

4. *The ill-founded susceptibilities of minorities*. In all situations of admitted insecurity, men are all too prone to find danger where it does not exist, or suppose discrimination where it is not present. This theme needs little elaboration here. A persecution complex is more easily acquired than dispelled. With a thousand changes in economic order, with endless points of personal disharmony over housing, employment, promotion, judicial procedures, and the rest, men are all too likely to read persecution into chance, or malice aforethought into reasonable deserts.

An Islamic State decides, for example, to reduce the number (chronic enough in all conscience) of national holidays and in the process eliminates Good Friday. A group of Christians discussing the matter finds an unfair anti-Christian discrimination. The State is said to be hostile to the cross. But wiser reflections prevail. Friday is half a working day already; representations may well obtain the privilege of Good Friday as an optional, communal holiday; there is economic need for curbing holidays and Good Friday anyway concerns less than one per cent of those involved. Perhaps, then, a truer attitude to the meaning of Good Friday would be to forgo a petulant complaint.

The point within this random (and actual) example is familiar enough. Minorities do not commend themselves by an assertiveness that is ill-balanced and quarrelsome. We are, by nature, more likely to

[1] See Wilfred Cantwell Smith, *Islam in Modern History*, 1957, pp. 275–6.
[2] Ibid., p. 281.

err from lack of meekness than from excess of it. Is it not, in the end, the way we take the real adversity, and the capacity we have to transcend the supposed adversity, which commends and measures the Gospel that has a mighty suffering and a blessed uncomplainingness at its heart?

These, and other, dangers spell the positive demand. We may note, in conclusion, a few final points that belong with that "genius as minority" which lives in the New Testament.

(*a*) Transcending the victim-mentality, we should reach out hospitably and joyously into the majority world. The creative minority, not intimidated by its quantitative inferiority, will strive to know the majority world. It will strive to explain its qualitative distinctiveness in terms that are intelligible to the majority community and the dominant faith, conceding gladly that the latter for the most part informs and determines the national thought patterns.

(*b*) This presupposes an inner intensification of life and devotion. The constant duty of the Christian minority is to be vigorously and assuredly itself. We cannot live co-operatively as Christians with the rest of men, except out of a fervent and vital Christianity. Constructive attitudes to national problems do not mean an abeyance of the Christian allegiance. Sympathy with Islam and its meanings does not involve a diluted Christianity. On the contrary. It is *out of* the fulness of the truth of the divine Lover that we may live *in* the power of his love for men. We shall not the better penetrate into the ends and meanings of Islam for getting apologetic or diffident about the incarnation and the cross. The virilities of truth and of love belong together. The ruling duty of any Christian toward any situation is to be in it authentically Christian.

(*c*) With this aspiration to know the majority, and to love them in being ourselves as Christ's, goes an alertness to the ways in which "good may be evil spoken of". The apostolic injunction is that we "give no offence in anything". Alertness is imperative where prejudices abound. Majorities have susceptibilities as well as minorities. Perhaps they arise in the field of medicine. Is the Christian activity in hospital and clinic soundly related to a wise commendation of the faith in the love of God that energizes it? Do we keep loyally to our Lord's own patterns, in which works of mercy were tokens of the kingdom but never of themselves reasons for accepting it? How far do we rightly assess and actively belie the frequent accusation that Christian medical ministry is a form of spiritual exploitation of the needy in the interests of conversion? Or it may be in matters of education. There are some accusers who say wildly that Christians have a sort of "black market" in education, that they run their schools at reduced rates for Christians out of fees paid by Muslims. The critics mean that Christian education is often available for Christians at lesser rates because the Churches give to bursaries made available for Christian students. In this way the community is only looking after its own, and there is no legitimate complaint. But situations of prejudice are not Christianly handled merely by denying charges. There has to be also a sensitivity to why people nourish prejudices and a constructive openness to dispel their falsity and disarm their menace.

(*d*) There is also the duty to be active with the majority in common campaigns for social good.[1] Let the minority demonstrate its mettle in initiating and fulfilling deeds of human ministry. The needs of the vast illiterate masses are a case in point. The ability to read, with resultant access to the world of knowledge, is part of that human dignity to which "love of our neighbour" is committed. Endless other realms of initiative await the vigorous and imaginative. Precedents show that it is usually "minorities" that get things done. In these practical realms many antagonisms can be silenced and the will to co-operation made plain.

(*e*) We must also refuse to capitulate to the political. There is more that matters in life than the political order knows or admits. So much of the recent past and the general scene in West Asia has been dominated by the political, to the unhappy abeyance, not only of theological thought, but even of creative philosophy, literature, and art. Too many problems are confronted as if the whole of their solution was political. It may be that this has been unavoidable in the process of dislodging and expelling western power and asserting independence. Independence is a political concept, valid enough in its limits. There are, however, other realms of life in which con-dependence is a much truer term. And, where the latter is acknowledged, minorities may be differently seen.

(*f*) Yet, finally, the claim of any minority must lie in its quality of life and thought. So we return to the New Testament. "It was not by any despairing withdrawal from city and market that they conquered the world; not by any proud isolation or selfish security; not by

[1] The theme of the final chapter.

any impatient violence: but by the winning influence of a gracious faith, they mastered the family, the school, the empire. . . . Pure among the self-indulgent, loving among the factious, tender among the ruthless, meek among the vain-glorious . . . joyous in hope among the sorrows of a corrupt society, they revealed to men their true destiny and showed that it could be attained." "Ye see your calling, brethren."

QUESTIONS FOR STUDY AND DISCUSSION

1. Formulate and discuss in your own local setting any occasions that have arisen in which Muslims have complained about Christian minority attitudes or behaviour.

2. Similarly, examine and clarify any recent occasions of Christian criticism or complaint about majority action or majority outlook. Have they been querulous, misguided, and petulant, or serious and genuine? If the former, what ways can you suggest of transcending them? If the latter, what attitudes would you suggest in seeking constructive remedies?

3. What quranic passages, and other elements in Islam, would you cite in justifying and commending to Muslims a concept of real toleration which includes freedom to become as well as freedom to remain?

4. What is meant by saying that the man who clokes his convictions rather than the man who lives openly by them is the one who really despises his fellow men?

5. Since it is understanding that begets understanding and sympathy that merits sympathy, what are the intellectual and spiritual duties of Christian communities towards Islam?

6. What, as you see them, were the New Testament attitudes to the Roman political authority and the dominant beliefs of Gentile religion?

7. What should be the Christian position in regard to the concept of the secular State?

8. What, in your view, is the true rôle of Christian Arab communities at the present juncture in Arab affairs?

9. What practical ways would you suggest of avoiding the victim-complex? How may Christian groups, despite unhappy precedents, racial complications, and economic precariousness, come by, and live by, the apostolic knowledge of "how to be abased and how to abound"?

22

"... or Turk"

COMPASSION IN COMMON

With his last words he wrote: "All I can add in my solitude is may Heaven's rich blessing come down on every one, American, English or Turk, who will help to heal this open sore of the world."

In pride of place on the tombstone of Livingstone in the nave of Westminster Abbey are these last words of his African journal: ". . . or Turk". Strange to think that there, in the lonely silence on the brink of the grave, the Muslim world came into the Christian liberator's mind as a potential ally.

"Turk" was of course the traditional word through four centuries of English literature to denote a Muslim. English writers from Shakespeare to the nineteenth century used the name of the typical Muslim power as a synonym for Islam itself. The sixteenth-century *Book of Common Prayer* has it in the Good Friday Collect with its petition for "all Jews, Turks, infidels and heretics", while Isaac Watts, renowned for his hymns, referred, in 1725, in his *Logic* to a "divine distribution of mankind into Turks, Heathens, Jews or Christians". Either of these two sources may have been in Livingstone's mind unconsciously as he wrote. For he was well reared in Scottish piety. If not, there were scores of other precedents to make him think of "Turks", not least in his own careful studies of the background history of African slavery.

Was that history partly to blame for the way he penned his plea? Is there something of a hope against hope in that last addition? Or a feeling that there was an evil so desperate that any potential partnership must be recruited to eradicate it? "Or Turk". . . "Americans" no doubt had precedence, not then because of their wealth, but because of their traditions. For Lincoln had been dead but eight years when Livingstone breathed his last. And "English" was a natural plea—the people of his own tongue. They would accept his legacy of sacrifice.

But "Turks" too should be invoked. Even the Ottoman stone should not be left unturned if it might produce a volunteer for compassion.

For compassion in common was what Christian Livingstone sought. Faced as he was with a humanity in bonds to cruelty he was prepared to find comrades anywhere if they would only share his vision. He would commend his mission more widely than the limits of the faith which generated and sustained it. The urgency of what he had in hand made him aspire to common action despite a differing faith. Yet there can be no doubting, either in deeds or diaries, that what made Livingstone was the Gospel of God in Christ, from which his every impulse sprang.

For that very reason, then, his parting words serve as a proper preface to a theme of thought and study which grows increasingly important in our midst. It may be argued that Livingstone's words were in a sense rhetorical, since there was at that juncture no prospect whatever of Muslim co-operation in his purposes. But with us the question is constant and real. To what degree, and in what terms, may the Christian person and the Christian community find a common front with Muslims in the tasks of human compassion? What spiritual and practical issues belong with ministry to the needs of men within a co-operation that is astride religious lines?

THE CHANGING SETTING

There is no need to argue the altered pattern of to-day's world. There were, even up to recent decades, many times and places where the Christian Church was the sole instrument of active and informed compassion in the context of human misery, disease, and squalor. Whole areas of human life and tragedy had no relief save that which might be found through Christian mission. This is not to ignore or deny the potential capacity for mercy and ministry in such faiths as Confucianism, Hinduism, Buddhism, or Islam. But, in large measure, in endless villages and through long years, those capacities were inoperative. Either through ignorance or apathy, or by the long ascendancy of witchcraft, fatalism, superstition, and sheer atrophy of the will and power to save, human suffering went unrelieved, unless, in its pathetic frailty of numbers and of range, the Church with Christ was on the scene. Mission had a near monopoly of responsible ministry to suffering. The education of the world in the will and power to heal and help was virtually in its hands.

We do well to take the full measure of this situation if we are to appreciate the changes to-day. That almost unshared burden of Christian sensitivity for humanity in trouble passes with contemporary developments to many shoulders. Political independence brings a new sense of state responsibility; patterns of social welfare under government authority extend; technology widens its empire with the spread of literacy and education in the sciences, medical and social; old evils in the mind, like witchcraft or lethargy, begin to give way before pride of new self-esteem; old cultures become alive to activist philosophies and see ancient ills with a more hostile eye.

It is well that it is so. For, at the same time, the range of human problems—on the unchanging pillars of birth and death, marriage and the generations—has incredibly widened and diversified. The Christian forces, always unequal to their undertakings for humanity, grow even more utterly so, with the accumulating complexity of human problems on every hand. Medicine, nursing, education, compassion—these must be the arts of all, and the capacities of soul that they require must be the obligation of all religious systems. Christian faith must rejoice to see its inner impulse to compassion operative, as far as may be, within systems of belief which deny, or ignore, the understanding of the divine nature in which that impulse has its final source.

The Gospel, which is that ultimate ground, must rejoice in every working of the will to serve, wherever it is evident in the increase of state responsibility for the social order, and of local, national, or personal action in the sphere of welfare. In measure it fulfils a Christian dimension even where in fact it displaces a Christian agency. Much of the professional skill and competence requisite to such action must still be sought in Christian, or at least in western, places. An actual Christian personnel, though in minority, must still be locally vigorous in the pursuit of compassion. The Church in mission gives thanks, on every ground, if its unbearable monopoly gives way steadily to a more widely shared mercy to humanity.

But behind this changing pattern there are some deep and unchanging issues. What are the grounds of compassion, the springs of mercy, or the resources of love? How is compassionateness related to belief? Can you renounce indifference to suffering and remain indifferent about God? Is compassion manward unrelated, in fact or in act, to compassion in God? Is there an equal competence for compassion in every religious system? Should a will to act *with* other faiths in such ministry argue an unconcern *about* what they teach? Must Christian co-operation in act imply neglect of distinctiveness in dogma? Or, in practical terms, what is necessary to constitute a school or a hospital Christian? Let us set these questions under three heads.

COMPASSION AND CONVICTION

It is at once clear on several grounds that what we are here calling compassion (in the fullest sense of an active response to human need) is deeply involved in what we believe and in why we believe it. In our concern to serve we cannot escape the effects and consequences of beliefs, religious or otherwise, already in men's minds and ways. On the negative side, many of the ills with which compassion must be concerned stem from religious error or breed in religiously sanctioned apathy. Compassion soon finds that there are no limits to the range of what it must attempt if it would fulfil itself. Its adversaries may be as much from religion as from bacteria, its burdens from superstitions more than from disease.

Communism has not failed to point out the baleful effects of some religious beliefs upon the social and economic order. But they can be illustrated from a very different source. In her *Reveille for a Persian Village*[1] Najmeh Najafi describes her valiant efforts to bring new health and life to the villagers of Sarbandan and tells how, in this quest, she was constantly confronted with the query as to which need was really first and foremost.

Was it simply sanitation, calling for plumbers and piped water indispensable to cleanliness? Or was it education, without which women would still pollute the open jube and no physical improvement would avail? Or was it nutrition, without which lethargic minds could never respond to the demands education would enjoin? Or was it economic action dealing first with the poverty and accumulated debts from which apathy and ignorance derived? Or was it a new village council, free from the bickerings and petty jealousies that impeded all worthy change? Or was all to be blamed on a government which did not care?

[1] Gollancz, 1958.

Clearly they all depended together: there was no one thing that could either come, or suffice, without the others. But the immediate point is that ultimately all go further back still into the beliefs by which wills are determined and the thoughts that shape them. There is no escape from the consequences of religious belief if we are concerned about compassion. There is no final emancipation from the ills men suffer which does not deal radically with the things they believe. The soul of salvation is always the salvation of the soul.

But this is the negative side—the roots of evils in false beliefs or their tolerance by imperfect ones. On the positive side there is the vital grounding of compassion in conviction. We have here one of the most sacred and exacting areas of Christian expression in the whole realm of inter-religious relationship.

The question is often raised in Christian circles, and elsewhere, about the compassionate capacities of Islam. How far are the convictions nourished and taught by the Quran capable of compassion? What dimensions of mercy in and with sacrifice or of loving kindness in humility, belong with the doctrines that make Islam? How compassionate, in other words, is the Muslim because he is a Muslim?

Observers have not been lacking who answer this question pessimistically. They point to an apparent callousness in Middle Eastern life, to a tolerance of suffering and an apathy about the toils of animals, an acquiescence in preventable misery, an absence of self-sacrificing love or self-humiliation in the doctrinal scheme of things.

Let us not oversimplify a bewildering range of questions. Times and places differ: generalizations distort. There are imponderable factors of personal temperament and external circumstance. There are the arrogant and the heartless in every context. Comparisons can so easily and subtly become self-patronizing. We are only safe if we keep our inquiry strictly to the content and emphases of Islamic dogma and history. And we shall be less likely to err if we give the benefit of every doubt.

Reveille for a Persian Village, already referred to, is a moving document of self-abandonment in the service of the needy. It deserves to be carefully studied. The reader will find a quality of self-renouncing ministry, worthy to be seen within the New Testament concept of "the second mile" (Matt. 5.41), and surmounting great odds by reliance only on the power of love and patience. The Christian reader searches the book eagerly for articulate associations on the writer's part of this vocation with Islam. The associations come to light. The initial impulse may have been nurtured while in America, and a Christian hymn[1] of that time is quoted. But the will to go abroad and study antedated the sojourn in the U.S.A. and this will came from compassion. "I decided to go to America. The picture of my life as it should be was taking shape but I did not know how to take the first step. *To learn I must leave* Teheran."[2] The Prophet's birthday, disciplines of Ramadan, prayer in crises of compassion and in the routine of the *Namaz*, the *Adhan* ("I heard the strident voices of all the mullahs in my life"),[3] the *sajjadah* and *tasbih*[4] and the *Fatihah*—all these figure in the author's portrait of her vocation.

In her pursuit of it she demonstrates a rare and rich capacity for pains, humility, and endurance, often memorably expressed, e.g. "If you wish people who must walk to trust you, go among them walking."[5] Here, then, is one of the most telling pieces of evidence as to the self-sacrificing goodness which may be sustained in and by Islamic conviction. It therefore sets the Christian reader to deep thoughts. Here he finds witness to the potential dimension of the *Rahmah* of God of which the *Fatihah* speaks. Patient service to the poor, the ignorant, the quarrelsome, the dull-witted, the superstitious is constantly referred in prayer to the wisdom, the mercy, the tenderness of God. It is a human loving kindness which consciously roots itself in the like conviction about God.

It is this which makes the Christian wonder all the more wistfully why there is so little indication of a sense in the author of Christian parallels and potentials. Is it that she is immersed in a cultural self-sufficiency that explains both her neglect of what is not her own and her exclusive satisfaction with what is? There is one remark seeming to suggest this: "I thought that *because I was a Moslem and loved the people* suspicion would not wall me out."[6] Yet, clearly, her Muslim behaviour was not simply tactical. If she had said "... because I was a Moslem and *knew* the people ..." it would be also right. But does she mean that there is no effective love possible across religious difference? If so, what becomes of the concept of humanity as one in its need? Or is it simply that, being Persian, she wishes not to be involved in the endless complications of religious issues? Or is it an indirect reproach to

[1] Ibid., p. 38. [2] Ibid., p. 6. [3] Ibid., p. 8.
[4] Ibid., p. 102. [5] Ibid., p. 108. [6] Ibid., p. 51.

the "mission" compassion that involves also a doctrinal desire for conversion?

It seems right to set these issues in the context of this remarkable book (the instances of which may God multiply) despite the danger of apparently studying a general question from a particular, and perhaps singular, case. For we are led here right into the final theme. Where so authentically as in the meaning of the cross do we find the divine counterpart of this essay in Muslim autobiography about compassion? Can there finally be an imitation on earth if the perfectly imitable is not in heaven? "We love because he first loved us", says the First Epistle of St John. It is finally in Christ's cross, rather than in the Quran's consensus, that we find the patterns which the author of *Reveille for a Persian Village* is following. Perhaps we should conclude that Christ has disciples in will who hold off from him in creed, who confess him blessedly and indirectly as a pattern of behaviour without seeing him to be the very disclosure of heaven.

Yet his Church can never, in all reverence and honesty, be satisfied with such a situation. Was not the very term "Son of Man", under which Jesus moved by one decision into both messianic achievement and the cross, intended to describe a consequent community of like-mindedness through grace, a generation of redeemed humanity re-made in the same image? This remaking of human nature comes through that unity with himself in his cross which only faith in who and how he is effectuates and ensures.

This, for the Christian, under the shadow of the cross, entering into Christ who "in us is the hope of glory", is the dependence of compassion upon conviction. The more sensitive we are in gratitude for all outworking anywhere of the meaning of compassion, the more concerned we become for its conscious discovery of Christ, in whom it is validated, secured, and multiplied.

COMPASSION AND COST

The source of mercy among men in the mercy of God toward men is clearly the first issue. But there is a second, having to do, not with the ground of such compassion, but with its continuity. If at the cross we learn authentically how God is love, this symbolizes the cost of such a pattern for ourselves. This is a way we cannot take cheaply: its price must continually be paid. "Be not weary in well doing" is no idle exhortation (Gal. 6.9) since goodwill is so easily wearied in this evil world. Ministry demands a staying power. Where can this be found?

A common feature of life in many parts of Asia and Africa is rural poverty and urban wealth. There is a wide gulf, not only in actual physical fact, but in imagination, between village and city. The young, the ambitious, and the educated are so readily drawn into the vortex of the urban world with its cinemas, its luxuries, its high salaries, and its glamour. It becomes a matter of extreme difficulty, and so of desperate urgency, to man essential services in rural areas. Doctors, nurses, teachers, social workers, emphatically prefer the cities. On this rock of personal distaste for sacrifice, many grandiose paper plans for rural betterment have come to grief. Absentee landlordism abounds. Governmental action tends to be remote (as indeed does the work of Point Four and the Foundations) for the reason that people can only be helped when they are helped to help themselves. This cannot be done by bulldozers, techniques, committees, vital as these are—but only by patient alongsidedness that is costly, exacting, tedious, and self-effacing. There is much of "know-how": little of the "be-there"—"be there", that is, in imagination, forbearance, and in the will to be identified. All the problems of humanity turn in the end upon human availability. The person is, in the end, the crux of all social action, on both sides—the person in need and the person in ministry.

Yet such persons in their yieldedness, are all too hard to come by. The acid test of any religious system, in the social field, is its ability to multiply their numbers and sustain their graces, when all the odds of the "principalities and powers" in our acquisitive, technique-dominated world are against these prerequisities of sacrifice and devotion. Najmeh Najafi's book takes honest stock of this fact and provides a forceful example of how it must be met.

Here, in all that has to do with the cost of compassion, stands the Gospel of the cross, in its unique relation to the need of the world. It is there that these inescapable necessities of love are in fact faced and satisfied in a divine dimension. The Gospel has to do with a way of salvation divinely undertaken and achieved, in which all that love knows of its travail on the human plane in men's hearts is found to be eternally the truth of the divine nature. Is not this the great argument of John 15 and Romans 5? "Greater love hath no man than this. . . ." "God commendeth his love in that. . . ." That love is love in giving all is a truth of realism in the human situation: it is also the secret by which God reigns.

Only in the Gospel is this fact found. It is the unique heart of Christianity. All other faiths are in these terms "cross-less". In the real world, the Gospel of the cross is truly and uniquely the source of a compassion which knows and embraces its cost. This is not to say that there are not random goodnesses in every system. Nor is it to claim that actual Christianity has unfailingly attained its own meanings. Indeed on the contrary.[1] Yet these practical failures do not disqualify the Gospel's meaning. They betray it. The meaning remains to condemn them.

For, in the end, all other systems, somewhere, abandon the necessities of love which God in Christ undertakes and through him teaches men to undertake. Communism, of course, abandons them at the outset; indeed, denies they ever have any rôle. The changes which it wishes to induce in the human situation, though real impulses to compassion may generate them, as in Marx at Manchester, are themselves compassionless since they are violent, compulsive, and unredemptive, and ride roughshod over mercy.

In its different way, Islam, as a coherent system of doctrine in history, also stops short of the full necessities of love. In the end it relies upon the State to actualize the good and chooses the imperial arm for the furtherance of its purpose. In the last analysis "war is better than *Fitnah*". It is truer to secure oneself than to be exposed, to assert oneself in mastery than to consecrate oneself in sacrifice.

It is not meant that states and laws and political action have no relative place in the ordering of this world. Nor that force within and behind these has no just rôle. But when these are invoked as ultimate, and displace the final efficacies of love of which the cross is the sign on earth and the pledge in heaven, then the full cost and victory of compassion are not known and won. Love cannot be itself in the human situation except in the shape of the cross.

[1] Cf. the words of Albert Schweitzer relating to the general reception in Strasbourg of his proposal to become a medical missionary: "In the many verbal duels I had to fight, as a weary opponent, with people who passed for Christians, it moved me greatly to see them so far from perceiving that the effort to serve the love preached by Jesus may sweep a man into a new course of life, although they read in the New Testament that it can do so and find it quite in order." *Out of My Life and Thought*, p. 108.

COMPASSION AND CO-OPERATION

Yet it will be loyal to it only in also being ready to engage in works of compassion that still lack these final divine grounds. It will be eager to co-operate with the will to compassion wherever it is found. Like Livingstone, it will not write off any potential partners in action because these have not yet seen the clue to all compassion in the cross.

To do otherwise would be false to actual need which can never be met in isolation and exclusiveness—because of its volume, as needing all, and of its nature in the present setting of nationalism. It would also be self-defeating. Imagine the Gospel wishing to withhold the benediction of giving rather than receiving. And self-defeat would be likely in another sense also. Much of the Gospel can only be learned in the desire to serve. Men and women have more likelihood of entering into the meaning of Christ when they will to be unselfish than when they are content to live only for themselves. For then they begin to enter realistically into the staying power that goodness must possess and the persistent exactions of ministry. By all means, then, let us welcome the widest co-operation in the fight against need, poverty, sickness, and wrong. Why do we always somehow assume that the first contact and decisive relation to Christ must be in the realm of doctrine? The disciples in the Gospels shared in Jesus' campaigns before they understood his identity. So it may be still.

The important practical aspects of this co-operation must be pondered and solved in every local setting. How do you ensure a Christian temper in institutional ministry when operating it with Muslims? Commitment and atmosphere are vital: do they necessitate a Christian majority? If so, how large? What is the Christian part in general enterprises of a national or civic kind for social betterment? How does one maintain a warm, constructive relation, such as joint action requires, with those among whom one must be at the same time a witness, and to that extent, in their eyes, a critic?

Clearly these are fine arts for which there are no easy or general answers, but only constant creative tension and travail. To withdraw into ourselves in effort, or to contract out of the Gospel in co-operating—both would be easy and each would be fatal. To hold them together is alone the full loyalty Christ expects. "And when thy glory dawns", we may each say to our Lord, dawns in act and dawns on systems, "I will be well content" (Ps. 17.15).

PRAYER

O Lord, who in this wide world of human finitude dost call us to loving kindness, help us to find our place in partnerships of compassion with men of goodwill everywhere. Grant us, also, in loyalty to the Gospel, to express in wisdom the heavenly goodwill for ever accomplished in the cross and ever active in the fellowship of the Son of Man, Jesus Christ our Saviour. Amen.

QUESTIONS FOR STUDY AND DISCUSSION

1. What other evidences exist, like that of *Reveille for a Persian Village*, showing a deep, sacrificial concern for human need tracing its inspiration specifically to Islam?

2. Is it fair to say that some people are better than the ultimate meaning and content of their dogmas, and that others are worse? Or is this an over-simplification?

3. What attitude to sacrifice and suffering can be found in the Quran? in Islamic institutions? in tradition and the *Sirah* (or prophetic biography)?

4. In what senses is the way of the cross truly unparalleled in the whole range of the religions?

5. Why must the Christian Church insist that in the end "the imitation of Christ" does, and must, depend upon faith and fellowship in him? Why is belief in the Gospel necessary to its full and sustained practice?

6. How, then, do you explain the often collapse of compassion within the community of faith in Christ crucified?

7. When you have come across occasions of cruelty (to men, children, or animals) and of callousness, indifference, and acquiescence in wretchedness, how have you reacted?

8. When traditional doors of Christian ministration to the sick or the ignorant are closed, what new ones can be entered or unlocked?

9. What practical problems have you met with in working co-operatively with Muslims in school or hospital or other enterprise, and how have you resolved them?

10. "Only love makes good the clumsy ignorance of 'know-how'." Consider this comment on mere technique and skill.

A Short Book List

The following titles, in addition to the works mentioned in the text and footnotes, will be found useful in pursuing the themes of the foregoing chapters.

Abdul-Hakim, Khalifa: *Islamic Ideology*, Lahore, 1951.
Anderson, J. N. D.: *Islamic Law in the Modern World*, New York, 1959.
Andrae, Tor: *Muhammad, the Man and his Faith*, New York, 1936.
Arberry, A. J.: *The Koran Interpreted*, London, 1955, 2 vols.
—— *Sufism*, London, 1950.
Bousquet, Georges H.: *La morale de l'Islam et son éthique sexuelle*, Paris, 1953.
Brown, David A.: *The Way of the Prophet*, London, 1962.
Burckhardt, J. L.: *Travels in Arabia*, London, 1829, 2 vols.
Calverley, Edwin E.: *Worship in Islam*, Mysore, 1925.
Dalman, Gustav: *Sacred Sites and Ways* (Chap. 16), trans. by P. P. Levertoff, London, 1935.
Dehqani Tafti, Hassan: *Design of my World*, London, 1959.
Dermenghem, Émile: *Muhammad and the Islamic Tradition*, trans. by Jean M. Watt, London, 1958.
Donaldson, D. M.: *The Shiʾite Religion*, London, 1933.
—— *Encyclopedia of Islam*, Leiden, 1913–38. New Edition, proceeding, 1954–.
Farmer, Leslie: *We Saw the Holy City*, London, 1944.
Fyzee, A. A. A.: *A Modern Approach to Islam*, Bombay, 1963.
Garlick, Phyllis L.: *Man's Search for Health*, London, 1952.
Gaudefroy-Demombynes, M.: *Le Pèlerinage à la Mekke*, Paris, 1923.
—— *Muslim Institutions*, trans. by J. P. MacGregor, London, 1950.
Grunebaum, G. E. von: *Muhammadan Festivals*, New York, 1951.
—— *Modern Islam, the Search for Cultural Identity*, Berkeley, California, 1962.
Guillaime, Alfred: *Islam*, London, 1954.
Hussein, Mirza Mohammed: *Islam and Socialism*, Lahore, 1947.

Jeffery, Arthur: *Reader in Islam*, Selections from the Standard Arabic Authors illustrative of the Beliefs and Practices of Muslims, The Hague, 1962.

Lammens, Henri: *Islam Beliefs and Institutions*, London, 1929.

Levy, Reuben, *The Social Structure of Islam*, London, 1957.

Morgan, Kenneth W. (ed.): *Islam, the Straight Path*, New York, 1958.

Neill, Stephen: *Christian Faith and Other Faiths*, London, 1961.

Oldham, J. H.: *Life is Commitment*, London, 1953.

Padwick, Constance E.: *Muslim Devotions*, A Study of Prayer Manuals in Common Use, London, 1961.

—— *Call to Istanbul*, London, 1958.

Rahbar, Daud: *God of Justice, A Study of Ethical Doctrine of the Quran*, Leiden, 1960.

Ramadan, Said: *Islamic Law*, London, 1961.

Rutter, E.: *The Holy Cities of Arabia*, London, 1928, 2 vols.

Schuon, Frithjof: *Comprendre l'Islam*, Paris, 1961.

Schroeder, Eric: *Muhammad's People*, Portland, Maine, 1955.

Sell, Edward: *The Faith of Islam*, 3rd ed., London, 1907.

Sharif, M. Raihan: *Islamic Social Framework*, Lahore, 1954.

Slater, Robert L.: *World Religions and World Community*, New York, 1963.

Stanton, H. U. W.: *The Teaching of the Quran*, London, 1919.

Tritton A. S.: *Islam Beliefs and Practices* London, 1951.

Voillaume, R.: *Seeds of the Desert*, London, 1958.

Watt, W. Montgomery: *Free Will and Predestination in Early Islam*, London, 1948.

—— *Muhammad, Prophet and Statesman*, London, 1961.

Williams, John A.: *Islam*, London, 1961.

Zwemer, Samuel M.: *Studies in Popular Islam*, London, 1939.

General Index

NOTE

The questions tabulated for study and discussion at the conclusion of the chapters provide a sort of index to their contents, especially of the larger themes not readily itemized in the alphabetical index. They occur on pp. 19–20, 29–30, 57–8, 66, 92–3, 102–3, 113–15, 124, 135–6, 150, 161–2, 170–1, 182–3, 193, 204, 214, 225–6, 238–9, 250–1.

Index of Quranic and Biblical References

QURAN